SHADOWS
IN THE
SKY

THE
HAUNTED
AIRWAYS
OF BRITAIN

NEIL ARNOLD

The
History
Press

This book is dedicated with love to Doris, the nan I never met but miss dearly X

First published 2012

The History Press
The Mill, Brimscombe Port
Stroud, Gloucestershire, GL5 2QG
www.thehistorypress.co.uk

© Neil Arnold, 2012

The right of Neil Arnold to be identified as the Author
of this work has been asserted in accordance with the
Copyrights, Designs and Patents Act 1988.

British Library Cataloguing in Publication Data.
A catalogue record for this book is available from the British Library.

ISBN 978 0 7524 6563 0

Typesetting and origination by The History Press
Printed in Great Britain
Manufacturing managed by Jellyfish Print Solutions Ltd

CONTENTS

ACKNOWLEDGEMENTS

I would like to thank the following people for their help and support: my mum and dad (Paulene and Ron), my sister Vicki, my nan (Win) and granddad (Ron), Jemma, Nick Redfern, Joe Chester, Sean Tudor, John Hanson, Dawn Holloway, Evelyn 'Missy' Lindley, Corriene Vickers and Jonathan Downes. Thanks to those at The History Press, the Centre for Fortean Zoology, *Fortean Times*, *Paranormal*, *Encounters*, *The Unknown*, Victor Harris, Karl Shuker, *Dead of Night*, *UFO Magazine, Fate*, Paranormal Database, *The Why Files*, *Sightings*, *Ghost Hunters*, *Strange But True?*. Thanks to all the newspapers mentioned herein, and particularly to the *Grimsby Evening Telegraph* for permission to reproduce the Schaffner story, and also a big thanks to Simon Wyatt, Alan Friswell and Adam Smith for the fantastic illustrations.

FOREWORD

BY NICK REDFERN

When Neil Arnold asked me if I would write the foreword to this very book – *Shadows in the Sky* – I quickly and enthusiastically said: 'Yes!' Not just because Neil is a good mate who shares similar tastes in music and embraces the idea of living life to the full, but also because – as is the case with all of Neil's books – his new one is a damned fine read!

There's often a danger that when compiling and writing a book on countless cases and incidents of a distinctly paranormal nature, the finished product can come across as being overly sterile and encyclopaedic. In other words: highly informative, but as downright dull as dishwater.

Thankfully, Neil is the sort of author who astutely realises that capturing the attention and imagination of the reader is as important as presenting the evidence. And that's what I like about Neil's work: he's a good, solid researcher, but one who also knows how to craft a fine and captivating account that is as factual as it is spellbinding.

And that's precisely what you get with *Shadows in the Sky*: a mighty and mysterious tome best devoured by candlelight on a thunderous, chilled night. If you happen to be in some spooky old house at the time, well, all the better!

So, with that said, what, precisely, is *Shadows in the Sky* all about? Put simply, it's a first-class study of strange, bizarre and, at times, downright terrifying phenomena seen in the skies of the green and pleasant British Isles.

No one should be surprised to learn that Neil devotes a whole section of his book to the controversy surrounding UFOs – and he does so in a fashion demonstrating that whatever the nature of the phenomenon, it's a very ancient and mysterious one. But, flying saucers and aliens are not the only things that pop up on Neil's radar. He also provides us with a fascinating body of data on issues that some see as being connected with the modern era of Ufology, including weird and enigmatic ghostly balls of light, and nineteenth and early twentieth-century sightings of 'phantom airships', unidentified balloons and much more. Neil even entertains us with stories of baffling falls of fish and frogs from the heavens above!

Then there are those ominous monsters of the sky – creepy winged creatures that sound like they surfaced straight out of the pages of an H.P. Lovecraft novel. Their names include the Brentford Griffin, the Owlman, and the Birds of Death. Truly, they are the stuff of nightmares.

Now that I have given you a taste of Neil's book, it's time to read on. Disappointed you won't be. After reading *Shadows in the Sky*, however, you may find yourself glancing upwards far more than normal, pondering and brooding upon the many and varied monstrosities and mysteries that lurk above …

Nick Redfern is the author of many books, including *There's Something in the Woods*, *Body Snatchers in the Desert*, *A Covert Agenda*, *The FBI Files* and *The Real Men in Black*.

INTRODUCTION

On 24 June 1947, Kenneth Arnold, a skilled and experienced pilot, was flying in his Callair aircraft in the vicinity of Mount Rainier, Washington, when he encountered something that would change mankind's perception of life as we thought we knew it. Whilst searching for a downed plane, Arnold was suddenly alerted by a flash of light and then nine boomerang-shaped objects appeared in the sky in a chain-like formation. In 1977 Arnold recalled, 'They seemed to fly in an echelon formation. However, in looking at them against the sky and against the snow of Mount Rainer as they approached, I just couldn't discern any tails on them, and I had never seen an aircraft without a tail!'

Arnold's sighting became known as the first ever official report of a 'flying saucer'. He hadn't described a saucer-like craft, but in 1948 Arnold wrote an article for *Fate* magazine under the title 'The Coming of the Saucers', and in 1952 a book Arnold wrote with Ray Palmer had saucer-like craft on the cover. These flying saucers would become more popularly known as UFOs (Unidentified Flying Objects). In their book *UFOs and Ufology*, Paul Devereux and Peter Brookesmith wrote that Arnold had initially thought that the objects were of military construction but what puzzled him most was their unusual formation in the sky. Arnold commented that each object seemed to move of its own rhythm and 'fluttered and sailed, tipping their wings alternately', whilst 'emitting those very bright blue–white flashes from their surfaces.'

Since Arnold's encounter literally thousands, if not millions, of people have come forward to not only report unidentified objects, but to claim to have photographed them, too. Whilst the majority of the evidence supporting the existence of unknown craft is inconclusive, there's no doubt that people are seeing *something* in the skies of the world that cannot simply be explained by weather balloons, known aircraft or natural phenomena.

A few years previous to Kenneth Arnold's sighting, strange objects, which became known as Foo Fighters, were reported in the skies at the height of the Second

The author. (Photograph by John Estall)

World War. UFOs, and the sub-genres they have spawned, have made folklore all the more entertaining: from tales of alleged alien abduction, to alien-constructed crop circles, and even cases of UFOs rumoured to have crashed in remote deserts or rural countryside. What is clear is that the phenomenon has embedded itself into our culture whether we believe or not.

Of course, the term 'unidentified flying object' has often been misinterpreted over the years. Any mysterious object in the sky can be unidentified until explained, but since the 1947 sighting thousands of sky watchers and investigators have proposed the theory that this planet is being visited by alien beings. This has resulted in conspiracy theories and what might be deemed irrational suggestions. In a sense the term UFO is restrictive, and what you are about to read proves that all manner of strange, aerial phenomena can in fact be considered an unidentified flying object.

Over the centuries the skies of Britain have been littered with unexplainable forms. Flying dragons, angels and other winged beings, balls of light, odd things pouring down from the heavens and even airborne ghostly manifestations had been recorded long before Arnold's sighting. One person's UFO could be another person's ball lightning – it's often down to perception. In this book I've decided not to regurgitate the thousands upon thousands of UFO reports, that would be pointless (and impossible); after all, this is not a UFO book. Instead, whilst touching upon a few unusual encounters over Britain – mainly involving pilots and strange objects – *Shadows in the Sky* looks at more diverse mysteries of the air.

The abundance of weird cases you are about to read suggests that the UFO phenomenon is only a small part of a very complex mystery that has plagued mankind since the beginning. It's unlikely that we'll ever come close to solving the perplexing riddle, but as long as we keep our eyes to the skies, these manifestations will continue to haunt Britain's airways.

1

ANCIENT UFOS AND
FLYING DRAGONS

THE FIRST UFO?

There has always been a sceptical view when it comes to sightings of strange flying objects in the sky. However, for centuries anomalous aerial phenomena has been recorded, and in many cases by reputable people. On 18 August 1783 Thomas Sandby, a founder member of the Royal Academy, was having dinner with a group of friends at Windsor Castle, Berkshire. After their meal they took a break on the castle terrace but were immediately drawn to an object in the sky to the north-east. The phenomenon was recorded in the *Philosophical Transactions* of 1784 by Tiberius Cavallo, one of Sandby's dinner guests, who wrote:

> I suddenly saw appear an oblong cloud moving more of less parallel to the horizon. Under this cloud could be seen a luminous object which soon became spherical, brilliantly lit, which came to a halt. It was then about 9.45 p.m. This strange sphere seemed at first to be pale blue in colour, but its luminosity increased and soon it set off again towards the east. Then the object changed direction and moved parallel to the horizon before disappearing to the south-east. I watched it for half a minute, and the light it gave out was prodigious; it lit up everything on the ground. Before it vanished it changed its shape, became oblong, and at the same time as a sort of trail appeared, it seemed to separate into two small bodies. Scarcely two minutes later the sound of an explosion was heard.

This remarkable incident, thousands of miles away and 164 years before Kenneth Arnold's Washington experience, proves that unidentified flying objects, whatever they may be, have been with us far longer than we realise. Thomas Sandy recorded that the size of the object was immense, possibly half that of the moon, and the fact that it changed shape, halted, then changed direction, suggests it was no natural phenomenon. Scientists and sceptics argued that the group of witnesses observed a meteor, but again, this is not how a meteor behaves, and many witnesses to UFOs over the years have come from astronomical and scientific backgrounds so should be able to identify a natural phenomenon.

BEWARE OF DRAGONS!

During the eighteenth century there was no mention of flying saucers or space aliens, yet reports of such anomalous objects persisted under different guises. Devereux and Brookesmith, again from their *UFOs And Ufology* work, comment: 'Meteors aside, during the centuries leading up to the Age of Reason one of the favourite explanations for strange lights in the sky was that they were dragons. Even the 1783 objects were referred to by some people as *draco volans*, the "flying dragon".' In my book *Paranormal London* I wrote of a curious incident which took place in 1882 concerning astronomer Walter Maunder. Whilst gazing into the depths of space from Greenwich Observatory he observed a disc-like object of greenish hue that moved at incredible speed across the sky. The disc headed in a north-easterly direction. Shortly after the incident via the pages of *The Observatory*, the Royal Astronomical Society, by coincidence, had asked readers to send in their stories of strange aerial phenomena. Walter Maunder responded with his account.

In 1741 Lord Beauchamp was said to have observed a small fireball (measuring only 8in in diameter) over Kensington in London. The following year over St James's Park a 'rocket' was reported by a fellow from the Royal Society.

In the year 1113 a group of French clergy, whilst travelling through Dorset in the south-west of England, recorded a seemingly far-fetched account of an encounter with a five-headed dragon. It had allegedly emerged from the foaming waters of Christchurch Bay, flown about the place and breathed sulphurous flames; the beast even destroyed a ship!

In 764 and 1222 dragons were said to have been seen over London; two years later, on 1 January, it was recorded that several monks in Hertfordshire observed a strange ship as it floated over their monastery; in 793 'exceptional flashes of lightning, and fiery dragons' were recorded from the skies of Northumbria; and flaming manifestations were recorded by a Scottish pastor who wrote in 1792 that 'many of the country people observed very uncommon phenomena in the air (which they call dragons) of a red fiery colour, appearing in the north and flying rapidly towards the east …'.

Looking back at such events, some scientists argue that what people were experiencing was in fact lightning and atmospherics resulting from severe storms.

Some of the first reports of unidentified flying objects described dragons. (Illustration by Simon Wyatt)

BIBLICAL UFOs AND MORE ...

In other parts of the world, reports of strange aerial phenomena date back even further. Hilary Evans' book *UFOs: The Greatest Mystery* records, '332 BC – While Alexander the Great was besieging Tyre, 'flying shields' appeared over the Greek camp'. The objects were described as round discs that flew in triangular formation, 'one larger than the others by about a half'. Both armies watched the incredible objects until the leading disc flashed tremendous light aimed at the city's defences which were said to have crumbled with ease. The besieging army flooded through the ruins until the city had been taken with success and then the discs, which hovered overhead throughout, zipped off into the sky.

According to Evans, in 66 BC the historian Pliny spoke of a strange incident which occurred in Rome during the consulship of Gneaus Octavious Gaius Scribonius. A spark was allegedly seen to have fallen from a 'star' and approached the Earth. The object seemed to be as large as the moon and it hung in the sky giving off a cloudy hue. The object then ascended and took on the form of a torch.

From fifteenth-century BC Egypt, in the annals of Pharaoh Thutmose III, there is mention of circles in the sky giving off a pungent odour; in AD 664 a great shaft of light swept across the sky over Barking in Essex; in AD 747 dragons that breathed fire were seen over China; and 153 years later in France a woman and three men emerged from an aerial craft and were allegedly attacked by locals. Then, in 1561 at Nuremberg, Germany, over 200 cylindrical objects were reported as spinning in the sky. From a century later Hilary Evans records, '1661 – A Belgian Jesuit missionary in Tibet, Albert d'Orville, saw a flying object shaped like a double Chinese conical hat: silently, it circled the city twice, then, surrounded by mist, vanished.' Four years later in the Russian village of Robozero, people leaving a church observed a bright ball of light in a clear sky.

Some researchers claim that what could be perceived as UFOs are even recorded in the New and Old Testaments of the Bible. The *Reader's Digest* book, *UFO: The Continuing Enigma*, under the section 'UFOs in the Bible', mentions the following examples:

> As I looked, behold, a stormy wind came out of the north, and a great cloud, with brightness round about it, and fire flashing forth continually, and in the midst of the fire, as it were gleaming bronze. And from the midst of it came the likeness of four living creatures. And this was their appearance: they had the form of men, but each had four faces, and each of them had wings. Their legs were straight, and the sole's of their feet were like the sole's of a calf's foot; and they sparkled like burnished bronze.
>
> Ezekiel 1:4-7

William H. Watson, writing on Ezekiel's unusual sighting for *UFO Magazine*, delved deeper into the incident and also gave a different account from Ezekiel, stating that, 'According to the bible, in 595 BC, the prophet Ezekiel had a most interesting encounter beside the River Chebar in the land of Chaldea (Mesopotamia or Iraq, if you prefer).'

It seems that Ezekiel saw a whirlwind which came from the direction of the north but this was no ordinary whirlwind. The object resembled a cloud but of some brightness and fire. From this object came four living creatures, which according to Ezekiel had 'four faces' and 'every one had four wings.'

The wings of these beings were stretched upwards, but each creature also used a wing to cover its body whilst another wing was used for the creatures to be joined to one another. Ezekiel claimed that their appearance was 'like burning coals of fire' and from the fire came forks of lightning. Ezekiel also mentioned a wheel-type object, of the colour 'beryl'… some researchers believe these creatures were in fact helicopter-type machines which boasted rings. Ezekiel mentions, 'As for their rings, they were so high that they were dreadful' and also full of eyes.

The wheels lit up as the creatures ascended from Earth and the 'firmament upon the heads of living creatures' were the colour of a terrible crystal. The noise of their great wings was said to have been heard, a sound akin to the rush of a great body of water. Had Ezekiel described an encounter with some form of ancient, extraterrestrial craft ? Or, over time, has such an account simply succumbed to exaggeration and misinterpretation ?

Watson, after citing the verse from Ezekiel, comments, 'If one didn't know that the above had been written about 26 centuries ago, one could easily believe that this was the attempt of an intelligent man to describe a flight of autogyros or helicopters, perhaps descending from some kind of carrier ship'.

... And lo, the star which they had seen in the East went before them, till it came to rest over the place where the child was. When they saw the star, they rejoiced exceedingly with great joy ...

Matthew 2:9-10

... Eli'jah said to Eli'sha, 'Ask what I shall do for you, before I am taken from you'. And Eli'sha said, 'I pray you, let me inherit a double share of your spirit,'
... And as they still went on and talked, behold a chariot of fire and horses of fire separated the two of them. And Eli'jah went up by a whirlwind into heaven. And Eli'sha saw it and he cried, 'My father, my father!' ... And he saw him no more.

2 Kings 2:9-12

And he said to me, 'What do you see?' I answered, 'I see a flying scroll; its length is twenty cubits, and its breadth ten cubits.'

Zechariah 5:1-2

As you will read in this book, many accounts of weird balls of fizzing light, fiery monsters and other aerial phenomena suggest that the UFO phenomenon is a sum of many parts and, as with the case of the quotes from the Bible, all down to interpretation. In the modern day we rarely, if at all, record sightings of dragons and chariots in the skies over Britain, but we do record a great deal of flying discs, cigar-shaped craft and the like. As we evolve as a race it appears so do the mysteries around us. Dragons are very much part of British and world folklore, but were they the first interpretations of what we now call UFOs?

One only has to look at ancient paintings and flick through old scriptures and text to read of strange symbols and signs in the sky. Weird lights, peculiar orbs, flaming chariots *et al* have been recorded from all over the world. Ancient Roman and Greek texts mention serpents, dragons, gods, angels and wonders of the sky and Britain, despite appearing as a small island (when in reality it is the seventh largest in the world), is not excluded from the weird activity that takes place among the clouds.

In worldwide UFO lore, especially since the 1960s, there have been numerous reports of close encounters with strange objects that have allegedly descended from the sky and landed close to our homes. Vehicles have reputedly been buzzed by UFOs and people claim to have been taken from their beds in the dead of night and taken aboard spaceships. Alien beings have also been blamed for inserting microchips and other foreign objects into the bodies of abduction victims. UFO witnesses claim to have been threatened and harassed by mysterious men in black (MIBs) shortly after their sightings. UFOs have been blamed for making crop circles in the fields of the United Kingdom, and also for mutilating cattle and other livestock across the globe. Some researchers believe that the extra-terrestrial occupants of such craft are working in cohorts with the government. Others theorise that UFOs and those Martians at the wheel are not from outer space but inner space, or some of the world's deepest lakes. Whatever the truth behind the flying saucer enigma, it is quite clear that such forms are nothing new.

Dropping in ...

One Sunday afternoon in the Kentish town of Gravesend in the year 1211, as recorded by English chronicler Gervase of Tilbury in *Otia Imperialia*, a strange ship appeared in the sky over a local church. The appearance of the craft naturally spooked those who had congregated for their Sunday worship, and those in attendance were made all the more uncomfortable when the object released an anchor, which clipped a tombstone on the way down. Moments later an individual emerged from the hovering ship and attempted to lunge towards the anchor to retrieve it. His actions were described as if he was swimming in the air. The church bishop ushered his congregation back into the church and the occupants of the object simply cut the anchor and glided away, leaving the weight in the churchyard as the humanoid clambered back into the safety of his craft.

Interestingly this story, or one very similar, has been connected to other English counties. For example, Robert Emenegger's *UFOs Past, Present and Future* comments: 'During the Middle Ages, similar experiences were recorded around the world. From Bristol, England, in the year AD 1270, comes one such account. A spaceship was seen, and it was said that its occupant scampered down a ladder, and was stoned and asphyxiated in the earth's atmosphere.'

Some researchers have argued that the story has been confused with another record made by Gervase of Tilbury, which, possibly in reference to Bristol, states:

This port is the one used by the most of those who travel to Ireland. On one occasion a native of that place set sail from that port for Ireland, leaving his wife and family at home. His ship was driven far out of its course to the remote parts of the ocean and there it chanced that his knife fell overboard, as he was cleaning one day after dinner. At that very moment his wife was seated at table with their children in the house at Bristol, and, behold, the knife fell through the open skylight, and stuck in the table before her. She recognized it immediately, and when her husband came home long afterwards, they compared notes, and found that the time when the knife had fallen from his hands corresponded exactly with that in which it had been so strangely recovered.

In the year 1211 a strange ship was said to have dropped an anchor in a Kentish churchyard. (Illustration by Simon Wyatt)

The story of an anchor appearing from the heavens also appears in Irish lore, from the borough of Cloera, where it was said that at the church of St Kinarus in AD 956 (although it has also been recorded as the year 1211) an anchor attached to a rope dropped from the sky. Something unseen above was dragging the anchor, which suddenly got hooked on the church door. A crowd gathered just in time to see the hull of a ship. Then, a man appeared to descend the ladder but panicked upon seeing the crowd and climbed back up the ladder. According to this legend the anchor was cut off its rope by the villagers and put on display in the church. The event was recorded in *Speculum Regale*.

French chronicler St Peter of Vigeois similarly claimed that an airship of sorts dropped its anchor in the centre of London in the year 1122. Oddly, in the 1857 work *Cumberland and Westmorland Ancient and Modern*, author Jeremiah Sullivan writes of another event bearing some similarities. Sullivan tells of a Mr Jack Wilson who, whilst walking home in an area known as Sandwick Rigg in the Lake District, observed a bizarre spectacle:

> He suddenly perceived before him, in the glimpses of the moon, a large company of fairies intensely engaged in their favourite diversions. He drew near unobserved, and presently descried a stee [ladder] reaching from amongst them up into a cloud. But no sooner was the presence of mortal discovered than all made a hasty retreat up the stee. Jack rushed forward, doubtless firmly determined to follow them into fairy-land, but arrived too late. They had effected their retreat, and quickly drawing up the stee, they shut the cloud, and disappeared.

In the concluding words of Jack's story, which afterwards became proverbial in that neighbourhood: 'yance gane, ae gane, and niver saw mair o' them.'

Another story pertaining to Irish folklore is mentioned in the fifth volume of the book *Darklore*. In his article 'Enchanted Islands and Ships in the Sky', Nigel Watson writes: 'Early Irish monastic literature has several accounts of "demon ships" in the sky ...'

The Book of Leinster mentions that during a royal fair at Teltown, County Meath the High King Domhnall, the son of Murchad in AD 763, allegedly observed a trio of unusual sky ships. Watson also states that according to the Book of Glendalough, the King Congallach, during the tenth century, saw a mystery aerial ship. A 'sailor' was said to have emerged from the craft wherupon he speared a salmon, which he then retrieved. Several guards of the king were said to have apprehended the cosmic sailor but he was released and floated back to his sky vessel.

There is another mention of this legend, which Bishop Patrick speaks of in *Mirabilia* (*Wonders*):

> There was once a king of the Scots at a show with a great throng, thousands in fair array. Suddenly they see a ship sail past in the air. And from the ship a man then cast a spear after a fish; The spear struck the ground, and he, swimming, plucked it out ...

Weirder still, in 1897 a similar story emerged from Texas in the United States, where it was claimed that the anchor lodged itself on the railroad track and a man in a blue sailor suit came down the rungs of the ladder, but then became scared by a jeering crowd. An almost identical story comes from Iowa, where it was recorded that at Sioux City a farmer had the garments he was wearing hooked by an anchor, which had dropped down from above. The man escaped by grabbing on to a branch of a tree.

How could such a tall tale, if it was just that, have travelled so far in miles and centuries? Oddly, the legend even connected itself to an eerie airship (or, as some call it, 'scareship') mystery, which plagued the USA during the late 1800s, and Britain during the early 1900s. On many occasions witnesses fled in fear from Zeppelin-type ships and other cigar-shaped objects, which on occasion would drop an anchor or grappling hook. The next section looks at some of the phantom airship panics, but it may be worth noting that some research-ers believe that such grappling hooks were used by the mysterious crew of the elusive ship to lift up victims. Were these anchors and hooks the earliest form of 'alien abduction'?

MORE HIGH STRANGENESS

The Milwaukee Journal of 8 July 1947, a couple of weeks after Kenneth Arnold's strange sighting, reported 'Queer things seen in skies as long as 150 years ago', and listed several British accounts. The journal's researcher Charles Fort stated that '... disks were seen in north Wales Aug. 26th 1894' and that four years later, on 27 October at 6.00 p.m. at County Wicklow, Ireland, 'an object that looked like the moon in its three-quarter aspect [had] moved slowly, and in about five minutes disappeared behind a mountain'.

In 1718 other accounts tell of an enormous, pear-shaped craft, said to have been bathed in a great arc of light, spotted over Northamptonshire; the object moved slowly and silently across the sky. Then from 6 March 1912 it was recorded that over Warmley, England, 'a splendidly illuminated airplane travelling at a tremendous rate' was observed. This strange sky vessel came amidst the airship panic, which you will be introduced to shortly.

The newspapers of the time put forward three main theories to explain such strange aerial objects: 1) that a secret weapon was being experimented with by the army and the navy; 2) that 'the disks actually come from Mars'; and 3), 'They are things out of other dimensions of time and space'. All three of these theories are still applied today by researchers keen to solve the so-called UFO mystery. However, as already stated in the introduction, high strangeness involving sky-related phantas-magoria has more than one answer and source. The stories to follow will prove this point. Even so, in many cases of unidentified flying objects, you'll find it's easier to blame the aliens!

In his book, *The Realm of Ghosts*, author Eric Maple wrote, 'In Elizabethan times the west of England must have been more in the nature of a foreign land than an integral part of the country.' According to Maple, the county of Cornwall possessed its own language and that the beliefs of the locals were inherited from Celtic ancestors who had fled before the advance of the Saxons

With regards to West Country aerial phenomena, Maple commented that locally there was a deep belief and respect regarding folklore and ancient tradition. Many Cornish legends pertained to the foaming seas, folklore shared with 'their kinsmen in Brittany across the channel.' According to Maple, tales of phantom ships frequenting the shores were rife in ancient lore and there were also stranger tales of ships taking to the air.

Why on earth should phantom ships, often connected with wild and stormy seas, be seen in the sky? Or were local folk simply seeing the same flying objects so many others had seen many years before, and after?

Speaking of spectral ships, Maple goes on to speak of another terrifying West Country encounter, from Cornwall to be precise, stating that many years ago, one crisp autumnal evening, a foreign ship had been observed off Cape Cornwall. Maple writes, 'There, she disembarked a man, not too willingly it may be presumed, for he stood swearing and screaming as the ship put to sea again.'

It seems, that according to legend, the man was a nasty pirate, so vile in fact that he'd been shunned by his fellow pirates and cast out of the boat. Understandably those on land soon began to fear this hideous man who was said to have lured unsuspecting ships onto the rocks by way of striding across the cliff-tops on horseback with a lantern attached to his back – as a way of distracting vessels in distress.

'What on earth has this got to do with unusual things happenings in the sky?' I hear you cry. Please bear with the tale and find out! Maple adds that the pirate would murder any seaman who made the shoreline, but his terrible crimes were to lead him to a bizarre death.

Many years later, according to Maple, this villain had an encounter with an aerial anomaly as he lay, close to death, in his remote cottage. The pirate, despite his malevolence, was in the company of the parson, the doctor and two local fishermen when suddenly a strong wind screamed across the marsh and peculiar, eerie voices could be heard swirling in the gales. The voices were said to have cried, 'The time is come, but the man isn't come'. It was then that a black ship appeared on the horizon, heading slowly toward the foaming shore, and above it hovered an ominous black cloud. The ship was said to harbour no crew, and somehow seemed controlled by the black mass above it. A black shadow appeared to be cast over the pirate's hovel and an air of malevolence seemed to seep through the cracks. The parson attempted to rid the house of the evil but to no avail, and as thunder roared and lightning cracked the dying pirate yelped, 'The Devil is tearing at me with the claws of a hawk.'

At that point a fork of lightning struck the house and the timbers began to burn. No prayers could save the pirate or his home. The parson, the doctor and the two fishermen fled the burning building and as they came out into the night air they could clearly see a small, dark cloud detach itself from the phantom ship and make its way towards the pirate's cabin. Once it had reached the house, the cloud hovered over the roof and then seemingly sucked up the soul of the pirate before drifting back to the ship which in turn floated back out to sea.

When the companions of the pirate returned to the smouldering cottage they found the corpse of the pirate, staring wildly into space. On the day of the funeral a terrible storm was said to have broken out and the coffin was struck by lightning. Maple concludes, 'Then all afire, it was lifted up by a whirlwind and conveyed like a great burning log through the sky to the Wrecker's Hell.'

From 1743 there comes a fantastic tale of a 'ship' in the sky at Anglesey, Wales. According to legend a farmer named William John Lewis, aided by a ploughboy, was ploughing a field near Holyhead when they were astonished to see a huge ship, or 'ketch', weighing around 90 tons, descend from the heavens. The object reached about a quarter of a mile from the ground but this was no spacecraft, it looked exactly like a ship of the sea. The object had vast sails and flags flying. Mr Lewis rushed to get his wife, but when they came back the ship, which was being mobbed by birds, sailed backwards towards the clouds. Lewis realised that what he was seeing was something extraordinary, but stated he had seen such a thing previously. He claimed that roughly every decade such a ship sets sail through the clouds, from the direction of the mountains.

A SIGN FROM THE HEAVENS

Some things that appear in the sky, whether malevolent or benign, apparently take on a different form depending on who sees them. A hovering black cloud in the sky which plucks someone from the ground could be perceived as a demonic visitor to one person, or as a UFO abducting a victim to another. Author Eric Maple speaks of other anomalous aerial phenomena in the form of symbols and signs. He writes, 'The outbreak of the cholera epidemic in 1832 was accompanied by the vision of a flaming sword seen by thousands in the sky over London.' The weird object – considered some type of omen – was said to represent the last symbol of the Victorian Age – the Crystal Palace, which a century later was said to have caught fire. Locals peered from their windows at a red light in the heavens and commented, 'It is a sign' – a sign that the old ways and the old world were doomed. The 'flaming sword' may sound extremely bizarre, but its appearance wasn't unique to the skies over Britain. On 13 November 1650 Rector Samuel Clarke recorded:

> … being Saint Andrews Day, a little before, or about sun rising, the sky opened in a fearful manner, in the south-west over Standish, a town five miles from Gloucester, and there appeared a terrible fearful fiery shaking sword, with the hilt upwards towards the Heavens, the point downwards towards the Earth; the hilt seemed to be blue, the sword was of a great length, shaking hither and thither, and coming lower towards the Earth: There was a long flame of fire towards the point, sparkling and flaming in a fearful manner, to the great astonishment of the spectators, who were many. At last the Heavens closing, the sword vanished, and the fire fell to the earth, and ran upon the ground.

Strangely, a sword-like object was seen a few centuries later in Manchester during the November of 1961. A Mr Burrows, accompanied by another witness, observed an unusual cloud formation positioned to the left of the moon. In the middle of the cloud could be seen an object resembling a sword. Suddenly, from the hilt of the sword emerged a peculiar submarine-type object. In the modern era, flaming objects in the sky could easily be perceived as UFOs from outer space.

In the November/December 1998 issue of *UFO Magazine*, a woman named Mrs J. Barnard, from West Sussex, wrote in with an intriguing letter of a strange aerial object. She commented that during 1951 she'd been taking a late evening stroll along a path at Hammonds Hill Farm in Hassocks, Sussex, when she spotted an unusual sight in the sky. Mrs Barnard had her camera with her at the time and snapped the aerial phenomena which she described as looking like a topless cross with arms and leg aflame. In her letter she stated that, '...it then rose at a phenomenal speed, upwards, then as quickly shot forwards and disappeared.'

Her letter concluded, 'At that time, I don't think UFOs and space ships were part of everyday language, and I certainly didn't come to think of it as something alien. I haven't seen anything similar since.'

Mrs Barnard's letter was accompanied by a small black-and-white photograph showing a blurred cross-like object in the sky. The editor of the magazine at the time, Graham Birdsall, replied, 'Reports of a strange flying cross phenomena were prevalent across many southern counties of England in the late '60s, but Mrs Barnard's account predates these by almost 17 years.'

Birdsall added that the photo which Mrs Barnard took may well have been the first ever photograph of an unidentified object taken in Britain.

Strange crosses in the sky have been reported since the Sussex enigma. In 1967 several witnesses, including police officers, observed a 'flying cross' in the Okehampton area of Devon. The sighting was featured in several newspapers across England under varying headlines, such as 'PCs chase flying cross', 'Police chase white flying light' and 'Saucer led us a chase, say police'. Police Constables Roger Willey and Clifford Waycott reported that they had pursued the unknown craft through rural back roads. Despite reaching speeds of 90mph in their patrol car they felt as if the object was toying with them. Willey commented that, 'It was star-shaped and I would say it was bigger than any aircraft'.

A few days later one newspaper headline commented, 'Flying cross was Venus, say boffins', after researchers from the Plymouth Astronomical Society came forward with their observations of the story. They claimed that the object appeared bright due to the fact that the police officers were viewing it through the windscreen, although why on earth police officers would waste their time chasing a planet is beyond me.

The flying cross was also observed in Sussex and then by an Evelyn Robson, from Salcombe Hill, which was reported in the *Sidmouth Herald*. *The London Evening Standard* of 27 October 1967 ran a story on the flying cross under the headline 'Refuelling Clue To Things In The Sky', with reporter Peter Fairley writing, 'That 'fiery cross' in the sky – seen by nearly a dozen reliable witnesses – may have a terrestrial explanation – aircraft refuelling.'

According to the article the US Air Force had come forward to state quite categorically that the unusual phenomena seen in the skies over south-west England could in fact be explained by several aircraft refuelling operations that had taken place all week. The array of lights, according to the Air Force, could be explained – the white light seen was in fact used as a way of illuminating the tanker, whilst the red lights seen near by would have come from the jets waiting to refuel. The newspaper added that the US Air Force were hoping that all reports of a 'flying cross' would eventually tally up with their night-time operations.

Around the time of the reported phenomena a Dorset vicar, sixty-two-year-old Revd Lawrence Ing, had been out in his vicarage garden at Stourton Candle, Near Sherbourne looking out for satellites on behalf of the International Committee on Space Research. He told the reporter that at 7.00 p.m. he'd been lying in a deck chair when he saw a cross-like formation in the sky. Reaching for his binoculars Revd Ing noted a bright light surrounded by seven or so red lights, some of which were flashing. He reported, 'It suddenly came to me that it might be a tanker aeroplane flying in close formation with other aircraft.'

On the morning of 7 December 1984 two postmen observed a huge aerial cross in Bideford, North Devon. Bill Taylor, one of the postmen, was cycling to work when he looked to the sky and saw, 'Two huge beams of light, like searchlight beams [phantom airships anyone? – see Chapter 2] which formed a perfect cross. The Moon itself was the centre.'

Ten minutes or so later the 'arms', which Bill reported as being thousands of feet in length, began to fade. When Mr Taylor got into work a colleague, Paul Downing, also commented that he'd seen the strange aerial phenomena. At the time meteorologists from Plymouth could not explain the mysterious cross of light.

Similarly, at 7.00 a.m. on the Christmas morning of 1977 a Mrs Alice Camburn, who resided at Whitstable, in Kent, looked out of her living room window and was stunned to see 'a large black cloud with a distinct crucifixion-like cross in the centre'. The amazing phenomenon lasted for around twenty minutes. Valerie Martin, who lived near Mrs Camburn, sketched the cross-like cloud, basing it on a painting Mrs Camburn had done. A comparable sky cross was observed in Folkestone, Kent, a few years later.

CITIES, ROADS AND FLAGS IN THE SKY

Charles Berlitz, in the second volume of his *World of Strange Phenomena*, mentions the bizarre phenomenon of 'castles in the sky'. Berlitz states, 'Every year from June 21st to July 10th, The Silent City of Alaska appears on the Mount fair-weather glacier.'

This phenomenon, according to Berlitz, is said to be visible for roughly two hours from 7.00 p.m. to 9.00 p.m. Bizarrely, the incredible sight is thought to be a 'mirror representation' of the city of Bristol, England, some 'twenty-five hundred miles away.' No one knows why this fascinating mirage takes place but according to Berlitz some experts believe it may be the 'result of lenslike [sic] layers of air', said to magnify scenes many miles away.

A flying 'cross' was seen in the late 1960s by police officers. (Illustration by Simon Wyatt)

A peculiar aerial cross, which appeared in the sky over Kent in 1977. (Sketch by Valerie Martin)

This extraordinary sky-related mystery is not as rare as one might think. Chief chronicler of the strange, Charles Fort (*Fortean Times* magazine is named after him), has recorded thousands of reports of anomalous phenomena over the years. In his intriguing book *New Lands* he notes: 'June 1801 – a mirage of an unknown city. It was seen, for more than an hour, at Youghal, Co. Cork, Ireland – a representation of mansions, surrounded by shrubbery and white palings – forests behind …' Peculiar indeed. He also records: 'Sept. 27 1846 – a city in the sky of Liverpool. The apparition is said to have been a mirage of the city of Edinburgh. This 'identification' seems to have been the product of suggestion: at the time a panorama of Edinburgh was upon exhibition in Liverpool.'

And what of space islands? In *Country Queries and Notes* of 2 August 1908, Fort described how at Ballyconneely, Connemara, on the coast of Ireland, the mirage of a phantom city appeared, '… different sized houses, in different styles of architecture; visible three hours.'

Fort added that the mirage was a mirror of some far away city, although, 'This apparition is not of the type that we consider so especially of our own data.'

Fort also mentions another piece of intriguing information from *Country Queries and Notes*; that on the night of 14 September 1908 over Gosport, Hampshire, a strange light came from an unseen moon. According to Fort's source a Mr David Packer, from Northfield in Worcestershire, had observed a luminous phenomena that he assumed was 'auroral'. However, after the photo had been developed it seemed as though the light had in fact come from an object that resembled the moon. This image was said to have been reproduced for *English Mechanic* and was said to show a very bright object almost identical to that of what we know as the moon. As in many cases of strange phenomena, whilst it was revealed on camera, it did not appear to David Packer's eyes.

Fortean Times, as *The News*, Vol. 1, No. 3 (March 1974), reports on 'A Road In The Clouds', that was originally mentioned in a work called *The Ley Hunter*. Via editor Paul Screeton, *Fortean Times* managed to contact the witness to the phenomenon – a lady who wished to remain anonymous but who told the magazine that whilst on a morning flight from Edinburgh, during the January of either 1972 or '73, she was looking out of the window of the plane at the clouds. The witness wrote that she was '…on the left-hand side of the plane as you face the engine'. The cloud cover had been very thick and bereft of breaks, and about thirty minutes before touching down at Heathrow Airport she was amazed to see, on the cloud below the plane, what appeared to be a single track road 'as though it had been cut with a digger and this was soft earth' and that flanking this phantom road were in fact clouds rolled back. The road was about the width of a lane and ran in a south-easterly direction for what appeared to be many miles until it was out of the reach of the eye. As the plane passed over the 'road' never altered its shape.

Lands, dragons, roads, ships and goodness knows what else in the sky! 'Surely not,' I hear you cry. And yet reports persist of such spectacular and eerie sights.

What of reports of a phantom sun? Or was it an unidentified stationary object seen over Hoo in Kent in 1974? A Mrs K. Mortley of Wylie Road wrote to the *Daily Mirror* of 17 September 1974 asking, 'Did anybody else notice the "sun dog" or mock sun, the other evening? There seemed to be two suns in the sky. My husband and I knew then that we were in for some rough weather. An old chap told us this weather sign some years ago.'

In their book *Strange Tales of Scotland*, authors McLaren, Livingston, MacFarlane and Griffiths write of an unusual 'flag' in the sky, which they believe may have given birth to the Scottish flag we know of today. Legend has it that the flag of Scotland (a white St Andrew's Cross on a blue background) may well have had its origination at Athelstaneford, a village situated in East Lothian. It is said that soldiers, about to go into battle, marvelled at an object in the sky. The king of the Picts, named Hungus, and the king of Scots, Achaius, were said to have prayed for divine help as they rallied against the Saxon king, and it was then that a great white cross appeared in the heavens.

From here on Athelstan lost the battle and the Scots carried the blue and white cross. The authors also mention that 200 years later a version of the tale speaks of how, 'Hungus and seven of his men were nearly blinded by a divine light. Then the voice of St. Andrew was heard from heaven. He said that the cross of Christ would move before them as they marched against the enemy and bring success in battle.'

Whether these types of phenomena were, or are, UFOs we'll never really know, but it seems very likely that such visions and forms will always play an integral role in the history of unidentified objects in the sky. Nevertheless, even the seemingly unnatural can at times be explained as natural, albeit in nature's most unpredictable way.

Haunted skies. (Photograph by Neil Arnold)

The perception of flaming crosses, spectral flags and ethereal cities could well depend on the individual, but when more than a handful of witnesses lay claim to seeing some type of sky anomaly, there really can be no other answer except to say that such images are not only unexplained, but possibly supernatural.

2

ANOMALOUS AIRSHIPS

PHANTOM FLIGHTS OF FANCY ...

During the eighteenth century the hot air balloon was invented. French broth-ers Joseph-Michel and Jacques-Étienne Montgolfier, who were paper makers, launched their balloon on 5 June 1783. The balloon, which was filled with heated air, lasted for only ten minutes, but by the end of the year hot air balloons were reaching several hundred feet in the air.

In 1784 a French general named J.B.M. Meusnier proposed several plans to make the flight of balloons easier, especially as those which were fuelled by hot air, helium and hydrogen tended to be affected by strong winds. By the middle of the nineteenth century another Frenchman, Henri Giffard, had built a cigar-shaped balloon measuring more than 114ft in length and 39ft in diameter. Powered by a 3hp steam engine, it could reach 5mph in speed. However, it wasn't until 1896 that airships, fuelled by a gasoline engine, really took off.

There are three types of airship. Rigid (having an internal framework), semi-rigid and non-rigid (those without a framework often referred to as blimps). In 1900 one Count Ferdinand von Zeppelin from Germany flew the world's first rigid airship. Zeppelin drew up designs for such a ship in 1874 after being impressed by the French and their use of balloons to deliver mail, and such plans were reviewed by a committee in 1894. Eventually, Germany began to use the airships for military purposes, especially when the First World War broke out in 1914.

Before the First World War, only twenty-one airships were manufactured. Strangely, despite their slow speed and the very few numbers in existence, air-ships would be reported from several parts of the world long before they became known as commercial craft. In 1896 a wave of 'phantom airship' reports came from the United States, starting in California. The weirdest thing about such ships being the fact they travelled at great speeds and appeared to be extremely robust.

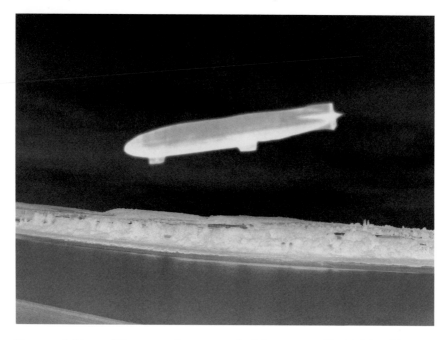

Phantom airships – of German or alien construction? (Image created by Neil Arnold)

Some of these ships were equipped with great wings, others seemed to be able to travel for hundreds, if not thousands, of miles. Many of the sightings were blamed on misidentifications of planets and clouds, some were deemed hoaxes, others hallucinations. Sceptics argue that there were in fact some airships being flown over the US as early as 1863, but in response to this those investigating the 'scare-ship' mystery commented that such craft seen in the skies were capable of feats far greater than those as yet realised by man's airship.

With no adequate explanations forthcoming to solve the airship riddle, newspapers began to blame possible invasion from aliens. As the *Saint Louis Post-Dispatch* commented, 'these may be visitors from Mars, fearful, at the last, of invading the planet they have been seeking'.

BRITAIN UNDER THREAT?

In 1909 the phantom airship craze swept through Britain and Europe. Were the cylindrical floating nightmares of military intelligence, covert craft sent to spy on us by an unknown enemy? Or were these craft constructed by extra-terrestrial beings? These are questions which persist in the realm of UFO lore.

During the early hours of 23 March 1909, a mystery object appeared over Peterborough in England. A policeman observed an oblong object, which emitted a buzzing noise and was equipped with a powerful searchlight. The airship flew at a height of approximately 1,200ft. The police constable, a Mr Kettle, reported the incident to a newspaper. Two nights after Police Constable Kettle's sighting, an Arthur Banyard observed a light in the sky at 11.00 p.m., 10 miles east of Peterborough. Mr Banyard told a newspaper, 'a few minutes of careful watching revealed beyond all doubt that it was an airship.'

On the night of 21 April 1909, a farm labourer named Fred Harrison observed an airship over Kings Lynn. Three nights later a strange object was seen over Ipswich, in Suffolk. The sighting was reported in several newspapers. The media didn't latch onto the full-blown scare until 15 May, however, after a Mr Egerton S. Free of Clacton-on-Sea in Essex reported:

> I looked up, and in the sky I saw a long, torpedo-shaped balloon, high up in the air overhead. It was a clear, fairly light night, and I could see everything almost distinctly. The airship was travelling swiftly in the direction of Frinton and showing two bright lights. I stood and watched it for some time until it disappeared.

Nigel Watson, writing in *Darklore*, Vol.4, added, 'The next day an India-rubber bag, which was presumed to have been dropped from the airship was found.' Mr Free described the object as looking like a large, albeit slightly flat football punctured by a steel bar that had been pushed right through it. Mr Free picked up the object – which wasn't very heavy – to examine it and noted the 'contrivance', to be 'about five feet long from end to end.' The central bar appeared to have been constructed of a hollow type of steel 'with an end round and flat like the buffer of a railway engine.' The football-type object measured approximately 3ft in length and appeared to be made of a hard, greyish rubber and emblazoned upon this in black were the words Muller Fabrik Bremen.

Strange objects dropped from unusual craft in the sky? Haven't we heard this somewhere before, regarding mysterious anchors?

When the object was investigated by the navy they identified it as a 'reindeer buoy', an object used as a gunnery practice target. However, things were to get even stranger for Mr Free. On 16 May his home was visited by two strange men. They looked around the area and spoke in a foreign tongue. The men stayed in the area for several hours, then left.

Some researchers believe the men were German agents hoping to recover the object dropped by the mystery airship. Such activity is reflected in the modern UFO climate, where it is often reported that areas where unidentified craft have been seen are investigated by mysterious agents, usually dressed in black suits. The biggest problem with the airship mystery, of course, was the panic that was about to ensue, especially with war just around the corner.

On 9 May at 11.00 p.m., a few days before Mr Free's encounter, an object with flashing lights was seen over Lincolnshire. The airship was estimated to have travelled at some 210mph because (assuming it was the same craft) it had been seen twenty minutes later over Southend. Then, on 13 May at 11.10 p.m., a Mr Graham and Mr Bond were making their way back from Teddington to Richmond, south-west London, when they observed a huge Zeppelin-type ship which they estimated reached more than 200ft in length and made a buzzing sound. The ship was very close to the ground at Ham Common. Both startled witnesses claimed they spoke with the two pilots and were given a pipe! David Clarke, contributing to Nigel Watson's book *The Scareship Mystery*, added that, 'Their story was given with every evidence of conviction...' after the witnesses reported that they were walking toward the central area of the common when Mr Graham asked his friend (Mr Bond) if they could sit for a while, as he had a stone in his shoe that had become very uncomfortable. It was then that they both heard a buzzing noise coming from behind them. Mr Graham initially thought the noise was emanating from a car but then saw a strange object floating close to the grass.

'What is that, an airship or what?' Mr Graham asked. He described the object as looking like 'a collection of big cigar-boxes with the ends out.'

The 'airship' was around 250ft long, according to the witnesses, and two 'pilots' were visible. The man at the front of the object seemed to be encased in a wire cage and when the occupants of the airship saw the witnesses they trained a searchlight upon them. The glare was so intense that neither Mr Graham nor Mr Bond could get a good look at the shape of the craft. The second man, who they said was situated in the centre of the craft, apparently looked 'like a German', and was smoking a calabash pipe.

Bravely, Mr Graham approached the ship and the German-looking pilot asked, rather hesitantly, 'I – am – sorry – have – you – any – tobacco ?' to which the witness replied that as it happened he did have an ounce or so and handed it over to the occupant of the airship.

The man took the tobacco from Mr Graham and offered him payment to which Mr Graham replied that this was not necessary. However, the pilot gave Mr Graham the pipe... According to a reporter from the *Star* paper, the pipe had been made in Austria but was available from a tobacconists in Fleet Street, London.

A few hours later, at 3.30 a.m. at Tottenham, two railway shunters reported seeing a strange craft, which headed towards Downhill Park. The unlit monstrosity made no sound and eerily glided off into the night. J.H. Stockman, skipper of a fishing boat, mentioned that the previous year, whilst out in the North Sea, he saw a large star-like object come out of the water in the vicinity of Lowestoft, Suffolk. Stockman called to a fellow crew member and they signalled to the object with a red flare. The object in the sky responded with a red flare. Stockman then sent a white flare up and the craft above responded with a blue one. In 1908 in Coventry, four men on the tramway at Foleshill reported that at 4.00 a.m. a searchlight was seen flashing from the sky. The light came from a huge object, which moved quickly towards the east, the quiet night only disturbed by the faint sound of a small engine.

Press influence suggested that the German military were spying on Britain. Nigel Watson confirmed these suspicions by adding that on 19 May 1909 a Sir J.E. Barlow, whilst addressing the House of Commons, asked if the Secretary for War knew anything regarding the alleged 66,000 trained German soldiers said to have been stationed in England, as well as the many thousands of Mauser rifles and millions of Mauser cartridges which were being stored at a cellar in the vicinity of Charing Cross in London. This rumour was dismissed by the Secretary.

On the same night there was a report of two airships travelling together. The *Western Mail* interviewed one of the witnesses, who claimed that whilst in the vicinity of Mumbles Head they had observed, at dusk, two elongated objects almost 100ft in length that had travelled over the Bristol Channel. The objects moved from north-west to south-east at great speed and after a few minutes the most easterly of the objects seemed to emit four white flashes which followed one another in quick succession and three slower flashes were given in response by the other object. The witness added, 'I also distinctly heard three sharp signals, apparently from a bell, answered by two more. The objects appeared to approach each other, and then disappeared travelling away from the observation point, at a considerable speed.'

A few hundred miles away at Berwick-upon-Tweed, Northumberland, another airship sighting took place. At 10.30 p.m. two railway signalmen were alerted by a buzzing noise and were drawn to a cigar-shaped object, which had two bright lights attached to it. A few moments later they saw another similar object and then both airships drifted out over the sea. An hour or so before this sighting, at Pontypool, South Wales, several people observed an airship, which was also spotted at Penygarn by two witnesses. Norfolk, Suffolk, Kent and Devon also experienced airship activity around this time.

On 20 May 1909 the *Meriden Daily Journal* reported 'Phantom Airship – England Worried Over Mysterious Nightly Invasions', stating:

> The mysterious aeroplane or airship, the alleged performances of which in or over England been mentioned, is becoming a perpetual nightmare. The newspapers for some time past have recorded daily the testimony of various persons who declare they have heard or seen it flying over the eastern counties and the North Sea. Now, this latest Flying Dutchman has turned up suddenly in the neighbourhood of Cardiff, where a wayfarer, according to his own account, saw a cigar shaped airship aground on the summit of Caerphilly mountain at about midnight yesterday.
>
> He tells a very circumstantial story. He relates how he watched the two men forming the crew apparently repairing the machine until they saw the watcher, when they hastily embarked and soared away. A local newspaper reporter went to the scene and found the ground had been torn as though by a ploughshare. Various printed papers, one in French containing technical directions, and numerous newspaper cuttings dealing with aeronautics were lying around. While some newspapers profess scepticism, all print the details. A large proportion of the public possessed with the anti-German mania are convinced that their arch enemy is among them.

Once the stories of the strange airships spread across the British Isles, the sky phantoms most certainly embedded themselves into the minds of the general public. Any area which may have been seen as a target for military opposition had some type of spy scare. In particular, many coastal regions harbouring docklands became a frenzy of activity as newspapers reported on the possibility of German invaders.

Many stories were of course false and the result of brief hysteria, whilst others were simply overblown accounts of sincere foreign people visiting places for their

GERMAN VIEW OF THE SCARE.

The Berlin correspondent of the "London Mail" writes on May 22nd :--

It is not too much to say that accounts of phantom German airships alleged to be flying over England and the North Sea, freely telegraphed here each day, are placing England and Englishmen in a ridiculous and humiliating light before the German people.

At first they regarded it as a joke, but to-day, as I will show, responsible leaders of German opinion, including writers well known to be friendly to England, are expressing disgust, astonishment, impatience, and some little alarm.

What every German knows is that no German airship has yet attained that perfection which would enable it to execute any sort of manoeuvre in any weather. The belief which prevails here is that some practical jokers are sending up balloons with lights attached, and these, seen through the frightened spectacles of a nation which has given itself over to panic, take the form of Zeppelins, Grosses, and Parsevals.

A very significant note of alarm is sounded from a friendly source—namely, Herr Friedrich Dernburg, father of the German Colonial Secretary and a publicist who has never tired of preaching the gospel of a cordial understanding with England. Writing in a recent issue of "Berliner Tageblatt," Herr Dernburg says:

The development of the relations between Germany and England cannot be observed without grave misgivings. The danger does not lie where it is often sought, in methodical antagonism between the policies of two empires, or in the belligerent ideas of their rulers and leading statesmen. It lies rather in the continual piling up of explosive material in the temperament of both peoples.

There is nothing quieter in the world than a powder magazine the second before it explodes. A spark falling suddenly in the midst of public temper can convert long-gathering exasperation into a conflagration. It is dangerous sparks of this kind which Englishmen term untoward events— events which nobody could foresee, which, without warning come to pass and stir and excite popular passions with elemental fury.

There has certainly been no lack recently of symptoms indicating what has been resting on the English national mind. For the most part our idea of good taste has simply been offended by what has been gossiped about nefarious German plans. In the consciousness that these tales are mere phantasies we shrug our shoulders. The invasion danger, the 40,000 waiter-spies, the airship cruising over England at night compel our ridicule.

But while we pass over these myths with nonchalance we overlook the fact that it is not our opinion which is concerned, but that it is the feeling thus spread broadcast over England which constitutes a very grave situation— that if to the popular phantasies some inflammable external incident should be added, even a peace-loving Government might be driven to take the most fateful decisions.

Let us imagine what would happen if such an untoward event should occur as firing by German warships upon English fishing smacks. Like a flash England would be aflame. Everything which had been accumulating in the shape of hostility to Germany would break into violent fury. A war party would be ready to place itself at the head of the movement and overthrow the opposition of the Government. Once again war would be decided before even the world had come to its senses regarding the incalculable consequences of such a decision.

Such a move, if directed against Germany, could conceivably have analogous consequences, for we also have no lack of unenlightened persons who would jump at an opportunity to put an end to the eternal pinpricks emanating from England. The danger of unexpected explosive incidents between Germany and England can be abolished by an arbitration treaty. Such treaties already exist between a number of States, but one is lacking between the very States which by universal consent require it most. I call it an insurance treaty against untoward events.

Colonist coverage of the 'scareship' paranoia, 3 July 1909.

own enjoyment or business. On 3 July 1909 the *Colonist*, Vol.LI, Issue 12581, ran the following story:

Phantom Airships in England – German View of the Scare:

The Berlin correspondent of the *London Mail* writes on May 22nd 'It is not too much to say that accounts of phantom German airships alleged to be flying over England and the North Sea, freely telegraphed here each day, are placing England and Englishmen in a ridiculous and humiliating light before the German people. At first, they regarded it as a joke, but today, as I will show, responsible leaders of German opinion, including writers well known to be friendly in England, are expressing disgust, astonishment, impatience and some little alarm.

What every German knows is that no airship has yet attained that perfection which would enable it to execute any sort of manoeuvre in any weather. The belief which prevails here is that some practical jokers are sending up balloons with lights attached, and these, seen through the frightened spectacles of a nation which has given itself over to panic, take the form of Zeppelins, Grosses, and Persevals.'

The 26 July 1909 edition of the *New York Times* also tried to play down the scare, under the heading, 'A Solution Which Will Bring Peace To Disturbed Englishmen' commenting that the airship scare was nothing more than the misguided adventures of an Englishman named Dr Boyd, an inventor, who'd be trying out his new machine with 'utmost secrecy'. According to the newspaper, on 18 May several witnesses in Belfast, Ireland, had seen a strange, long-bodied ship sporting brilliant lights over the Channel. However, the ship, said to have belonged to Boyd, was part of the inventor's longest trip which from shore to shore was believed to have taken in some 90 miles. Boyd apparently travelled at 32mph 'without striking any pear trees'. The ship, described as measuring over 120ft in length on a 300 horse power, did not match the machinations of the alleged Zeppelin ships said to have been causing panic across the country.

So, with an inventor allegedly parading through the skies in his own phantom airship, it's no wonder panic and paranoia was on the agenda.

This sequence of events was exploited in 1909 by several filmmakers. As Nigel Watson wrote, 'The fear of airships that made the defence of Britain by our navy useless was played on in *The Airship Destroyer*, directed by Walter R. Booth. This shows an enemy ship bombing railway lines and shooting down British aeroplanes.' In 1910 Booth also made *The Aerial Submarine*, a movie in which two children are kidnapped by pirates. Whilst unloading their strange craft the villains of the piece are photographed by the children. Thankfully for the children, their father finds their camera and when the film is developed alerts the authorities as to what has happened. The captain of the ship is a sinister femme fatale who sends out an order to have an ocean vessel torpedoed but after the pirates get too greedy on board the sunken ship, a British naval submarine is sent to deal with the baddies. Of course, the naval submarine isn't able to take to the sky like the pirate vessel and soon the good guys are under siege from the aerial craft, but, whilst fleeing over a mountain range one of the villains accidentally drops a cigarette, causing a huge explosion in which the pirates are killed but the children are fortunate to escape.

Despite being a fictional account, the film seems to echo many alleged true cases pertaining to mysterious craft and their occupants. Watson, in *The Scareship Mystery*, notes that in 1901 a ten-year-old boy observed two small men, adorned in military attire, who had spilled out of a box-like object in the area of Bournbrook, West Midlands. The men, who were wearing helmets, were spooked by their watcher and quickly scrambled back into their craft and, with a whooshing noise, shot out of sight.

THE SHEERNESS SCARE

In 1912 a strange object was seen over Sheerness (Isle of Sheppey), in Kent. The *New York Times* of 18 November 1912 reported, 'Sure Zeppelin Ship Sailed Over England – British believe strange craft hovering over navy port on Oct. 14 was German.'

The article stated that belief was rife that the ship which appeared over Sheerness on 14 October 1912 was of German origin. At the time the rumours were confirmed from a Hamburg dispatch which stated that the ship was a 'new Zeppelin naval airship, with Count Zeppelin and twenty-one men aboard', which, 'flying in a haze, passed with great speed over Borkum and Norderney on the North Sea on the afternoon of Oct 14 at a height of 4,500 feet.'

According to sources little was known about the outward voyage of the airship but at 2.00 a.m. on 15 October it had returned to Kiel then continued on to the Prussian island of Fehmarn, in the region of the Baltic, then headed south toward Johannisthal, close to Berlin. The 'official' account given out by the Germans stated that the ship headed out on 13 October, and arrived at Johannisthal during the afternoon of the 14th. The newspaper added that, 'The suggestion has been made in British naval circles at Portsmouth and Sheerness that the official date was changed and the actual time of the voyage officially put back twenty-four hours.' One thing was known for sure: that during the time of the airship scare, no British machine was in flight over Sheerness. Further enquires also proved that the craft was not of French origin either.

Whatever strange machine had appeared in the skies of Kent in 1912, there was clarity on one point: no other country possessed an airship that was in any way capable of such a voyage and in such a duration. The newspaper concluded that if indeed it had been the Zeppelin over Sheerness, according to all available evidence, the craft would have had to have travelled from Friedrichshafen to Borkum – some 437 miles, then from there to Sheerness – covering 293 miles, then from Sheerness on to Fehmarn, covering 456 miles then from Fehmarn to Johannisthal – 162 miles – with a speed at over 43mph. Owing to the conflict of dates, it is not possible to give the time taken for the different stages. But it is officially admitted that the ship was in the air for thirty-one hours, which would give an average speed of just over 43mph.

A Berlin dispatch stated:

> The new Zeppelin, known as the L1, is the only German airship which could possibly have been hovering over Sheerness on Oct 13 and 14. She made her first long distance flight in 31 hours from Friedrichshafen to Berlin about that time. Her detailed movements were never made public, as the cruise was the official trip for the Admiralty and therefore secret.

The information furnished to the press states that the trip began at Friedrichshafen at 8.30 a.m. on 13 October and ended at Johannisthal on 14 October. The Admiralty wireless station at Norddeuch, on the German mainland south of Norderney, reported that the *L1* sent in a wireless signal 'from a great distance at about 7 o'clock on the evening of Oct 13'.

The vessel's wireless range has a radius of between 300 and 400 miles. The version provided for the press added:

> A fog prevailed throughout Oct 13 to such an extent that the exact determination of the airship's position was impossible. The fog having cleared during the late hours of the afternoon, the vessel found itself sailing north rapidly over Osnabrueck. At an altitude of only 200 feet, less than a mile away, the vessel left the mainland in the early hours of the evening between Borkum and Norderney, and continued its trip across the North Sea.

In 1912 a phantom airship was said to have flown over the marshes of the Isle of Sheppey. (Photograph by Neil Arnold)

Passed Over A Warship

The lights of Heligoland were said to have served as a guide. The crew easily distinguished the lights of a passing passenger ship, and discovered the lights of a warship. The mainland was said to have been reached again at about 2 AM on Oct 14 near Buesum, after Kiel had been passed. The L1 then crossed the Baltic so far that the coast lights of Denmark could be discerned, whereupon Count Zeppelin, who was at the helm, turned about. Throughout the early hours of the morning of Oct 14 the vessel is said to have battled against strong counter winds. Coming from the North, the L1 next sighted Lübeck at 9 o'clock and headed for Berlin, which was crossed at 2:30 pm. An hour later she was standing at the Johannisthal flying camp.

Nigel Watson, again from his book *The Scareship Mystery*, in the chapter 'Did a German Airship Fly Over Sheerness in 1912?', explains that considerable alarm was indeed caused by the unknown craft said to have travelled over Sheerness in Kent. On 18 November 1912 a statement on this incident was made in the House of Commons when MP for Brentford, Mr Joynson-Hicks, asked the Secretary of State for War, a Colonel Seeley, if he knew anything regarding the night of 14 October and a Zeppelin.

According to Watson the matter was passed to the First Lord of the Admiralty, Winston Churchill, who wrote, 'I have caused inquiries to be made and have ascertained than an unknown aircraft was heard over Sheerness about 7.00 p.m., on the evening of 14 October. Flares were lighted at Eastchurch, but the aircraft did not make a landing. There is nothing in the evidence to indicate the nationality of the aircraft.'

Watson goes on to describe how Members of Parliament were not able to comment on the situation until 27 November. Strangely, although a few people came forward to say they had heard the mysterious craft, no one who'd seen the object came forward.

At the time, those who heard the peculiar buzzing noise assumed it was coming from the Naval Flying School at Eastchurch. As the *Daily Mail* commented, 'A score of people in all parts of town agree that the noise was heard. It first came from above the dockyard; the people in the streets [of Sheerness] stared up in the belief that a belated naval aeroplane was passing, and the noise appeared to pass away towards Queenborough and the sea.'

According to Nigel Watson, a Mr B.G. Wade, a naval tailor and resident of Blue Town, stated that on the day of the strange buzzing noise sailors had come into his shop and told him that, whilst on their ship, HMS *Actaeon*, they'd seen an airship that had a searchlight and another red light. The majority of the witnesses who experienced the Sheerness incident reported hearing a buzzing noise, but at most only saw a light moving through the sky.

Interestingly, the Sheerness Heritage Centre has on file a photograph of the mystery object seen in the skies over the island. Although nothing more than a flash of light, the photo certainly proves, to some extent, that some type of mysterious object was over the Sheerness. The website for the Heritage Centre states:

The panic that followed wasn't because the British were unfamiliar with aircraft, although flying machines other than balloons were not a particularly common sight [In fact, in 1911, England's first rigid airship, the *RI-M*, had been destroyed even before it could be tested]. What bothered Britons the most, once their government assured them that the Sheerness craft wasn't one of theirs, was the fear that Germany controlled the skies. There was nothing they could do about it either, and nightmare visions of enemy airships destroying Britain began to infect the national consciousness.

Watson, in conclusion to the mysterious airship panic, stated that although no 'specific airship was found guilty of causing the incident', a Royal Flying Corps officer felt there had been a moral to the story, that being that the British had, rather embarrassingly, been shown to be quite pedestrian in their military aeronautics and that '...there seems very little prospect of any advance being made as long as responsible Ministers give public utterances of their being content to wait to pick the brains of foreigners.'

At the time, compared to other countries in Europe such as Germany and France, Britain's defences in an aerial sense were pretty dire. Twelve aeroplanes divided between the army and navy and two small airships hardly compared to the 250 military planes owned by the French and over 100 owned by the Germans, twenty of which were airships.

Of course, after the whole Sheerness panic there is still the possibility, as in the phantom airship enigma as a whole, that some sightings (if not all, according to some researchers/sceptics) were nothing more than hoax and rumour. As a possible result of hysteria the airship wave was pretty potent, especially as war loomed so close. Hoax, hallucination or real, it doesn't matter; the arrival of war simply provided many Britons with the information they'd already guessed at – that the Germans were on the march towards England.

The 20 February 1913 edition of the *Grey River Argus* ran the headline, 'Phantom Airships – Disquiet In England – Germany's Successful Dirigible – London Feb 8 – Commenting upon the mysterious dirigibles that have recently been making their appearance in different parts of the country, the *Daily News and Morning Leader* remarks that the visits of foreign airships are becoming unpleasantly frequent.' The paper went on to say:

> It would seem that they can elude observation at pleasure, which raises a disquieting doubt as to whether some don't escape observation altogether. This aerial espionage is an intrusion which we have a right to resent. Our sovereignty goes up in the sky and down to the centre of the earth. We need legislation to assert our rights, and also an aerial police.

The article concluded that, 'A good deal of prominence is being given to the fact that Germany now has a fleet of eighteen military airships, while Britain possesses none'. On 25 February 1913, the year before the war broke out, Prime Minister Asquith met aviator Claude Graeme-White to discuss the airship panic. The fact that three days before an airship had been seen by Captain Lundie and his second officer over Leeds, added some credibility to the sightings.

In 1912 there had been several reports of unusual aerial craft, one emerging from County Derry where an old lady reported seeing a strange light that gave off a sulphuric odour. On the night of 2 November 1912 in Leith at the Firth of Forth, Scotland, a male witness observed a speck of light travelling towards him as he stared from his window at 11.30 p.m. The object was cigar-shaped. Another object appeared a short while after but this time was described as having a crescent-moon-shaped body. Mysterious lights were seen all over the country, from Hampshire to Scotland.

Kent was visited once again by a strange flying object, this time on 4 January 1913. Mr John Hobbs was inspecting a road in Dover when he heard the sound of an aircraft engine. When he looked up to the sky he saw a light, which moved quickly across the sky towards the sea. At the time the incident echoed the Sheerness scare, with a majority of witnesses stating that they'd only heard the ship instead of seeing it. The local press stated that a French airship was to blame for the reports, but the weather at the time was considered too rough for an airship to navigate.

Shortly after the Dover sighting, a strange light was seen over Ireland and credible witnesses, such as police officers, came forward to report their sightings. A red light that moved erratically was observed in Swansea, and areas such as Great Yarmouth, Essex, Manchester and Yorkshire experienced similar reports. Not all described airships; a large number described fast-moving lights.

On 3 April 1913 the *Lewiston Morning Tribune* stated that a mysterious German airship had been caught in Luneville, France. According to the newspaper 'The German officers aboard the airship explained that they had been lost in the clouds and did not know they had crossed the French frontier'.

The city of London seemed to be a hotbed of airship activity, particularly in 1914 when phantom airships were seen over Hendon, Brixton and Woolwich. On 7 November 1914 two police officers watched a huge airship drift over Bromley. Some of the reports received more publicity than others, as is usually the case when a panic or mystery overstays its welcome without resolve. In 1905, a few years before the airship scare, it was reported that the sky over Wales had been full of strange, misty objects, although one report commented that an object 'like an iron bar, heated to an orange-coloured glow' had been suspended vertically.

During 1914, as war broke out, it was reported that over Hertfordshire strange objects resembling 'dumb-bells' were seen in the sky. The objects were first observed in September but the following month, on 14 October, a black, spindle-shaped ship was seen crossing the sun. An Albert Buss saw the object over Manchester and described it thus: 'Its extraordinarily clear-cut outline was surrounded by a kind of halo, giving the impression of a ship plowing [sic] her way through the sea, throwing up white-foamed waves with her prow.'

The phantom airships and the panic they caused lasted far longer than a majority of mysteries before and after them, and there's no doubt that their presence caused a great deal of alarm. Of course, looking back at such reports we are now, in the modern day, able to shed more light on such a mystery, and there is also that

A phantom airship. (Illustration by Simon Wyatt)

tendency to put such unexplainable flying objects alongside the UFOs of today. Many researchers believe that those cigar-shaped anomalies of the early 1900s were in fact something akin to UFOs, and not military craft, especially when the enemy (the Germans) were also being plagued by strange aerial phenomena. Those mighty sky ships, which moved so gracefully and were able to turn at speed, surely could not have been the same labouring Zeppelins which the Germans had manufactured – could they? Maybe the Germans led us to believe that the only ships they offered could travel at around 30mph, but maybe, just maybe, they were testing out secret military craft like many of the world's superpowers do today. It seems highly unlikely that space beings were floating through the sky in those vast machines, especially when we consider that only thirty or so years later they were allegedly zipping through the skies of Washington in slim, stream-lined vehicles, which would become known as flying saucers.

However, there could be a remote possibility that the ancient reports of fiery chariots and pulsating lights were the original UFOs, and that the airship-type objects were another type of alien craft, manufactured by an unknown race to mimic our own.

These types of panics will always have this effect. One only has to look at the *Bakersfield Californian* of 19 April 1918 for an example of this:

Phantom Airship Sets London All Agog With Wonder

All London was talking today about the latest rumour – the landing in England last night of an American airplane after a non-stop flight from New York with twelve passengers. The authorities declared there was no basis for the story but this denial served merely to give it additional currency.

EVOLUTION OF UFOS

Author Nick Redfern, writing for Issue 31 of *Paranormal* magazine, looked into the evolution of UFOs and studied the way such forms alter over time, in the same way humanity does. It is intriguing to note that as every century passes, so do the shapes of UFOs – and also human perception of them.

UFOs in the modern climate appear as sinister black triangles in the sky, almost mimics of the stealth aircraft that for a long while were themselves a secret subject. In the past they have appeared as or alongside the phantom airships just described. They were the Foo Fighters of the early 1940s, and then the saucers of the later '40s. UFOs have been described as ghost rockets, as fiery balls and those weird chariots from Biblical and Medieval times.

The big question is, however: can such forms be manifestations of the human psyche? Do we somehow create such forms, unintentionally, perhaps through fear? Are UFOs the product of mass hallucination or covert government experiment? Maybe UFOs do not exist at all in the extra-terrestrial sense. Perhaps those airships and the like alter as mankind does, suggesting that such objects have a far deeper meaning than we give them credit for. Maybe such mysterious forms aren't from the distant galaxies of outer space, but from the deeper, more complex void of inner space…

3

GOODNESS, GRACIOUS, GREAT BALLS OF FIRE (AND LIGHT!)

JUST A LOAD OF OL' BALLS?

In the November/December 1998 issue of *UFO Magazine*, an article appeared entitled '101 Possible Explanations For UFOs'. Among theories put forward were jet trails, fireworks, ghost rockets, frauds, laser lights, research balloons, orbiting satellites, street lights, flares, helicopters, kites, blimps and even monsters! One of the most common explanations for such eerie lights is called ball lightning. This intriguing phenomenon still eludes the explanation of scientists.

Brian Handwerk, for *National Geographic* of 31 May 2006, wrote, 'People have reported seeing ball lightning – [a] rare phenomenon that resembles a glowing sphere of electricity – for hundreds of years.' Whilst Graham K. Hubler, a physicist at the US Naval Research Laboratory in Washington DC, said, 'There's certainly no consensus. I don't think that anyone knows what it is … Most scientists feel that the proper model hasn't been found yet.' Surveys estimate that 1 in every 150 people believe they have seen ball lightning. Hubler is one of them. He describes seeing a glowing, tennis ball-sized formation hovering nearby, which 'drifted along a few feet above the ground'.

According to an entry on the website Wikipedia, ball lightning is 'a hypothetical atmospheric electrical phenomenon of which little is known.' The entry explains that this term typically refers to luminous, usually spherical objects and that they tend to vary dramatically in size, 'from pea-sized to several metres in diameter.' It goes on to say that ball lightning is 'usually associated with thunderstorms, but lasts considerably longer than the split-second flash of a lightning bolt, leaving behind the odour of sulphur.'

On 21 October 1683 at Widecombe-in-the-Moor, Devon, a severe storm rattled the local church. A huge ball of light, measuring 8ft, blasted the building, causing four people to die and more than sixty to be injured. The glowing sphere entered

Woodcut showing the 1683 Widecombe-in-the-Moor phenomenon.

the church and split into two. One of the orbs smashed pews and windows before eventually leaving the church in a trail of sulphurous smoke, whilst the other fiery object vanished within the building. After the event, some of the congregation were quick to blame the apparition on the Devil, claiming that the fire was indeed 'flames from Hell'. In 1809 the British ship HMS *Warren Hastings* was said to have been 'attacked' by three peculiar balls of light, resulting in the death of two crew members and mild burns for another.

Ball lightning is a relatively regular phenomenon, recorded for centuries all over the world, particularly from Russia, Sweden and the United States. Such orbs of fire are unidentified flying objects in the truest sense. We know they exist, we've seen them fly and hover, and yet we cannot identify their origin. Some even appear without the clap of thunder. The already briefly mentioned Foo Fighters of the Second World War may well have been similar enigmatic balls, but again, such mysterious objects may exist as a space ship to one individual, and to another some type of devilish manifestation. They have always been with us.

The descriptions of ball lightning vary wildly. At times such forms are said to take unpredictable trajectories, other times they simply hover. In some cases the balls of light have been known to explode or simply fade to nothing. Ball lightning has been said to travel through the walls of buildings; rise from marsh ground; and float high in the sky. In shape they are not confined to spheres but have been reported as oblong, tear-drop shaped or hazy blobs; and whilst at times such light forms are said to travel silently, many reports describe the objects making a fizzing, popping or crackling sound. At times they are dull in their appearance, while at other times they dazzle intensely. In folklore such manifestations sit alongside the will o' the wisp, spook lights, corpse candles, orbs and other mystery light phenomena. No one knows where such forms originate from and such lights can melt into various other phenomena, i.e. UFOs, ghosts.

The will o' the wisp, also known as Jack-o-lantern, is said to be caused when the oxidation of phosphine and methane – produced by organic decay – gives off photo emissions. When phosphine comes in contact with the air even small quantities can ignite, and together with methane can cause short-lived fires. The will o' the wisp can also vary in size – its biggest being that of a football – and can be quite an eerie sight when experienced on a fog-enshrouded moor. In folklore the form was said to appear to a lonely traveller and lead him astray. Fooled by the appearance of the glowing object, the weary rambler was often said to be led to his death on the treacherous moor, or completely lost at the very least. The wisp is always said to appear out of the reach of its pursuer. Some folklorists believe that the will o' the wisp is a spirit of the dead. In the United States, similar spook lights are seen alongside old railroad tracks and roads, although there appears to be no boundary for such forms.

In the modern climate the will o' the wisp is said to resemble orbs. Orbs are often considered, by paranormal enthusiasts anyway, to be the first form of a ghost. These small, glowing balls often elude the naked eye but are frequently picked

A mysterious orb-like form. Could these aerial phenomena be modern-day interpretations of the fabled will o' the wisp? (Photograph by Neil Arnold)

up on digital cameras. This suggests that the orb phenomenon is a sum of several parts, being dust particles, moisture, etc. Ghost hunters disagree and claim that orbs signify the presence of a spirit, even though some photographs show thousands of such orbs. Strangely, orbs in photographs, as we know them today, rarely featured before the advent of the digital camera.

Their reputation is something akin to 'rods': peculiar objects, again filmed and photographed the world over, which have flitted into ghost, but mainly UFO, lore. These objects are rarely seen by the naked eye but often turn up on video and photographic equipment and appear as fast-moving, rod-like objects with a fluttering appendage. Again, sceptics argue that such rods are simply the effects of clever cameras picking up insects and all manner of objects in the atmosphere, but some researchers who have studied the phenomenon believe that rods could be anything from unknown sky serpents to, of course, unidentified flying objects.

Whatever the answer, rods, orbs, will o' the wisps and ball lightning all run a similar path, in that they are unexplained by science and often classed as supernatural. For instance, in British folklore the will o' the wisp is connected to the lore of fairies and other ethereal beings. These orbs are said to not only be the spirits of the dead, but to take the form of monsters such as hellhounds and winged entities. Maybe the fact they exist in often remote parts gives them an air of the sinister, leaving our minds to work overtime when we happen to experience them. In Welsh folklore the will o' the wisp is known as fairy fire. In the West Country the light is known as the pixy light, and to follow one means you are being pixy-led.

From Australia to South America these lights, whether as ball lightning or will o' the wisp, are known to haunt the air of strange places. The following accounts suggest that these eerie lights haunt the night air in abundance …

A LISTING OF LIGHTS

Over the course of six months in 1915, Dartmoor's foggy fens and quagmires were being plagued by mysterious balls of light, which naval intelligence officers originally thought may have been a German spy signalling from the hills towards the sea. However, further investigation into the Devonshire enigma revealed that the light was in fact a peculiar white orb, which emerged from the marshes within the vicinity of an old tin mine. The light would drift across the murky moor then fade into nothing after about twenty minutes.

Two years previous to this, at Ironbridge in Shropshire, there were several accounts of a ball of light moving over houses within the hamlet of Linley. In 1927 at Upstreet in Canterbury, Kent, peculiar small balls of light were seen dancing in the air and over trees in an orchard. These types of incidents were nothing new. Charles Fort, writing in 1919, commented, 'In the *Monthly Weather Review* there is an account of ball lightning that struck a tree. It made a dent such as a falling object would make.' The following year a man from Southport, Merseyside, was washing up with his cousin when they saw a big fiery ball suspended over the telephone wire.

In *Ghosts of the Ghost Club 2010*, a Joan Bygrave wrote of a strange ball of light, which she and her husband experienced one evening in the 1950s as they were travelling through an area of Oxfordshire. There had been a heavy bout of rain and as they drove along the soaked lane they noticed that behind them the road had become illuminated. Joan's husband was expecting a fast-moving car to overtake them and so slowed his vehicle, but no car came by. Looking behind, Joan was surprised to find the road was now in complete darkness, then was suddenly shocked by the appearance of a ball of light, some 2ft in circumference, which floated over the roof of the car. The object drifted down the windscreen and over the bonnet, and then sped to a distance of about 20ft away before vanishing into thin air. Joan commented in her story, 'Both my husband and I were utterly astounded by what we had just witnessed. Yet this was the period when there was a new and rapidly growing interest in UFOs and we both felt it might be wiser to keep quiet about the experience.'

On 11 June 1987 a cottage situated at Cwmyglo, Gwynedd, in North Wales, was struck by a thunderbolt that destroyed the chimney. Local villagers reported that just before the strike a red ball of light was seen zipping through the sky. Those who lived in the house stated that when the bolt from the blue struck, it was as if a bomb had been dropped on the property. In their excellent book *Modern Mysteries of the World*, husband and wife team, Janet and Colin Bord, recorded that one night in

A nineteenth-century image of ball lightning. (Image courtesy of Wikimedia Commons)

1961 a Mrs Doris Will of Cheltenham, in Gloucestershire, was enjoying watching an atmospheric thunderstorm from her kitchen window when she suddenly felt as if she was being watched. Mrs Will turned to look behind her and was amazed to see a fireball had entered the kitchen. Terrified she ran upstairs but the ball of light followed in hot pursuit and sped by her. In her state of panic, Mrs Will followed the ball and then watched in horror as it shot out of an open window and made a noise like crashing thunder.

In Coventry, West Midlands, during 1952, a man taking an evening walk through country lanes was confronted with a peculiar ball of light the size of a golf ball, floating in the air. The witness originally thought that the object was a soap bubble and looked around to see if any children were hiding somewhere and blowing bubbles across the road. The object approached the witness at a height and hovered above him, before moving away in the opposite direction. The witness immediately blamed 'floaters', which are small pieces of debris which occur in the vitreous jelly of the eye. Rubbing his eye the witness was shocked to see the object still in view, and that it was now accompanied by several more. The bubble-like orbs seemed to swarm around the witness, as if observing him, and then gradually moved away, all forming into one bigger bubble.

Janet and Colin Bord believed the bubble was something akin to a will o' the wisp. During October of 1974 at Aveley, in Essex, a family travelling home in their car came face to face with an eerie blue light and then a spooky green-coloured mist, which seemed to envelope the vehicle as they made their way along the remote lane. The car began to stutter and the usual short trip home eventually took them ninety minutes. Bizarrely, after being interviewed by a researcher the family claimed they'd been abducted by weird creatures. Just over ten years later, at 5.45 p.m. on 6 February 1985, a nursing assistant travelling in the small Cornish village of Colan encountered a strange yellowish blob, which appeared by the roadside. The object measured over 10ft in length and appeared to be bobbing up and down; its edges were somewhat hazy. The object made its way along the fence line of the nearby RAF base, at one point turning green and then purple before completely vanishing. Peculiarly, the witness had previously encountered the phenomenon known as ball lightning but thought that this particular object was something completely different.

Indeed, what may at first be perceived as ball lightning could in fact materialise into something completely weirder. Author Alasdair Alpin MacGregor once recorded that many years ago a doctor from Edinburgh had been staying at an old inn on the Isle of Skye. After taking in a delicious supper he decided to go for an evening stroll along the shore. It was here that he observed a strange light – which at first he took to be a flare – out in the bay. After a short while the light seemed to approach the shore. The doctor described it as a 'globe of light – a light such as one might see hanging from a lamp-standard in a modern city [hence the name Jack-o-lantern for these type of weird illuminations].'

The light reached the edge of a ridge and suddenly blinked out, as if one had switched a light off. Suddenly, and to the astonishment of the doctor, now in its place stood the spectre of a woman clutching an infant at her chest. The figure moved with haste across the sand and then, in an instant, vanished without trace.

When the doctor returned to the cosy confines of the inn he mentioned the manifestation to the inn keeper who said that many years ago a ship had been wrecked on the shore and among the shattered timbers were found the body of a woman and her child.

In his book *The Ghost Book*, Alasdair speaks of several spook-light encounters; one such form is said to skip across the surface of Loch Rannoch and two other lights have been reported over Loch Tay. An eerie sight to behold, whatever your perception of light-related mysteries.

MacGregor also speaks of 'corpse candles' seen in the small township of Taagan, situated close to Loch Maree. The lights are said to appear when there is going to be a death. At one spot, known as Holly Pool, the lights have been seen and, interestingly, in the same area many years ago two local children were said to have drowned. MacGregor also speaks of ghost lights at Upper Loch Torridon and Loch Carloway. Many of these stories are connected to areas where a death has occurred, so they could be an extension of a haunting.

One particular will o' the wisp legend concerned two chaps who were returning home to Stoneyfield one night after a visit to Stornoway. Upon reaching a crossroad both men went their separate ways. One of the men observed a strange light in the distance and the next day spoke to his friend about the curious ball. Both men agreed that there was indeed an eerie light, with one of the witnesses stating that he'd tried to overtake it with his pony. Two days later the farmer, who was the father of one of the witnesses, died by drowning at Stornoway harbour.

In 1890 a ghost light was seen at Luing, situated in the Firth of Lorne. A James Campbell was travelling home one night through the small glen of an island known as Duiletter when suddenly, up ahead, appeared a bright light. The object was moving along the line of a stream and so Campbell attempted to follow it. At one spot the light then ceased in its motion and completely vanished. The next morning a local man named Livingstone was riding his horse through the area when the bridge beneath him collapsed and he and his horse perished in the stream, the horse crushing Livingstone as the waters rose around them.

MacGregor also records that one night, in 1938, two men poaching on the murky Barvas moor observed a strange light. Originally they thought that other poachers were in the vicinity but, when the men approached it the light blinked out. The men entered an old hut but there was no sign that it had recently been occupied and so left the building. Suddenly, they noticed a glow behind them and looking back to the hut noticed the inside illuminated. Both men decided to approach from different sides, but again, as they got to within a few feet the light blinked out and when they went inside there was no sign of anyone. On the third occasion that the hut became illuminated the men fled, as ghostly music floated from the building.

Ball lightning, ghost lights, will o' the wisps – whatever you want to call them – clearly inspire many differing interpretations. Are they intelligent? Are they simply unexplained natural phenomena? In the November 2008 issue of *Paranormal* magazine, a Lillian Dutton of Broughton, near Cheshire, wrote in with an interesting tale concerning unusual light phenomena. She wrote that once, as a girl of nineteen, she'd been residing at a house in Latchford, near Warrington and had been employed by a local company that manufactured gas ovens.

During late July 1938 Lillian was looking forward to a week off – this had been the time when the Factory Act had been passed and factory workers permitted one whole week's paid holiday. A friend of Lillian's, named Edna, had been made secretary by the company and was also looking forward to her annual holiday, in which she hoped to visit France – and so she'd gone out and purchased some new clothes. One afternoon, Lillian and her father were heading off to work after a lunch break when the weather turned extremely humid and it started to rain. They were then both startled by a loud bang – far more severe than a thunderclap – and a bright flash which seemed to light up the sky. As the rain battered the pavement Lillian got to work but there was no sign of Edna. When Edna finally arrived she was, according to Lillian, 'as white as a ghost'.

When Lillian and several other members of the factory staff asked Edna what was wrong she replied, 'Oh, I've lost all my beautiful holiday clothes'. According to Edna, when Lillian heard the terrible bang, a fireball had zipped down Edna's chimney and rushed straight at the makeshift wardrobe Edna's father had made, and which held all her clothes. The ball of light ripped through the clothes, burned the curtains and carpet, then tumbled out of the front door into the rain-soaked street.

Lillian added that back in those days it was quite traditional to leave front doors and windows open during a thunderstorm – just in case a fireball had entered a house and exploded!

Lillian concluded in her letter that many people saw the fireball exit Edna's house and that the heat which emanated from it was so intense that it cracked glass and burned wood. Although Edna lost all of her clothes to the ball she described as looking like a big 'flaming sun', she may well have escaped being torched alive due to the front door being open.

The fourth issue of *Encounters* magazine, February 1996, spoke of two encounters with unusual balls of light. One story emerged from Buckinghamshire and was reported by a Mel Donovan. He stated that at 6.15 p.m. on the evening of 18 November 1995, three golden balls had arranged themselves into a triangle formation on the horizon. The orbs emitted a golden, pulsating light. Mel ran into the house to fetch his video camera and whilst he was away his wife reported that one of the lights had seemingly vanished as only two were now in view. By the time Mel had returned, armed with his camera, one of the golden balls moved close to the other and then it too vanished, leaving one object left. The object hung in the air for some time and then completely vanished. On a perfectly clear night this was a spectacular sight to see. Seven days previous, on 11 November, a strange ball of light was photographed in the New Forest in Hampshire. The glowing ball was situated approximately 20ft from the ground and illuminated the path and woods around it, even though the photo was taken during the afternoon in the area of Emery Down. After a photograph was taken (which appeared in an issue of *Encounters*) the ball completely vanished.

In 1969 at Oxendon in Northamptonshire, a youth walking across the fens one summer's night was frightened by a flaming column, which appeared to rise from the marsh. Strangely, in the same area a female witness described how one night she was awoken from her slumber by a phosphorescent light, which appeared at her bedroom window before zipping off across the foggy marsh. In the same year the *Yorkshire Evening Post* reported on 9 October that a bluish white light, which transformed into a figure, floated from the top of Spotforth Castle, Wetherby, and motioned towards them.

On 8 August 1975, in Staffordshire, a woman was in her kitchen during a severe storm when suddenly a sphere of light appeared over the cooker. The ball of light zoomed towards her. The woman reported, 'The ball seemed to hit me below the belt and I automatically brushed it away. Where I had touched it, there was a redness and swelling on my hand. It seemed as if the gold wedding ring was burning into my finger.' After the fiery assault the glowing globe exploded with a bang and charred the woman's skirt, leaving a small hole.

In Issue 155 of *Fortean Times* magazine, Robert Halliday catalogued an impressive list of fireballs from the year 1783 using material obtained from the *Bury Post*. The list included an account from 30 June in which the *Post* recorded an event from Mattishall – a village 12 miles from Norwich – concerning a man who had been 'pasturing his horse' when a large fireball dropped down from the sky, scorching his stockings. The newspaper also spoke of several other fireball events from between 21 August and 4 September 1783 although Halliday commented that, 'at the time it was generally agreed that the sightings didn't correspond with conventional meteors, and few people suggested that this was what they were.'

The newspaper mentioned an account from Bury St Edmunds one night between the hours of 9.00 and 10.00 p.m. in which a ball of light was seen approaching the vicinity of Angel Hill – a public square. The object was in view for around thirty seconds before it split into smaller lights and then broke up into three glowing balls. After just short of a minute the balls of light disappeared out of sight. Although the fireballs were out of sight a strange rumbling noise was heard and a boy taking water from a well in the cellar of a house confirmed this.

The *Bury Post*, which had a representative at Thetford, in Norfolk, learnt that the gentleman was standing on the town bridge at 9.15 p.m. when the ground began to shake. According to the witness, 'About a minute after, perceived in the northwest something resembling the Moon, which appeared to rise out from a cloud. This fiery meteor proceeded in a semicircular form, in a very rapid state towards southeast when it disappeared.'

According to Halliday's listing, another strange light was seen 6 miles away at Ixworth, north-east of Bury St Edmunds. The slow-moving fiery ball appeared to brush the tops of houses as it travelled from north to south, leaving a trail of flame. The object then burst into pieces over a nearby meadow. A rumbling noise followed the explosion and many windows in the vicinity began to shake. Some researchers believe that the types of fiery objects as recorded in the Bury St Edmunds area were meteorites.

In 1908 in Tunguska, Russia, it was believed that a huge meteorite crashed to earth. A large column of blue light was seen to move across the sky and a few minutes later a terrible explosion wiped out most of the surrounding area, flattening trees in its wake. Researchers in the UFO community believe that it was a UFO that had hit the hills north-west of Lake Baikal. Some claim that no crater was found at the site, suggesting that a meteorite could in fact be ruled out of the incident.

According to folklore, strange balls of light, such as will o' the wisp and ball lightning, have been known to pursue weary travellers on foggy marshes. (Illustration by Simon Wyatt)

In Britain strange aerial lights are connected to what are deemed to be sacred sites. An area in Shropshire known as the Fairy Stone is said to have unusual energies. Many years ago a farmer observed a peculiar set of lights around the grass area of the stone. The farmer approached and tried to kick the lights and they seemed to attach themselves to his limb. When the farmer fled the area and reached home he noticed that there were many small holes in his trousers.

In Issue 27 of *Paranormal*, author and researcher Paul Devereux described many ancient sites said to experience light phenomena. One such place is Castlerigg, a Neolithic stone circle situated in the Lake District. Devereux wrote of an engineer named Theobold Sington who was taking a stroll with a friend in the area shortly after the First World War, when the pair saw a light that moved very quickly. At first they thought it belonged to a bicycle but when it was joined by several other lights they thought different, especially when one of the objects approached them. As it neared it grew brighter and they estimated it to measure some 7ft across. The light wobbled then faded from view, but the witnesses kept an eye on the lights in the distance, which continued to dance near the stone circle.

Devereux also spoke of another megalithic site said to be haunted by weird lights. He wrote, '... the 5,000-year-old dolmen of Dyffryn Ardudwy, near Barmouth on the west coast of Wales, was at the centre of bizarre effects: luminous columns sprang up from the ground around it and startled witnesses could see small balls of light rising up within the columns.' Devereux, who has investigated many ancient sites across Britain, has given these aerial light phenomena names such as temple lights, church lights and earth lights.

In December 1922 a farmhand named William Neale experienced several spook lights in the churchyard of All Saints church, at Burton Dasset, 10 miles from Warwick. Several locals gathered in the misty churchyard after Neale reported seeing odd lights dancing over the graves and over the nearby hills. Many witnessed the dancing globules, which varied in colour from white to a reddish-blue.

On 15 February 1996 the *Dundee Courier* reported that dozens of motorists travelling on the M9 in west-central Scotland two days earlier had called police to say they'd seen a house-sized fireball zoom across the horizon, leaving a trail of fire. The Civil Aviation Authority said they'd no record of any fireball. On the same day, strange fireballs were reported from the Inner Hebrides island of Jura. Luminous phenomena, earthquakes, meteorites and heavy storms have often been connected, although there is no proven relation between the effects.

In 1843 at Guernsey a huge, luminous object was observed and described in the *Guernsey Star* as resembling '...a clouded Moon.' Two days after this object appeared, a remarkable earthquake shook Guernsey. Oddly, the day of the earthquake the weather had been fine, although it had been reported from the sky that a myriad of colours had begun to appear. In 1884 an earthquake shook Colchester, Essex, at 9.18 a.m. and was felt in parts of London. Similarly, at the time, a strange object appeared in the reddening sky. In a handful of cases concerning rare accounts of earthquakes in Britain, there has been mention of strange objects seen in a multi-coloured sky.

Writing for a magazine called *The Unknown* in the July 1987 issue, researcher S. John Saunders described strange visions in the sky as possible misinterpretations of natural phenomena such as '...the near-luminescence of the sea, magnetic storms, reflection or refraction caused by swirling vapour, or ignis fatuus (will-o'-the-wisp).' However, could such natural energies be responsible for sightings of ghostly armies and phantom craft in the sky? Of course, it's never that simple, but some atmospheric conditions and anomalies may be explained by events elsewhere in the country, or the world even. For instance, the Guernsey quake and light phenomena was believed to have connections with a quake that shook Lisbon in Portugal. And Charles Fort, in his *New Lands* book, wrote, 'Night of July 31, 1813 – flashes of light in the sky of Tottenham, near London. The sky was clear. The flashes were attributed to a storm at Hastings.' Hastings is situated in East Sussex. Fort also notes that the town of Comrie in Perthshire, Scotland, was prone to earthquakes, possibly dating back to 1597. During some of the quakes strange luminous objects were reported and in one incident 'a large luminous body, bent like a crescent, which stretched itself over the heavens', was also recorded.

On 2 September 1786 there is a report of a hurricane developing in England that resulted in a bright ball of fire being seen. On 17 December 1852 at 4.55 a.m. a severe storm hit Dover, on the coast of Kent. At the same time a triangular cloud was seen, measuring some 40ft square. The object had a long tail and a dull red nucleus. An explosion then took place somewhere in the sky and the object faded after being in view for thirteen minutes. In 1868 the Radcliffe Observatory of Oxford reported that an object, which looked like a comet, was seen sailing through the sky. However, the object changed its course, moving westward, southward and then north, so clearly not exhibiting the behaviour of a comet or meteorite. The following year a police officer had reported several stories pertaining to strange rumblings heard in the skies over Harlton, Cambridgeshire. Around the same time, parts of Essex, Sussex and Norfolk experienced the same noises. On 22 January 1869 the *Standard* of Norfolk reported that something of an unknown nature had spooked flocks of sheep in Swaffham and that something (not mentioning what) had been seen in the sky. An object described as an extraordinary meteor was then observed at Bristol, and around the same time several small earthquakes had taken place countrywide. Such strange sky quakes have also been blamed for extremely bizarre weather – falls of strange rain, huge lumps of ice – as described in Chapter 7.

In 1895, on the day of 24 August, a luminous object was observed in the sky over Donegal, Ireland. A young boy called Robert Alcorn saw the object drop from the sky and explode close by. His instinct was to shelter his face with his hands, but the explosion shattered his fingers. No substance from the explosion could be found in the area – could this object have been ball lightning? A week later, on 31 August 1895, an object described as luminous, and considerably larger than Venus, was seen

Meteor storms have been held responsible for some strange aerial phenomena. This image is an 1833 woodcut of a shower.

over Oxford. The object emerged from behind some trees and moved eastward without a sound. At the same time, in London, a similar object was seen moving eastward. Some suggested the object was a fire-balloon. Another report from the same time mentioned that an object in the area was star-shaped, whilst a motorist in Scarborough reported seeing a 'shooting star'. Author Charles Fort believed the objects to be meteors. They were also observed in Kent and in Bristol.

An earthquake-related ball of light was mentioned in October 1661 in the areas of Worcester and Hereford. So astonishing was the phenomenon that two church wardens had the incident published in a pamphlet entitled 'A True and Perfect Relation of the Terrible Earthquake', after monstrous flaming objects were seen in the sky. Bizarrely, there is mention that at the same time a Mrs Margaret Petmore fell in labour and:

> … brought forth three male offsprings all of whom had teeth and spoke at birth. Inasmuch as it is not recorded that the infants said, and whether in plain English or not, it is not so much an extraordinary birth such as, in one way or another, occurs from time to time, that affronts our conventional notions, as it is the idea that there could be relation between the abnormal in obstetrics and the unusual in terrestrics. The conventional scientist has just this reluctance toward considering shocks of this earth and phenomena in the sky at the same time. If he could accept with us that there often has been relation, the seeming discord would turn into a commonplace, but with us he would never again want to hear of extraordinary detonating meteors exploding only by coincidence over a part of this earth where an earthquake was occurring, or of concussions of this earth, time after time, in one small region, from meteors that, only by coincidence, happened to explode in one little local sky, time after time. Give up the idea that this earth moves, however, and coincidences many times repeated do not have to be lugged in.

Worcester was subject to another weird light during a quake on the night of 17 December 1896. Dr Charles Davison recorded that a luminous object in the sky 'traversed a large part of the disturbed area'.

For every seemingly explainable meteorite there is a ball of light that travels through houses and scorches garments. For every atmospheric orb of marsh gas there is a glowing craft that leaves a trail and yet changes direction – long before aircraft were in the skies of Britain. On 10 May 1902 in south Devon it was reported that a great number of highly coloured objects were seen. The year 1905 was of interest to Arthur Mee, who in the *English Mechanic* wrote that over Cardiff on the night of 29 March there had been seen by several persons 'an appearance like a vertical beam of light, which was not due to a searchlight or any such cause'.

Some may argue that these fiery balls and luminous objects are confined to the depths of history, but this isn't the case. On 18 July 1973 the *South Wales Echo* reported that a fireball had exploded in Cathays Street in Cardiff. There had been no thunderstorm at the time. Then on 22 December 1973 a fireball terrified residents of Windsor, Berkshire. The object was seen in the sky and locals jammed the police switchboards. The fireball was said to have dropped into Windsor Great Park but a police search uncovered no object. The following day a huge, bright four-pointed star-like object was seen over Gainsborough in Lincolnshire. A Mrs Edith Hart and her husband reported that the object moved slowly towards Middlefield School at 3.42 p.m. A Met Office spokesman said the object must have been a meteor, although Mrs Hart disagreed. At 3.15 p.m. on the same day in the same area, a Mrs Tacey reported a bright light that made no sound. Almost at exactly the same time, but in Yorkshire, a Mr Blenkin, whilst walking with his daughter, claimed he saw a break in the clouds and in this opening could be seen a 'bright incandescent light with a tail on it'.

Around the same time, a green and white light was seen over Westmorland and Cumberland, resulting in a police investigation. *New Scientist* of 24 January 1974 investigated the mystery which was said to have taken place on the evening of 27 December 1973. According to the magazine the moonless night was disturbed at 9.07 p.m. by a 'brilliant fireball' which illuminated the whole of northern Britain. The magazine stated that the phenomena had been reported from as far and wide as the Shetland Islands, Manchester, Dublin and North Wales. Witnesses described seeing an object that had a 'deep green head set in a teardrop shaped coma' and having an orange-red tail.

On 15 January 1974, the *Gainsborough News* reported on a mystery explosion around 5.00 p.m. The local RAF denied any involvement and the police couldn't explain it, although the sound of thunder had been heard earlier that afternoon – whether it was connected no one will ever know. Eight days later, on 23 January, a giant fireball was reported from a village in the Berwyn hills in north-east Wales. A huge explosion was investigated by mountain rescue people, but to no avail. Strange flashes in the sky were also reported, but a Dr Hindley commented that for a meteor to have made that noise it would have to have weighed in the region of 20–30 tons. He said, 'A meteor of that size would have made a fireball so large it would have lit up the whole country and woken up half of Britain.' Two months later at Hurley, Warwickshire, a strange star was observed close to the moon by a couple driving. After stopping at traffic lights the couple noted the object had vanished.

The News of November 1974 reported on a couple of interesting ball lightning incidents. The most intriguing, which took place in August, concerned two climbers clambering to the summit of Bidean-nam-Bfan in Glencoe, Argyllshire. John Graham and Jimmy Alexander stated that the weather was fine when they observed a ball of orange light the size of an orange, which appeared a few feet behind Mr Graham. The ball danced up the ridge in a bouncing motion and at the same time a thunderstorm broke above. Mr Graham seemed to hit the floor with a thump as a crackling noise ensued. Climbers further down the mountain described hideous lightning; it took them over an hour to descend. Four hours later Mr Graham was seen by a doctor. His main wound was a small purple spot on his head, which was circled by a fiery ring.

The following year, someone claimed to have actually seen where ball lightning comes from. A Mr R. George of Exwick Road, Exeter, wrote a letter to the *Daily Mirror* (which appeared on 16 February 1979). Mr George stated that he'd been sitting writing a letter during a severe storm when something came through the window, flashing. The object 'cut across the table, then, about six inches from the table, a golden or yellow ball some five inches round appeared.' The object then vanished as quickly as it had arrived.

However, the main issue with the ball lightning phenomena is actually proving that what you are experiencing is, in fact, ball lightning. Something as yet to be understood by science is simply without label, but one thing is clear: these types of cases refuse to go away.

On 18 March 1979 a strange explosion rocked Marlborough in Wiltshire. Much of the activity centred upon the grounds of Marlborough College where, at 2.00 p.m., students were finishing their lunch when the building shook and window-panes exploded. It was claimed that something unknown had ignited in the sewer and destroyed the ash tree situated over it. College bursar Jack Ashbury commented, 'There was a tremendous flash of lightning which zipped across the River Kennet, right up to the Bath road'. A local man named Keith Lovatt said that whilst walking his dog he'd seen a ball of light 'just like the arc of an electric welder', which rolled over the crowd, missing the witness by inches. Five hours later a huge ball of light was seen over parts of the West Country and Wales. Lifeboats were called out to investigate the incident at Solent (not the first time lifeboats would be called out to investigate mystery lights, see 'Phantom Flares', p.60). One object, described as 'blue-green in colour' fell from the sky, turning orange during its descent.

On 4 April at Caversham in Berkshire a bright red ball of light was seen crashing to the ground by several residents. One witness, of Graveney Drive, commented, 'It was in the distance, behind some trees and was coming down quite slowly. It looked [bright red] like the flames a rocket gives out, but instead of going up it hit the ground.' Another witness saw a flash of light and then ran for cover as all the windows in his house began to shake. Later investigations revealed that the catches of the windows had been sheared off. During the autumn of the same year, two fist-sized balls of orange light spooked two workmen from Hartlepool Borough Council, who had been decorating a house at Brierton Lane on 25 October. The ball of light was described as coming from the sky and fizzing past the arm of witness Terence Kelly before disintegrating. On 16 December the *News of the World* reported that a resident of Guildford, Surrey, named Jim Philpotts was woken up from his nap by a bang, as if a light bulb had exploded. Jim was startled to see a ball of light hovering at the foot of the stairs. The object was approximately 12in across and it faded away after a short time, leaving a 'strong chemical smell'.

AWAY WITH THE FAIRIES?

There is of course the alternative theory regarding ball lightning, which, however far-fetched, simply proves that the mystery is a sum of many complex parts. Earlier we considered fairy lights, as well as objects of fire, that seem to display intelligence. Well, in 1856 at the Vale of Neath, South Wales, a young man named Ronald Rhys was travelling home from the farm he worked at when suddenly he heard a 'whooshing' sound. Staring across the dark field the witness was startled to see

A woodcut depicting ball lightning entering a room and spooking a family.

an eerie light and decided to go and investigate. Ronald stepped inside the light and found himself suddenly floating. According to the legend, he was not seen for seven days. His employer enquired locally but could find no trace of him and assumed Ronald had quit his job. Until seven days later, when Mr Rhys casually strolled back into his job as if nothing had happened. Naturally, he was questioned by his employer who noticed that Ronald's skin had turned a strange bright pink. Finally, Ronald realised that he'd been missing for one whole week and told his employer what had happened. Of course, Ronald's employer thought he'd been at the drink, although Ronald wasn't the type of person to make up strange stories. Ronald vaguely recalled how he entered a surreal dream world where he was being probed by hordes of tiny people that were armed with tiny swords and extracting blood from him. The dream became rather grisly when Ronald explained that one particular being, who was green with a bald head, had cut into his stomach and removed his innards. Ronald claimed that after the experience he woke up in the field. His employer may have scoffed at such a story if it wasn't for the fact that Ronald's hair was falling out rapidly and his body was covered in terrible scars.

Another incredible story comes from the files of Nick Redfern, respected author on UFOs and folklore. In his book *Three Men Seeking Monsters* he tells the tale of Alistair Baxter who, in 1968, investigated the mystery of Scotland's Loch Ness Monster. Equipped with binoculars, notepad and camera he sat loch-side for nine weeks hoping for a glimpse of the elusive beast, but he got far more than he bargained for. During the fifth week Baxter recalled how one night, whilst sleeping in his tent alongside the inky waters, he was awoken by a peculiar humming sound. He was looking for the source of the sound when suddenly a bright light the size of a football came into view and hovered about 15ft above the ground. The object slowly made its way through the trees towards Baxter and then shot off into the night sky where it stopped and hovered over the loch. Baxter, although startled, eventually nodded off again, but at breakfast he was approached by three men dressed in black suits. The men seemed to appear out of nowhere and they questioned him as to whether he'd seen anything strange in the night. Baxter replied that he hadn't and one of the men told Baxter, 'We might return'. The men strolled off into the woods. According to Redfern, Baxter was a credible witness who held a position of responsibility in a mining company. He was terrified by his experience at Loch Ness.

In September 1989 a Kent man actually filmed the elusive phenomenon known as ball lightning. Ray Cahill, a resident of Ashford, was awoken by a terrific thunderstorm and decided to grab his video camera to film the event. As windows rattled and lightning streaked from the sky, Ray shot a few minutes of footage until the storm passed. The next day, Ray watched the video and was astounded to see a fiery red object on the film. This footage was shown on the television show *The Why Files*. On the same programme, presenter Dave Barrett interviewed a Professor Roger Jennison who claimed that many years previous, whilst on a plane, he'd seen a 'beautiful ball of light' glide up the aisle towards the air hostess. Moments later the air hostess rushed to Mr Jennison, collapsed on his lap and with a gasp said, 'Did you see that?'

PHANTOM FLARES

The *Sunday Mirror* of 14 October 1973 reported on the 'Riddle of the ghost SOS flares', after several peculiar lights – thought to be distress flares – had been reported off the Kent coast. The lights had been so frequent that, according to the newspaper, lifeboats, coastguards and inshore rescue craft had been continuously disrupted after investigating the 'phantom flares' which were never proven to have an origin.

A Dungeness lifeboat coxswain named Tom Tart told the newspaper that on two occasions his team had been called out to investigate distress signals and despite the visibility being perfect there was no trace of anyone in distress. Police at the time believed that a gang of smugglers were operating along the shore and possibly sending out flares to distract authorities from their clandestine operations, but this was never proven either.

The article concluded that, 'A Department of Trade and Industry spokesman said, "There have been too many examples of people firing distress flares when they are not in real distress. But some of the recent calls cannot be explained that way. They are a mystery."'

Phantom flares – quite rare, but not a unique occurrence, as Charles Fort recorded in 'False lights of Durham' from 1866. *The News* of April 1975 also

Ray Cahill, who in 1989 filmed ball lightning during a storm at his home in Ashford, Kent. (Photograph by Neil Arnold)

spoke of similar flare-like objects, mentioning that on 21 November 1963 a coal ship named *Thrift* had arrived at Blyth, Northumberland, some eight hours late. According to the crew whilst coming from Aberdeen on 20 November at 6.00 p.m. they had observed a 'pulsating red light' on the port side which hovered around 30ft above sea level. The object then disappeared from view. On 30 April 1974 a lifeboat out of Skegness searched the Lynwell area for five hours after the appearance of a mystery red flare but could find no trace of a boat in distress. A coastguard spokesman believed the RAF had been responsible and been involved in a flash-bombing exercise.

During July 1974 another search took place on the Norfolk coast, and combined the resources of the Gorleston lifeboat at sea and coastguards and police ashore, but was abandoned after two hours. Brian Coleman, a coastguard, reported he'd seen red flares to the north – which were confirmed by other witnesses. When nothing turned up it was believed to be a hoax. Five days later, a white 'flare' was observed off Souter Point lighthouse, at Marsden, Northumberland. Lifeboats investigated the area for over two hours until the search was called off.

There was also mention of mystery flares from Anglesey in January 1975, whilst yellow flares were seen on the Welsh coast in the vicinity of Llantwit Major. In the same issue of *The News*, under the heading of 'Fireballs Or Whatever They Are', the editors mention another peculiar case – sent to them by roving reporter Steve Moore – who found that on 5 November 1938, residents of central and north-west London observed a 'very bright object which moved from south-east to north-west'. The fiery object, which had a red, drop-shaped head and a greenish tail, zipped through the sky unlike any firework and was said to have been six times the size of the moon! As the object reached the skies over Hampstead it fizzled out – more like a firework!

It is also mentioned in the *Express & Star* of 24 June 1974 that from Shifnal, Shropshire, a 'mysterious glowing object' was sighted independently by two waiters employed at the Park House Hotel. At Merioneth, in North Wales, sixty-four-year-old George Longworth reported seeing a 'blinding sun', which flashed over his vehicle leaving a trail of 'eerie grey powder' in its wake. George, who was accompanied by his wife, cousin and granddaughter, also reported seeing an antenna on the object. Dr Patrick Willmore, of the Global Seismology Unit in Edinburgh, commented that 'the description could fit that of a fireball, which is a floating, bright, electrical object – but the odd thing is the grey powder which fell from it'. Strangely, Dr Willmore failed to mention the antenna.

By this point one can see how it can be difficult to decipher between 'genuine' ball lightning (not that anyone can explain this particular phenomenon), 'phantom flares' and what we deem UFOs. On 28 December 1974 the *Western Mail* from Cardiff reported 'mystery flares' at Dyfed in Wales, where in the past a lot of UFO activity has been observed. On this occasion a Cyril Hughes reported to police he'd seen a 'ball of red fire which also gave off a red glow' that fell from the sky towards the river. Mr Hughes was brave enough to drive to the area to search for the object, but in the darkness could find no trace. Several other witnesses came forward to report a similar object in the surrounding area.

PORTENTS OF DEATH

The News of April 1975 reported on an investigation into mysterious marsh lights, stating that in 1967 £5,000 of recording equipment was being taken to a remote part of south-west Ireland in order for a team of experts, led by physicist Dr Wilfred Forbes to investigate 'one of the strangest, most inexplicable mysteries of all time', known to the locals as 'The Lights of Crusheen'.

The lights, according to Forbes, were said to be 'uncanny flames in the sky' and said to centre upon the small island of Inchicronan. The lights, in certain conditions are said to float ashore during times of disaster and death. According to *The News*, 'Twin flames, that have been seen "for centuries", are said to bob along about 6ft from the ground as though being carried by invisible torchbearers.'

During his investigations Dr Forbes has, according to the article, interviewed over twenty people and mentions 'hundreds of reliable witnesses' with photographs even having been taken of the forms.

The lights have become the stuff of folklore and appear like enormous 'candle flames' said to hover atmospherically over the murky lake and misty marsh, and then at times of disaster, move along a rocky ridge (which is completely submerged in winter) connecting the island (which is barren, occupied only by the ruins of Inchicronan Abbey, and Crusheen cemetery); then they follow the road into Crusheen, and are said to loiter near or inside any household in which a death or disaster is said to occur. Although sceptics argue these marsh lights are merely the result of atmospheric phenomena, the local priest also adds potency to the legend by professing to believe the tales.

A peculiar incident pertaining to eerie lights and impending disaster was also recorded in *A Description of Caernavonshire* (1809–1811) by Edmund Hyde-Hall, who wrote:

In the winter of 1694, we are told by Penant (Thomas Penant's *A Tour In Wales*) an extraordinary phenomenon was exhibited to the neighbourhood. A mephitis, or pestilential vapour resembling a pale blue flame, arose out of a marshy tract called Morfa Bychan, and traversing the channel, here 8 miles wide, rested upon Harlech and its environs. Sixteen rocks of hay and two large barns were consumed by its action, and the village was so poisoned that the cattle and sheep browsing upon it perished in great numbers. The season of motion with it was night time, and for a second summer it reappeared, but less frequently and with diminished strength. The most curious facts attending it were perhaps the facility with which it was dispelled by any noise, and the impunity with which it could be traversed by human beings. Its cause is attributed, with what correctness I give no opinion, to a fall of locusts near Aberdaron, by the corruption of which the vapour is supposed to have been engendered.

FLYING JELLYFISH!

UFOs, if we go by the thousands of reports made across the world, clearly vary in size. Even the most drunken witnesses couldn't make up some of the bizarre objects seen in the skies of the world, so how on earth genuine and sober witnesses manage to see so many varying shapes of craft remains a mystery. Even so, the *Bournemouth Evening Echo* of 22 October 1969 reported that an Alastair Mackenzie, manager at the Suncliff Hotel, was having a coffee with his wife and daughter when they noticed something fluttering in the sky. Taking to the veranda, the family stood agog as a strange, jellyfish-type object, just measuring 5in across with a slight glow, floated by. The object was only in view a few seconds and drifted out towards the sea and gathered pace, all the while remaining about 30ft in the air.

On 14 January 2009 *Your Local Guardian* ran the weird headline 'Pink jellyfish in sky sparks UFO speculation in Merton', after a Wimbledon resident reported that they'd been looking out of their window in the direction of Merton Way when a large 'bright pink jellyfish' object appeared. The manifestation was surrounded by a pinky haze and it hovered close to some pylons in the distance for a few minutes but by the time the witness scrambled to his camera the object had vanished.

The *Kent Today* of 4 April 1999 ran a strange story about a motorist who reported to police that a jellyfish-type object in the sky had seemingly pursued her as she travelled along the M2 with her husband. The mysterious flying 'thing', which she described as being lit from beneath, hovered over her car for some 15 miles until they reached their Gravesend home and then ran inside to report their encounter to police. The witnesses told police that the 'UFO' disappeared within the vicinity of Blue Bell Hill but enquiries by the officers, including PC Dave Wisdom, drew a blank. The most likely explanation for the object is that it was laser lights projected from a local nightclub

On 14 April the *Gazette & Times* reported that two couples returning from the coast on Good Friday had observed an object they described as 'like the bottom of a jellyfish', which circled close to their vehicle as they neared the turn-off at Faversham. The story ran for a couple of weeks despite the fact that a nightclub in Maidstone had put on a laser show, which when reflected off the clouds looked like a set of swirling lights. Whether this fully explained the mystery we'll never know, but on 28 April the same newspaper reported that a Mr and Mrs Brown from Wormshill were settling down for the night when Mrs Brown noticed something odd in the sky. She called her husband and he went outside to get a better look at the object. He told the newspaper, 'It was a clear night and there was nothing in the sky to suggest where the lights were coming from. It rotated from left to right in a three-quarter circular motion. It was there from 9.30 p.m. and it was still there when we went to bed at 10.30 p.m.' The following day Mr Brown asked friends and neighbours if they'd seen the strange object, but his investigations drew a blank.

In UFO lore there is an obscure theory put forward to explain some of the more unusual forms of unidentified flying objects. Could such jellyfish-type entities and the like be unknown creatures? This observation may appear even more far-fetched than the possibility of extra-terrestrial beings invading the planet in their saucers, but when you consider the vast vacuum of space, and how unexplored the regions of the cosmos are, the possibilities are endless. As will be explored in Chapter 6, 'Monsters from the Sky', there have been an overwhelming number of reports – as there are for ball lightning, phantom airships, etc. – to suggest that the sky is haunted by all types of anomalous phenomena. Many authors for over a century have commentated on reports of weird luminous lights, flying feathery objects and the like, but not until the 1940s were such forms perceived as alien craft.

In the December issue of *Fate* magazine, a chap named Bessor, in an article entitled 'Are the Saucers Space Animals?' stated that UFOs could be 'a form of space animal, or creature, of a highly attenuated substance, capable of materialization and dematerialisation, whose propellant is a form of telekinetic energy.'

Many researchers have looked at this theory and believe such forms, often invisible to the naked eye, can change shape and even colour, akin to a cosmic chameleon.

This may seem the stuff of science fiction, but when one considers the vast variety of species in the greatest oceans of the world, and how little we have explored the watery realm, the definition of space takes on a whole new, almost terrifying meaning because we do not know what type of life exists 'out there'. To cast a sceptical eye and scoff at the limitless arena we call the universe would be insane, and perhaps more so than accepting the possibility that every now and then we mere mortals do in fact have eerie encounters with flying jellyfish and the like. Without jumping to conclusions that we are seeing and experiencing manifestations from the outer edges of heaven, or claiming that pilots must be observing demons from some wicked otherwordly plateau, it could still be that some of these encounters involve forms of life as yet unknown to science.

For added atmosphere, and as an apt way to end this chapter, you might delve into Sir Arthur Conan's Doyle's fantastic fictional work *The Horror From The Heights* in which a monoplane pilot named Joyce-Armstrong encounters an incredible sky form of sorts. The monster of the skies is described by the pilot as like a jellyfish, 'bell-shaped and of enormous size – far larger, I should judge, than the dome of St Paul's'.

With the 'gorgeous vision' passing gently over his head, the pilot marvels at its grace and fragility and then finds himself among a fleet of similar sky forms, some large, some very small, drifting on the breeze, all displaying a pinkish hue. Whilst such wonders may never cease in fiction, what are we to make of similar albeit apparently factual accounts experienced by pilots and others over the years? Some 'thing' is up there, but of which plateau or planet does it belong?

4

PILOT ENCOUNTERS WITH UFOS

Kenneth Arnold's 1947 sighting over Washington, although bizarre, seemed a one-off at the time; no one realised quite how frequent such encounters between pilots and unidentified flying objects would become. Although the pilots of the Second World War reported seeing strange lights in close proximity of their planes, once the occasional report surfaced of pilots possibly being buzzed by such mysterious craft it was clear that something very weird was going on. When strange events across the world take place, civilian witnesses in general are disbelieved, but when so-called 'credible witnesses' come forward to speak of their encounters it sheds a whole new light on a mystery. Police officers, government officials and the like are deemed credible witnesses, although in my view anyone can be credible and anyone can be crooked. Even so, in the world of the UFO situation the pilot is considered to be a very reliable witness.

The January/February 1995 issue of *UFO Magazine* also looked at how pilots' accounts are considered to be very trustworthy, stating, '...military and civilian pilots have provided extraordinary accounts of UFO activity over the last fifty years from throughout the globe.'

The magazine also states that whilst sceptics are quick to dismiss reports of UFOs from general members of the public, when it comes to pilots 'it beggars belief to argue that in every instance, the pilot in question made a mistake, and that a perfectly logical and conventional explanation can account for the experience...'

SKY PHANTOMS OF THE 1950S

I have lived in Kent – the 'Garden of England' – all my life and became interested in stories of pilots and their alleged encounters with strange aerial objects when I read of a story from the early 1950s concerning a flight lieutenant named Terry

Johnson. On 3 November 1953 Johnson, accompanied by Flying Officer Geoffrey Smythe, was flying over the West Malling area of the county. They were seated in a Vampire night fighter as part of a reconnaissance mission. At 30,000ft, whilst flying in a northerly direction, Johnson observed a bright, circular object which did not appear on the radar of his compatriot. The peculiar incident, which only lasted for thirty seconds at 10.00 a.m., puzzled the pilots a great deal. They were unsure if they should report the incident in case of ridicule, but were quite surprised at how seriously the matter was treated, especially when they were questioned by Squadron Commander Furze who then took the details and gave them to the station commander, Group Captain Hamley. Even more bizarre for Johnson and Smythe was the fact that Commander Furze said he too had seen a strange unidentified object whilst on a bombing mission over Berlin during the Second World War.

Mr Johnson, interviewed by the *Kent Messenger* in regards to his UFO encounter, stated, 'We were called up to the Air Ministry to give a full report of the incident to the Duke of Edinburgh's equerry. We were told that Prince Philip was interested in flying saucers.' Details of Johnson and Smythe's encounter were released to the press forty-eight hours later. At the time there appeared to be no Official Secrets Act on 'flying saucers', but all that was soon to change when UFOs became household names and the thorough investigations of the government and Ministry of Defence began.

Although the Johnson/Smythe incident was released to the media, and also backed up by another sighting, shortly afterwards the Air Ministry came forward with a differing statement, which claimed that what Johnson and Smythe had seen was in fact a meteorological balloon. There were two main issues with this change of comment from the officials:

1) They had made the two pilots seem rather foolish by stating that the object was nothing more than a balloon, even though such pilots were trained to be able to observe and identify different aerial objects.
2) When authorities change their statements regarding such phenomena, it often makes the subject seem even more suspicious!

On 24 November the Johnson/Smythe sighting became a debate in the House of Commons.

On 21 October 1957 at 9.18 p.m. Flying Officer D.W. Sweeney, who was flying a Meteor jet from RAF North Luffenham, was said to have had an encounter with a UFO over RAF Gaydon, which is situated in Warwickshire. At an altitude of 28,000ft Sweeney had to take evasive action to avoid the object. Sweeney then approached the object but, suddenly, it disappeared. The incident was tracked on radar and confirmed by RAF Langtoft. On 1 May of the same year the *Western Mail* reported, 'Flying Object Baffles R.A.F.' after an unidentified object appeared on radar as it made its way west along the English Channel. Two supersonic Javelin fighter aircraft were sent out by the RAF, but to no avail. The object was last seen over Dungeness in Kent.

In 1959 the Air Ministry recorded an unidentified flying object from over London Airport. The object was seen by four 'reliable' witnesses and remained in the area for more than twenty minutes. Although an air-traffic control officer observed the object through binoculars, it did not appear on the radar. In the March 1997 issue of *Encounters* magazine, a B.A. McCann submitted a UFO incident pertaining to 1954 in the skies above the North Sea, involving a pilot of a Meteor who when at an altitude of 40,000ft had a weird encounter with several unknown objects. Oddly, the radar team at Bawdsey in Essex had failed to pick up the objects, described as being whitish-yellow in colour but according to the pilot the formation of lights were straight in front of him at close proximity of about 10 miles. With the Meteor powered to intercept the foreign objects, the control tower still could not confirm any other presence in the air, and yet this formation was clearly showing on the airborne radar. McCann added, 'The night fighter had been 50 miles east of Lowestoft flying north at the start of the inter-

There are numerous cases on record of pilots observing UFOs. (Illustration by Simon Wyatt)

ception', but the plane was lacking fuel and was going in the wrong direction from its base at West Malling in Kent. However, the crew of the plane were fully aware that there was a base in Norfolk, at Coltishall, should they run into any fuel problems.

The crew continued their hot pursuit of the five lights but when they got to within half a mile something extraordinary occurred. The lights began to blip out – one by one, as if they'd been bulbs in the night sky switched off by an unseen hand. The night fighter crew streaked straight through the area the lights had been but there was nothing, only the inky blackness of the night sky. With their search proving fruitless the crew turned back and the next day they prepared their reports for the Air Ministry, yet rather oddly they never received any sort of feedback regarding what had happened in the air.

Three years later, during May 1957, a pilot named Milton Torres was ordered to shoot down an unidentified object that was reported as travelling at speeds of more than 7,600mph! From the Royal Air Force base at Manston in Kent, Torres took to his F-86 D Sabre jet after an object was seen hanging motionless in the sky and then reported as moving erratically. The report of the incident didn't emerge until decades later when top secret files were released by the UK government. Torres claimed: 'I was ordered to open fire even before I had taken off. That had never happened before. I was only a lieutenant and very much aware of the gravity of the situation. The order came to fire a salvo of rockets at the UFO. The authentication was valid and I selected 24 rockets.' With lock on, Torres prepared to fire when suddenly the object completely disappeared from radar. The following day Torres was questioned by a gentleman who he had never seen before and who didn't identify himself. Although at the time there was tension between the West and the Soviet Union, a UFO expert commented that maybe the UFO had been a 'phantom aircraft' created on Torres' radar as a secret project to test Soviet air defences. This brings to mind the 'phantom airship' panic of an earlier chapter.

In 1958, one year after the Torres incident, a Mr Todd reported he was doing his National Service with the RAF as a radar operator in a quiet area of the UK. One morning, at 4.00 a.m., Mr Todd and his colleagues were relaxing in their headquarters when his attention was caught by a particular 'echo' coming from the Derbyshire region. 'I aimed the height equipment at this echo and to my amazement, discovered it was flying at around 60,000 feet! No ordinary aircraft would travel at this altitude yet it was moving in a way that suggested aggressive or hostile action.'

Mr Todd recalled that he watched the object for some thirty or so minutes but when it descended to a height of approximately 20,000ft it halted. The craft was below the altitude for terrestrial aircraft and yet it made no attempt to sneak under the radar.

Gradually, the object began to rise again; 40, 50, 60, 70, 80 and then to 90,000ft, or as Mr Todd gasped: 'Seventeen miles above the earth!' The object eventually went off the radar. Mr Todd, after finishing his shift, asked the NCO in charge what he thought the object was. He refused to comment on the matter but didn't question Mr Todd's observational skills.

During the middle of August 1956 at Lakenheath, near Cambridge, RAF and USAF personnel witnessed a series of strange objects on their radar. On 13 August at 9.30 p.m. radar at Bentwaters station picked up strange phenomena. First was an object travelling at a speed between 4,000mph and 9,000mph! The object was on the radar for around thirty seconds. A few minutes later, three more objects were picked up on radar travelling in a triangular formation at 1,000ft. Suddenly, twelve more objects began following the front three at a speed of approximately 125mph. One of the objects was estimated to be bigger than a bomber. It hovered in the air then suddenly vanished. A T-33 fighter was asked by the RAF to check on the object but no contact was made. At 10.00 p.m. the radar picked up another fast-moving object and personnel on the ground also saw a peculiar light. This was confirmed by a C-47 aircraft, which picked up the object below it.

Staff at Bentwaters made contact with Lakenheath Airfield, who reported a visual sighting of the strange object, and further into the night more ground personnel reported seeing two white objects merge into one and then completely vanish. The written report from the airport described an object moving at 'terrific speeds and then stopping and changing course immediately'. At 12.00 p.m. an RAF Venom jet equipped with a nose radar took to the sky from RAF Waterbeach and the radar picked up three objects. The pilot of the plane was directed to intercept but lost the object in a brief chase. Staff at Lakenheath then spotted another object and the Venom jet attempted to intercept this one but, bizarrely, the unidentified object turned on the tail of the jet and reversed roles, and chased the jet. The pilot in the jet returned to base to refuel and was then aided by another Venom jet, but this plane had to return to base due to an engine fault.

CLOSE CONTACT

At 9.00 a.m. on the morning of 11 January 1973, a building surveyor named Peter Day filmed a strange light moving across the treetops of a wooded area on the Oxfordshire/Buckinghamshire border. Forty minutes later a US Air Force jet crashed to the ground; the pilot thankfully survived by ejecting. No connection was made at the time between the light and the crash of the plane.

In December 1980 one of ufology's 'greatest hits' took place in the Rendlesham Forest area of Suffolk. Much has been written of this case in books and magazines, making it one of the strangest yet most well-known cases of an alleged UFO involving military personnel. At the time, RAF Woodbridge was being used by the US Air Force and several of the staff employed at the base witnessed something so spectacular that it is still causing debate over thirty years later, and will continue to do so in the future. Interestingly, RAF Bentwaters (already mentioned) sits just north of the heavily forested area.

The incident was sparked off when guards noticed mysterious lights descending into the thick forest at 3.00 a.m. on 26 December. Servicemen thought the lights belonged to a downed airplane – this was never found – and later one of the personnel stated that what he'd observed was of unknown origin. Over the course of the next few days all manner of high strangeness would occur in the vicinity of the forest and the airbase as the area was scrutinised. Many witnesses, including Fred A. Buran, Airman Edward N. Cabansag, Master-Sergeant J.D. Chandler and Jim Penniston (all of the 81st Security Police Squadron) and Airman First Class John Burroughs (of 81st LE), all gave witness reports of what they experienced. Orford lighthouse sits a few miles away and sceptics argued that what the servicemen had seen was this light. This was dismissed by the witnesses, especially as the following day they had discovered strange burn marks on the ground and impressions in the soil, which suggested some type of object had sat there.

When a case involves several military personnel, one has to wonder just what type of object was observed during the early hours of 26 December 1980. If it wasn't a UFO then what type of covert operation was taking place, and one that several officers clearly knew nothing about?

On 13 January 1981 Lieutenant Colonel Charles I. Halt – deputy base commander at the time – submitted a memo to the Ministry of Defence. In it he wrote, 'I believe the objects that I saw at close quarter were extraterrestrial in origin and that the security services of both the United States and the United Kingdom have attempted – both then and now – to subvert the significance of what occurred at Rendlesham Forest and RAF Bentwaters by the use of well-practised methods of disinformation.' This memo caused quite a stir and over the years the case and some

Rendlesham Forest in Suffolk. In 1980 strange lights were reported in the skies by credible witnesses, such as military personnel. (Courtesy of Nick Redfern)

of the witness statements have come under a degree of criticism, but one thing is beyond doubt – the Suffolk police of that night did receive a report from the desk of RAF Woodbridge, which stated that an object, possibly a UFO, was being investigated.

This case, over the years, has caused a lot of controversy and limited space does not enable a thorough look at the case, but it is recommended that for further details those interested should read *Left At East Gate* by Larry Warren and Peter Robbins, or any number of well-sourced UFO literature by respected authors such as Timothy Good and Jenny Randles.

During the October of 1985 a strange aerial object reportedly buzzed Newcastle Airport. The witnesses, an air traffic controller (who should of course be used to identifying different aerial objects) and his assistant observed two objects above the airfield: one was described as being quite bright, the other more dull in intensity. This sighting was confirmed by a separate witness who was outside the airport. Two years later it was reported that a customs officer at the airport observed a golden-orange, cigar-shaped craft. During the same year another witness reported seeing an object of blue and amber lights which they watched for almost twenty minutes. Researcher Gordon Rutter mentioned that after several sightings within the vicinity of the airport, RAF Boulmer were contacted. The squadron leader commented in a letter that they were 'unable to confirm or deny' the reports, which is a rather bizarre statement which initially arouses suspicion. During October 2000 there were more sightings over Newcastle. One involved an object that seemed to be on course to hit a plane that was due to land at the airport. A witness, Mr Atwill, was so concerned about what he'd seen that he contacted the airport.

Another alleged UFO and terrestrial craft collision was reported in *Alien Encounters* magazine, Issue 18, November 1997. A reader submitted a report that on 28 June 1995 at approximately 10.00 p.m., in the region of St Michael's Abbey, Farnborough, in the county of Surrey, a brilliant yellow object had been observed in the clear night sky. According to the witness, '...the craft was easily visible as it hung for some twenty seconds' and when it began to dim two small white lights could be seen flanking the craft. The witness was then shocked to see the object vanish into thin air and four or so minutes later a large military helicopter began sweeping the sky. The chopper scanned over the Surrey Heath area and headed off towards the Ministry of Defence land. By this point the witness was watching with some excitement through binoculars when the unidentified object suddenly reappeared right in front of the helicopter. '...there seemed to be only a few feet between them', the witness added, until the object veered off towards some trees and the helicopter headed over Maultway. The sighting experienced by the witness was confirmed later that year by an ex-RAF man who, in conversation with the witness stated that he'd also seen the UFO, the same summer, whilst he'd been relaxing in his back garden. According to the RAF man the object made no noise and after half a minute vanished. And in the words of the RAF man, '...(it) was definitely not a plane or any other man-made object.'

In the same section of the magazine a reader named Frank Berry of South Yorkshire wrote of a weird incident, which took place at Harlyn Bay, Cornwall, during early 1997 whilst he and his family were on holiday. At 11.45 p.m. one evening he, his brother and father were fishing from the beach of the bay when they observed a bright orange light hovering approximately 200ft above the cliffs. The object, although appearing quite still, seemed to have a trail of smoke emitting from it. The following morning the family saw smoke billowing up from the area where the UFO had been seen and military helicopters and military powerboats swarmed around the area. Had some type of space craft crashed in Cornwall, or was this a secret military exercise gone wrong?

In 1990 a diamond-shaped object was not only investigated by officials at the Ministry of Defence, but the UFO was photographed as it neared an RAF jet. The incident took place over Pitlochry, Perthshire in Scotland. The event was one of over 1,000 noted and released more than a decade later by the Ministry of Defence. According to the BBC website, the unusual craft in the photo could not be identified by military experts. In the same year six RAF Tornado jets flying over Germany reported encounters with a strange craft.

THE SCHAFFNER MYSTERY

Another file, released in relation to the mysterious death of a US Air Force pilot over the North Sea on 8 September 1970, stated that Captain William Schaffner had misjudged his height as he was practising shadowing low-flying targets at night. This dismissal came after it was suggested by some UFO researchers and the media that Schaffner's last recorded radio message was to report seeing a conical object that was followed by another craft that resembled a glass football. In Issue 5, Vol. 11 of *UFO Magazine*, UFO investigator and former police sergeant Tony Dodd wrote an in-depth article on the Schaffner mystery under the title of 'The Fatal Flight of Foxtrot 94', in which he stated that a British radar station, Saxa Vord, which was used to scan the skies over the North Sea, a time when, '... the cold war was at its height with Russian aircraft making regular flights into the North Atlantic to test reaction from NATO fighters'.

According to Dodd's research, at 8.17 p.m. a radar operator had made contact with an unknown craft that was travelling over the North Sea somewhere between the Shetlands and Norway. The radar controller monitored the object for a few minutes as it travelled at a height of 37,000ft on a south-westerly direction. The object was recorded as travelling at a speed of 630mph. The object then altered direction, turning 30 degrees to head south, its altitude ascending to 44,000ft and its speed to 900mph. Two Lightning Interceptors searched the skies over the North Sea for the object but suddenly its speed was recorded as 17,400mph which completely stunned those monitoring from the radar tower. The fact that this high-speed object had infiltrated the air space had been a huge concern for NATO commanders and so more fighters were scrambled, this time from a base at Keflavik in Iceland.

The object was behaving like no known terrestrial craft, and each time a fighter jet drew close to it, it somehow managed to blink off from the radar, only to then reappear in a different area. At 9.45 p.m. Captain William Schaffner took to the sky, with Dodd adding that, '...four Lightnings, two Phantoms and three tankers were already airborne and they were joined by a Shackleton from Kinloss...'

The mysterious events that were about to unravel over the North Sea would eventually be broken by the *Grimsby Evening Telegraph* who featured the alleged original transcript between Schaffner and the controllers at Staxton Wold who had latched on to the object as it travelled 90 miles east of Whitby.

The *Grimsby Evening Telegraph*, after the event, recorded the series of bizarre events which Captian Schaffner was to become involved with. According to the newspaper Schaffner had reported to the control tower that he had visual contact with the object but when asked to describe it responded, '...nothing recognisable, no clear outlines. There is bluish light. Hell that's bright...very bright.'

Schaffner confirmed that all instruments within his plane were functioning and that he was coming alongside it. At this point, with the object was around 600ft away. Schaffner commented, 'It's a conical shape, jeeze that's bright, it hurts my eyes to look at it for more than a few seconds.'

Schaffner moved closer to the mysterious object, getting to within 400ft when he told the base that there was another object close by, something resembling 'a huge soccer ball', but constructed of what appeared to be glass.

The object then began to descend, and Schaffner dropped his plane, confirming that the glass-like object was still within the vicinity but then something bizarre happened.

'There's a haze of light. Ye'ow... it's within that haze. Wait a second, it's turning...coming straight for me... s**t... am taking evasive action... a few... I can hardly...', it was then that the radar tower lost contact with Foxtrot 94. From here Dodd records that, according to the radar controller, the two mysterious objects merged in to one. The object then became stationary 6,000ft above the North Sea and then sped towards Staxton at a rate of 900mph. A few moments later Staxton were back in touch with Schaffner.

Schaffner: 'GCI...are you receiving? Over.'

Staxton: 'Affirmative 94, loud and clear. What is your condition?'

Schaffner responded that he was feeling dizzy and that his instruments were malfunctioning. Staxton ordered Schaffner to then turn 043 degrees and to descend to 3,500ft, and Schaffner acted in accordance.

When Schaffner seemed to regain his senses the radar controller enquired as to how the fuel levels were looking to which the groggy pilot replied, 'About 30 per cent GCI'.

It was then that the controller asked Schaffner exactly what had happened. Schaffner responded, 'I don't know, it came in close... I shut my eyes... I figure I must have blacked out for a few seconds.'

Shortly afterwards a Shackleton took to the air over Flamborough and circled Schaffner's plane. At that point Schaffner asked the station, 'Can you bring me in GCI?' but the response from the controller seemed a little strange.

'Er... hold station, 94. Over... Foxtrot 94 can you ditch the aircraft? Over.'

This question perplexed Schaffner who reported that the plane was now handling fine and he was ready to land, but again the controller at Staxton asked if the aircraft could be ditched.

Schaffner seemed hesitant, 'Yeah… I guess', he stated, and at that point the Shackleton was contacted and told by the station that Schaffner was to abort the plane.

At this point the mystery deepened. For between six and seven minutes all contact was lost with Captain Schaffner.

The next words from the Shackleton pilot were unnerving, 'He's down GCI. Hell of a splash… he's down in one piece though. Over.'

The Shackleton circled the area, scanning the black waters but there was no sign of the plane or pilot. Then, a few minutes later the Shackleton pilot recorded that 'The canopy's up…can't see the pilot, we need a chopper out here GCI.'

With no sign of Schaffner, there was increasing concern that he may be down in the icy waters freezing to death. No flares or other distress signals had been sent out. At Staxton the controller continually asked the Shackleton pilot if there was any sign of the pilot. Each time the answer was 'negative' but, rather oddly, the canopy of the plane had now been reported as being shut.

Staxton Wold sent up a Whirlwind chopper from Leconfield, but again, there was no trace of Captain Schaffner.

Despite a two-day search of the area Captain Schaffner was never found. According to Dodd, a few weeks later the *Evening Telegraph* reported that 'the fuselage of the aircraft had been located on the sea-bed' but the ejector seat was still in the aircraft and so investigators believed that the body of the captain must have remained in the cockpit.

On 7 October the divers from HMS Kedleston investigated the wreckage on the seabed and stated that Captain Schaffner's body was still in the cockpit. However, when Foxtrot 94 was wrenched to the surface and sent to Binbrook, there was no sign of Schaffner. The whole operation seemed to have been carried out with a degree of secrecy. Even more bizarre was the fact that when the interior of the plane was checked over, several of the instruments, normally found in the cockpit, were completely missing and there was a strange, unpleasant smell. According to Dodd, 'The ejector seat also seemed to be "wrong", there was a suspicion that it was not the original one fitted to the aircraft…'

Another bizarre aspect was the fact that whilst Schaffner stated that his aircraft was handling fine, he was still told to ditch it. When Dodd contacted the Ministry of Defence regarding the incident he was told that it had simply been an unfortunate accident and did not involve any type of unidentified flying object. Strangely, other witnesses came forward to speak of strange lights in the sky at the time. However, two fellow pilots begged to differ.

Lightning pilots Mike Screten and Furz Lloyd were flying on the night of the incident. According, once again, to Dodd's article, Screten stated on the night of the loss of the Foxtrot – being 8 September 1970 – he'd been up in the air with 23 Squadron based at Leuchars. He commented, 'I remember the initial report of the loss of the aircraft well; at that stage I only knew that the pilot was missing and I knew that Binbrook was undergoing its annual Tactical Evaluation.'

Screten added that on the night '…the pilot had been shadowing an airborne early warning Shackleton from 8 Squadron based at Lossiemouth.'

A crew member reported that he had last seen the navigation lights of the Lightning passing to the rear and below his aircraft. When Schaffner failed to respond to any radio transmissions from ground control and an airborne bomber a search was initiated but when no trace of Schaffner or his plane were found the search was abandoned until the next morning. No wreckage or other signs were discovered during the next morning's search but two months later a mine sweeper employed by the Royal Navy detected the missing aircraft – which was virtually intact – sitting on the seabed. The oddest detail about the crashed plane was the fact that the canopy was still attached to the plane and the seat dinghy and ejector straps still in place. However, Schaffner's body could not be located anywhere. Screten was quick to dismiss any element of mystery, commenting that from his own experience Schaffner had possibly become disorientated during his night flight and been confused by seeing stars and lights from fishing boats in the North Sea. One would argue of course that if pilots are prone to such misinterpretations on a regular basis then surely they should not be flying?

The explanation for the missing body was that the plane had possibly hit the water at a certain angle and at slow speed, avoiding breaking up. Furz Lloyd commented that, 'Evidence from the wreckage suggested that he (Schaffner) unstrapped and stepped over the side.'

Was it possible an experienced pilot such as Schaffner had simply died somewhere in the cold blackness of the North Sea, even though, as Dodd stated, 'It does not make sense that a pilot would abandon his main life-saving equipment, knowing that immersion in the cold North Sea would drastically reduce his chances of survival.'

According to Dodd the story was a mess, nothing added up. More than fifteen years later a reporter named Pat Otter attempted to look into the case but drew a complete blank, mainly due to the fact that his normally helpful contacts at the Ministry of Defence seemed hesitant to assist in any way. Otter turned to Bob Bryant, a Northcliffe Newspapers Aviation correspondent who, over the years, had built up several contacts in the RAF and USAF, but again, the investigation drew a blank. Why on earth did a seemingly routine case involving a possible 'ditching incident' seem to be taking on a sinister tone?

Otter, when speaking to Dodd, stated that, 'A man who came forward to the *Evening Telegraph* told us he had been a member of the crash investigation team who had gone to Binbrook to inspect the recovered aircraft.'

However, even this team of investigators were treated rather oddly by those seemingly in the know of what had actually happened on that dark night in the North Sea. Why the cover up?

Furz Lloyd commented, 'Evidence from the wreckage suggested that he unstrapped and stepped over the side.' The freezing night-time North Sea would have presented an environment in which it was impossible to survive, especially with no life raft. 'This accident was a unfortunate error of judgement which cost an American pilot his life – not some stranger than fiction tale.'

Wreckage of Captain Schaffner's plane. (Photograph courtesy of *Grimsby Evening Telegraph*)

Judging by the fact that several unusual craft had been observed in the sky at the exact time of the incident, it seems that Captain Schaffner had indeed experienced a close encounter with a UFO. The eagerness of the crash investigators and Ministry of Defence to hush-up the incident raises even more suspicions. Some claim that the only anomalous phenomena that night were atmospherics. Whatever the case, if Schaffner's words were in any way close to those mentioned in the *Evening Telegraph* it seems highly unlikely that an experienced American pilot succumbed on the night of 8 September 1970 to natural phenomena.

Even more bizarre was the fact that Schaffner's encounter was not unique. On 7 January 1948 Captain Thomas F. Mantell, an experienced twenty-five-year-old Kentucky Air National Guard pilot, died when he allegedly flew in pursuit of a UFO over Kentucky, in the United States. Whatever the cause of Mantell and Schaffner's deaths, these two incidents have embedded themselves into UFO lore.

MORE ENCOUNTERS

On 21 April 1991 Alitalia flight AZ284, captained by a Mr Zaghetti, was flying from Milan, Italy, to Heathrow Airport when a missile-like object zoomed overhead some 1,000ft away. Zaghetti and his cockpit crew saw the object for around four seconds and estimated that it was around 3m in length, was light brown in colour, displayed no exhaust flame and headed straight for their aircraft before shooting upward. Three months later, *UFO Magazine* reported that the head of Civil Aviation Authority's Safety Data and Analysis Unit, a Mr B.H. Dale, had declared that despite several investigations into the matter it had not been possible to identify the object after the theory that it was a missile had been ruled out. Also, according to the Ministry of Defence at the time, there had been no reports of any space activity which may have explained the sighting of the object and there was no possibility that it had been a meteorological balloon, and so the investigation was closed and the object listed as a UFO – Unidentified Flying Object.

Was this object some type of military missile, which had accidentally been released to shoot down flight AZ284? If so, why was this event covered up, and with a UFO of all things. Or maybe, just maybe, Captain Zaghetti and crew had seen an alien craft, but if so, it seemed rather strange that such an event was admitted to as the UFO enigma and the politics within are riddled with tales of alleged conspiracy and cover up. However, when a pilot and crew comes forward to openly state that they've had an unexplainable encounter, there appears to be no way for the authorities to hush the experience up.

Pilot encounters with UFOs happen frequently, and there are also those passengers who come forward to report their sightings, too. In 1998 a Mrs Susan Clarke of Bradford, West Yorkshire, was returning from her summer holiday from Cyprus when she caught sight of a strange object close to the Airtours jet. Considering this was Mrs Clarke's first ever flight, on which she was accompanied by her husband, this would have been a rather unnerving sight.

The couple were sat by a left-hand side window, which gave them an amazing view of the moonless sky. Mrs Clarke was alerted by a flash in the sky. She thought to herself that perhaps it had been caused by strobe lights on the wing but when she looked down at the clouds 'it appeared as though someone was shining a very bright light, illuminating the underside of the clouds.'

Susan Clarke described seeing an object the size of a golf ball, if held at arm's length. 'I turned to my husband to tell him, but he wasn't in his seat. So I continued to look out of the cabin window at this soft light illuminating the clouds, when suddenly the light went out, just as though someone had turned it off.' When Susan's husband returned she quickly told him about the strange object she had witnessed but he had already seen it and in fact it seemed most of the passengers and crew were aware of the light. Oddly, what Mrs Clarke's husband and the crew had seen did not match her description. Of course, sceptics found it easy to argue that the light must have been some type of trick of the light or reflection.

Pilots, however, are not prone to such misidentification. In January 1995 a close encounter between a Boeing 737 and an unidentified craft was reported by the pilot of the plane. The incident took place close to Manchester Airport. The mysterious object flew so close to the Boeing 737 that the flight crew ducked their heads! The information on the sighting was released by the Ministry of Defence and reported by the BBC on 5 August 2010. The pilot, again considered a very credible witness because of his position, submitted a detailed report of the sighting to the Civil Aviation Authority, stating that the passenger plane was approximately 4,000ft up over the Pennines when something flashed by the cockpit window. The object sped by the right-hand side of the plane. One officer on board reported the object was 'wedge shaped' and may have had a black stripe down its side. The captain and first officer drew a sketch of the object. Coincidentally, on the same day a witness on the ground observed the object, which they also sketched. This image was also released by the National Archives.

UFOs have been known to 'buzz' British aircraft. (Image created by Neil Arnold)

During the year 2000 a dramatic high-speed chase took place over Sussex. The crew of a police helicopter had seen a glowing object at a height of 1,000ft and gave chase across Brighton. Sergeant John Tickner and a paramedic named Sean Mitchell followed the amazing object on thermal imaging equipment for three minutes. Mr Tickner commented, 'We were flying back from Beachy Head ... we didn't expect anything to join us. Not for a moment did we believe it to be anything sinister ... We thought it was funny though, so we chased it around for three minutes and were laughing and joking about little green men.'

In 2002 a disc-like object was photographed flying behind a Lancaster bomber over Withersnea, Yorkshire. The plane was taking part in a Battle of Britain fly-past on 15 June when the photograph was taken. Five years later, during June 2007, an airline pilot named Ray Bowyer came forward to report his dramatic encounter whilst flying for Aurigny Airlines. The sighting was mentioned in *Pilot* magazine. Bowyer stated that whilst flying over Alderney, of the Channel Islands, a cigar-shaped object, whitish-yellow in colour, was stationary at 2,000ft. Bowyer commented, 'I thought it was about 10 miles away, although I later realised it was approximately 40 miles from us ... It could have been as much as a mile wide.' The drama of the sighting didn't end there, either. Bowyer claimed he spotted another object in the distance. Two passengers confirmed the sighting and later another pilot, this time of Blue Islands Airlines, also claimed to have seen a strange object.

The Sun newspaper of 20 June 2008 spoke of a UFO flap over Wales during the first weeks of the month. The report claimed that a UFO flew straight towards a helicopter on 8 June as it was preparing to touch base at St Athan Ministry of Defence Airfield. The pilot reacted quickly to evade the approaching object, then took off in hot pursuit of it across the Bristol Channel and as far as the north of Devon. Three policemen observed the unidentified craft, which they described as being 'flying saucer shaped' and having a ring of lights. South Wales police confirmed the sighting, but the Ministry of Defence didn't. In fact one of their spokesmen allegedly came forward to comment, 'We've heard nothing about this. But it is certainly not advisable for police helicopters to go chasing what they think are UFOs.' One theory put forward at the time was that the object was in fact Chinese lanterns, as some had been released in the area. Such lanterns are often confused with UFOs as when released they rise gently into the sky as an orange, orb-like structure and then gradually fade.

Five months later *The Telegraph* of 21 November reported, 'Police helicopter avoids colliding with UFO, report claims', after a pilot had come forward to speak of his unnerving encounter over Birmingham in the May of 2008. The helicopter pilot was accompanied by two other police observers who at the time were carrying out routine surveillance over the city centre. All three witnesses reported seeing a craft about 100ft away, which had blue and green lights. The object circled the helicopter and immediately the pilot thought the craft was a radio-controlled object, but a search of the area with a thermal camera did not confirm this. The British Model Flying Association also ruled out the possibility of a model aircraft as the object recorded was flying too high.

There are literally hundreds of reports from across the world of pilots and RAF personnel having sightings and radar encounters with unidentified flying objects.

Many a witness has feared for their job and their reputation, should they come forward to speak of their observations. This seems a sorry state of affairs. Many years ago a former American Air Force press chief named Al Chop commented that there was a US Air Force regulation in place, which stated that any pilot who reported seeing a UFO to the media was subject to receiving a $10,000 fine. It seems that this was the US Air Force's way of keeping the information within the ranks of the company, so that their own personal investigations could be carried out without media disruption or drama. In some cases it is believed that pilots and crew members were not allowed to report their sightings in case it damaged the reputation of the airline they were employed by.

Former British Airways (BA) captain Graham Sheppard is one of the few pilots who have come forward to report their encounters. He commented that when he was interviewed for the *Today* programme regarding his sighting, several officers at British Airways heard his remarks in connection with having seen a UFO. As a result of the programme, Sheppard claimed, he was called in by the chief pilot to explain himself and 'to be advised in no uncertain terms that if I did any further media in this respect, that I would be dismissed.'

Sheppard added that he was told that being media friendly would damage the reputation of the company he was employed by, and that speaking about UFOs did not comply with British Airways' policies.

Graham Sheppard retired from BA in 1993 and became a freelance pilot; he was then free in the sense that he could talk about his airborne encounters. Despite being accused of hallucinating and lacking any experience in meteorological phenomena, Sheppard stands by his word that what he has seen in the skies are anomalous objects and not misidentifications of natural objects.

On 22 March 1967 Sheppard experienced his first UFO sighting. Whilst flying over the Bay of Biscay at 24,000ft he observed a brilliant bright light, which was confirmed by a fellow officer. The object was stationary at first and the officers began looking at a star chart to identify it when suddenly it moved to the left of the plane and began to change colour. When the object began performing amazing aerobatics the crew realised this was a bizarre form before their eyes. After the sighting Sheppard and his fellow crew were briefed by a senior captain in a room at Heathrow Airport. Sheppard was advised that it would compromise his career if he spoke of the sighting again.

Sheppard was to experience yet another UFO, however: this time whilst flying at 25,000ft from Scotland back to London. At the time he'd been chatting to a co-pilot when the controller at Preston radar gave an alert call of unusual nature. 'You have unidentified traffic in the airway, fast-moving, opposite direction,' the controller stated, and with that Sheppard and crew looked out of the window in time to see a disc-shaped object which sat 200–300ft below the plane. Sheppard reported that the craft was '… like a hubcap shining in the sunlight with a raised centre.'

The object was estimated to measure about 30ft across and was moving at approximately 1,000mph.

Despite discussing the disc-shaped craft with his crew and family members, Sheppard chose not to go public. Years after the incident Sheppard appeared on the

American television show *Sightings* and openly discussed his previous encounters. This is something that a majority of pilots have been reticent to do.

Whilst those of an untrained eye may be prone to inaccurately describing terrestrial aircraft and natural phenomena, so leaving the UFO mystery vulnerable to debunking by sceptics, it must surely be fair to say that when involving military personnel and aircraft pilots – used to identifying different aerial objects – such encounters can no longer be easily dismissed.

Nigel Doughty, in his 'Ghost Pilots of the Sky' chapter for the *Weekend Second Book of Ghosts*, reported on a very strange encounter from 1942 during the Second World War, when a Lancaster bomber and its crew – or, what was left of them as most were dead or injured – were coming back from a raid on Germany. The plane was a wreck, and it had begun to splutter as the coast of Britain revealed itself through the bank of fog. At this point the air-gunner rushed for cover as a

As well as being blamed for abducting humans, mutilating cattle and creating corn circles, flying saucers have also been held responsible for causing panic in British airspace. (Illustration by Adam Smith)

light flashed up ahead, bizarrely spelling out the identification letters of the flight commander. According to Doughty, 'The delighted air-gunner followed that "light of salvation" through the swirling fog', and then the clouds broke and there, before them, was the runway of the airfield. When the plane landed the air-gunner scrambled out of the plane and upon greeting the ground-staff said, 'Thank God, the flight commander led us back...', only to be told that the commander had been shot down in flames...

Speaking of ghostly airmen and the like...

5

PHANTOM AIRCRAFT AND THEIR GHOSTLY OCCUPANTS

When one considers how intricate life is, then surely there is a possibility that after what we call death, there may be some 'other' place for our souls to roam. Many people believe that death is the final frontier, but a great many of us share a faith that after our life has expired we'll rest in a place and be guided and comforted by those who have departed before us. Some may dismiss such a notion, and yet one cannot so easily dismiss the thousands of cases across the world in which people claim to have experienced some aspect of the afterlife. Whether by the visitation of what we call a ghost, or through some type of near-death experience, there are an overwhelming number of encounters that seem very genuine. Spirits of animals, apparitions on roads, phantom vehicles, water-related ghosts, shades of the past, noisy ghosts, poltergeists, *et al*: the list is endless.

As already discussed, the sky above us is clearly beyond the full reach of science and imagination. What it produces in its nature is bizarre enough and, like the Earth below it, it also conjures up surprises. In the supernatural world there appear to be two types of spirit. A recording, or 'stone tape', is a spectre that, for example, could be a ghostly monk with a tendency to walk through walls without once acknowledging the stunned witness who observes it. Then there is the other type of spook: that which is able to communicate with those in the present day, meaning it may converse with a witness, stare at them, touch them or certainly be aware of the surroundings to the extent that it opens a door rather than walks through it.

Of those spirits that have been documented, one of the most unusual mysteries pertains to that of phantom transport. One would not usually associate a car or bicycle with having a soul, and yet why is it there are so many cases of phantom buses, ghostly cars and, of course, phantom coach and horses? What I've always found odd is that we rarely, if at all, hear a report concerning a phantom coachman floating along the road bereft of his coach and horses. Why do we never observe a ghostly driver without his car? It is as if these recorded spirits, however old they may be, display some type of human intelligence, or perhaps the human mind fills in the blanks. This chapter focuses on one of the most intriguing types of ghosts, the phantom aircraft, and of course the ghostly occupants of such a mode of transport.

SOME PHANTOM AIRCRAFT …

In April 1947, two months before Kenneth Arnold witnessed strange aerial objects over Washington, another mystery was unravelling in the skies over England. The *Lowell Sun* newspaper, on 30 April 1947, reported, 'Ghost Plane From East Air Mystery In Britain – RAF Night Fighters Unable To Intercept Craft Flying At High Speed,' after several reports of a 'midnight ghost plane' which was said to have baffled the Royal Air Force. According to the report eyewitnesses had reported seeing a strange object which first appeared on radar in January as it zoomed across the coast of East Anglia at some 30,00ft. Travelling at speeds of more than 400mph the object was said to have come from the direction of the Continent and then disappeared somewhere inland, never making its return flight. On a few occasions after a sighting RAF fighters were sent out to trail the object but the searches proved fruitless.

The *Yorkshire Post* at the time commented that, 'Radar has plotted some strange things in its time, from children's kites and raindrops to formations of geese, but it surely never plotted a stranger thing than this.'

The article concluded that the RAF had listed the object in their records as X362 – the 'X' a symbol for unidentified.

During 1995 a phantom 'blazing plane' was reported by a man in North Yorkshire. The witness phoned the North Yorkshire fire service on 16 November to state that there was an aircraft in difficulty, but when an RAF helicopter was dispatched to the scene there was no trace of the craft. Police officers carried out a daylight search in the Appleton Roebuck area, but again, this proved fruitless. The witness, who was interviewed and believed to be telling the truth, stuck to his story. Strangely, this type of report is made on an occasional basis. Witnesses usually describe seeing a plane, often a wartime bomber, plummeting to the horizon. Rarely do witnesses describe any explosion, but sometimes sounds of the engine hum and propeller blades are heard. When police and fire services are called out to search an area they rarely find any trace. Has the witness suffered a bout of hallucination, or are they one of the few to have experienced a ghostly plane re-enacting its final descent?

One place which seems littered with tales of phantom planes is the Peak District of Derbyshire. This upland area of central and northern England covers a vast amount of land, talking in Greater Manchester, Cheshire, Staffordshire and South and West Yorkshire. In 1951 the Peak District National Park became Britain's first national park and each year more than twenty million people are said to visit. The National Park covers more than 550 miles. Imagine a panoramic

Tony Ingle, who observed a ghost plane over the Peak District in 1995.

view of rolling fields and windswept moorlands; it is a perfect setting for a foggy ghost story or two.

Tony Ingle, a retired postman from Sheffield, was holidaying in the Peak District in 1995 when one afternoon, at about 4.30 p.m., he took a stroll with his dog Ben at Aston Lane at Hope. Mr Ingle was never a believer in the paranormal but what happened on that evening as he approached the railway bridge shook him to his core. Around 40–50ft above the ground a Second World War plane approached the pair. Mr Ingle's dog bolted off down the lane and a sudden change in atmosphere took place. As the mystery plane drew closer Mr Ingle, who was standing agog, noticed that although the propellers were turning the plane made no sound whatsoever. The plane then suddenly veered off behind a hill as if taking a steep dive. Mr Ingle commented, 'I waited for a crash or an explosion but nothing came.'

Tony was extremely curious and so went to the brow of the hill to investigate but could find no trace of the phantom plane, just a field of sheep grazing peacefully.

Paul Freestone of Air Atlantique commented, 'We have eleven Dakota in use, none were flying at the time' and the RAF, who owned one Dakota, stated that although theirs was airborne, it was elsewhere in the country, 150 miles away. So, did Mr Ingle see a ghost plane? Intriguingly, on 24 July 1945 a crew of six American airmen boarded their C47 Dakota at Leicester East. They were due to go to Scotland on an administrative mission. Before they took off they gave a lift to RAF serviceman John Dunlop Main, who wanted to go to Scotland to visit his mother. Tragically, the plane crashed in the valley where Mr Ingle had seen the Dakota vanish. All aboard were killed. In 1995, as reported in the *Sheffield Journal* of 1 June, a plaque commemorating the dead was unveiled 1,800ft up on Bleaklow moor.

When Tony Ingle's story appeared in the local newspaper it prompted several people to come forward and tell of their sightings of phantom planes over Derbyshire. In 1948 an eight-year-old girl named Audrey Twigg, whilst on a day out with her mother, spotted a phantom plane that her mother couldn't see. Strangely, the area where Audrey saw the plane is the exact spot that a nineteen-year-old pilot crashed his plane. In March 1994 a Mrs Bishop was taking a walk along the Castleton Road when she was startled by a plane that was flying so low that she felt the need to duck. The aircraft made no sound whatsoever and dipped into a field.

Mrs Bishop waited for an explosion that never came. Fifty-one years previous, in 1943, a farmer reported how he had observed a Wellington bomber, en route from Stratford-upon-Avon, that flew into a bank in a field. Five airmen were killed. The field, even to this day, bears the marks of where the plane hit. This spot sits exactly where Mrs Bishop saw the plane dive.

In 1948 at Bleaklow a B-29 bomber crashed. In 1994 a researcher into the ghost plane phenomenon found a ring embedded in the soil at the spot of the crash after a bout of heavy rain. He sent the ring back to the United States. The researcher was contacted by two enthusiasts interested in the wreckage of the plane and so one misty afternoon he took them to the moor. When he showed them the area of the crash both men ran in terror. When he finally caught up with them he asked what on earth had scared them so much. The two men told the researcher that as he was looking through the pieces of wreckage a figure dressed in full airman regalia appeared from out of the fog.

On 24 March 1997 a USAF Dakota plane was sighted over the village of Bolsterstone, which is 10 miles away from Mr Ingle's encounter. Police responded

All manner of military ghost craft have been seen in the skies over Britain. (Illustration by Simon Wyatt)

to a flood of calls from confused witnesses who'd described that between 9.00 p.m. and 10.00 p.m. a low-flying plane was in trouble. Witnesses described some peculiar flashes in the night sky and then a pillar of smoke which rose into the air but despite a search team of more than 100 police and seven mountain rescue teams, no wreckage was found. The mystery 'crash' prompted an investigation by several researchers and this appeared as an article for *UFO Magazine* of May/June 1997, under the title 'Night of the Phoenix.' In the article it was stated two Balderstone residents had observed a low-flying plane which headed over the moors at 10.15 p.m. Police were alerted when it was reported that a red glow and smoke had been seen to spring from the direction the plane was heading. A local group of people who were hoping to observe the comet Hale-Bopp saw an object that was trailing smoke and then shortly afterwards a gamekeeper named Mike Ellison and his wife Barbara heard 'one hell of an explosion' which was said to have shook their home in the vicinity of the Strines Inn public house.

Many people believed a plane had crashed and so searched the area expecting to find smoking wreckage but to no avail. A police officer responded to calls made by several witnesses in the Woodhead area of a 'plume of smoke' and motorists travelling on the M1 even contacted *UFO Magazine* to report that fire engines and ambulances had been seen racing towards the area of the alleged crash.

The story soon took on a dramatic twist when a woman named 'Emma' phoned UFO researcher Max Burns to report that she'd seen a triangular craft pass over her house at a height of approximately 300ft. The object had pink lights on its curved frame and, on its underside a blinding blue light. For an hour after her sighting the witness said she felt unwell. 'Emma' also reported that six military jets sped across the sky minutes after the mystery object had gone over.

The boggy moors were thoroughly searched by police and rescue teams but to no avail. On 27 March *UFO Magazine* stated that Graham Birdsall (editor of the magazine) was contacted by journalists at Yorkshire Television's Leeds HQ, as they'd received video footage which they needed advice on. The footage appeared to show strobe and navigational lights of a light aircraft. Despite the seemingly 'hush-hush' nature of proceedings, a Dr Milton came forward to state that the object under investigation was military aircraft, Concorde or a 'bolide' meteor. *UFO Magazine* stated that researcher David Clarke, 'was told by RAF Linton-on-Ouse and the Ministry of Defence in London that nothing untoward had been seen on radar and apart from the rescue helicopters, no military air exercises had taken place on the Monday night'. The meteor theory was looking more likely …

The RAF later told the newspapers that a meteor shower had been responsible, but aviation historian Ron Collier was quick to comment that for many years people had been reporting seeing planes going down on the moors yet without any sign of a crash. He added, 'It's a mystery and it's just one of those things that will probably never be solved.'

For *UFO Magazine* the biggest issue was the amount of resources used in finding the phantom of the moors. The magazine concluded, in regards to Mr Collier's statement, 'it was all a mystery never to be solved', that this was unacceptable: '… taxpayers are left to pick up a huge bill, and over 100 mountain rescue volunteers spent a fruitless night on the moors, can we really afford to be complacent about such matters?'

The Peak District has always had a reputation for hauntings. One specific area, known as Dark Peak, has been known for occasional mystery lights, which have appeared to a number of witnesses over the years. The rugged landscape, according to some researchers, could be a haven for UFO activity, but folk who consider themselves to be more grounded believe the phantom lights are nothing more than atmospheric conditions – some of these anomalous lights having been already mentioned in this book. Even so, there's no natural explanation for what some people have witnessed.

A mother and daughter driving late at night through Dark Peak were spooked by five golf ball-sized white lights, which appeared on the dashboard of the vehicle. The lights then moved to the back of the car but when the frightened witnesses reached civilisation the lights dissipated. On another occasion a woman driving through the valley of a night was amazed when the whole sky suddenly lit up as if it was daylight, but much brighter. When she rushed home to tell her husband he didn't believe her but a few years later the woman's friend and many other witnesses reported seeing huge, bright lights on the moor. A search party was organised in case a climber had become lost on the moor, but when they reached the spot there were no lights or sign that anyone had been there.

The village of Calver has also experienced ghost plane activity. A lady named Caroline reported that she and her sister had seen a phantom plane on three occasions in the last few years. Each time the plane was silent despite its rotating propellers, and each time it flew so low that it almost touched rooftops. On one occasion the plane was witnessed at night and appeared in great trouble, until it simply vanished.

In Issue 145 of *Fortean Times*, Alan Murdie, chairman of The Ghost Club, wrote an interesting letter regarding a ghost plane from the 1930s which came from the notes of author Elliot O'Donnell. The tale, which pre-dates the Second World War, was described by O'Donnell as, 'One of the oddest hauntings I have ever been called upon to investigate', and concerned a plane which 'was said to hover at midnight over the spot where a plane had, some time before, crashed.'

The plane, a 1929 Vickers Vanguard, was described as having broken up in the sky at a height of 4,000ft and hit the ground at an area called Ferry Lane. A few years after the crash, O'Donnell claimed, several reports were made of this phantom crash, but when people rushed from their homes to look for wreckage they found nothing.

According to Murdie, O'Donnell listed several credible witnesses, including a Captain W.J. Gibson, who was in his bungalow with his wife when they heard the plane crash just 400 yards away. This noise took place four nights in a row just before midnight. This phantom plane crash was confirmed by their next-door neighbour, a Mrs Harding, who told O'Donnell that she'd got out of bed to investigate the phantom crash and heard the exact same sounds as when she was on a boat in the Thames and a Captain Scholefield's plane had come down in the vicinity of the river.

O'Donnell's notes add that, 'Not only was the phantom plane heard, but some residents told me they actually saw it, and that it was 'surrounded with a leadenish blue light'.

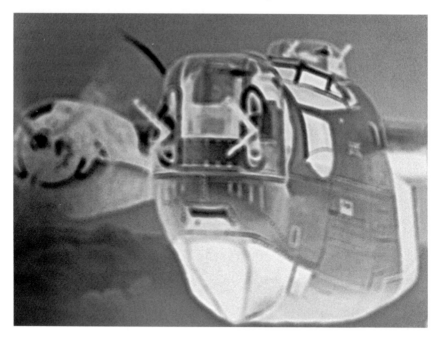

'Watch out, watch out, there's a phantom plane about!'

What secrets do the dark skies of Britain hide?

Eerily, in some instances where the plane was about to crash, dogs in houses nearby would start to howl. A Miss Turpin of the Anchor Hotel was another witness who claimed to have heard the drone of the plane and upon looking up to the sky saw a 'white and misty' aeroplane.

Murdie concluded that, 'According to O' Donnell, worried residents suggested holding a religious service at the site of the crash to try and lay the ghost, but 'after making half a dozen regular appearances the phantom plane suddenly stopped its visits and was not seen again'.

Another phantom aircraft sighting took place in the 1930s, this time at Wirral in Lancashire. A man driving a bus towards Hoylake observed an aircraft in the sky above that seemed to be in difficulty. The driver was so concerned that he pulled the bus over to the side of the road and called on the conductor to take a look. Both men watched in amazement as the plane swooped down to the waves. Immediately the men reported the incident and a lifeboat was sent out to seek the wreckage, but there was no trace of the plane.

RAF Hemswell, according to its website, was a Bomber Command Station situated between Lincoln and Scunthorpe. It was opened in 1937 and closed in 1967. Comedian and actor Michael Bentine told researcher John Stoker that he'd heard the sound of a Vickers Wellington bomber in 1976, even though the airfield had been disused for nine years. This particular haunting differs from some other phantom planes in that no aircraft is visible, the only sign that it could be drifting overhead is the sound of the engine and the propellers. Bentine, who was famous for his role in the television show *The Goons*, served in the Second World War. Bentine also had the gift of psychic power but was always reluctant to use it.

During an episode for a Channel Four show in 1984, however, he reported he'd visited an airfield which was once used by Polish airmen and was asked if he could pick up any spiritual presence within the location. Although Bentine was reluctant to investigate the area – which was deserted – he did manage to pick up the presence of a dead pilot and felt that the ghosts were at peace. Bentine added, 'In a way it helped me to exorcize those faces I had seen over forty years before.'

In the February 2003 issue of *Fortean Times* there appeared a small snippet regarding a 'Ghost Jets Scare' after several incidences since June 2002 of 'ghost' aircraft having appeared on air traffic computer screens at the new national control centre at Swanwick, Hampshire. The mystery planes were being held responsible for the garbled radar messages received from the North Sea sector, and also for the false symbols which seemed to suggest genuine aircraft were being followed by other aircraft. According to the article, 'The glitch is the latest of a series encountered at the £623 million control centre since it opened in January', but, rather bizarrely, the problems of 'ghosting' never occurred at the old centre which was situated at West Drayton.

During the early 1980s a Danny Litherland, whilst on holiday with his parents and brother at a caravan park near Colwyn Bay, North Wales, had a strange experience. One day when standing with his father in the garden of the caravan, they both spotted a low-flying Second World War bomber. 'It seemed to be making some erratic movements on its way inland. The memory is very vivid:

A ghostly bomber glides silently overhead. (Photograph by Neil Arnold)

I recall the sun glinting off the plane, but no sound,' Danny reported to *Fortean Times* magazine. The plane headed off towards Llysfaen but so acute was its angle that, according to Danny, '... it would have been very difficult to pull out of the dive; besides, I doubt that people would carry out stunts in such a plane'. Danny and his father waited for the explosion but no sound came. Immediately, they jumped in the car and drove to the area where they thought the plane would have crashed, but there was no sign of it.

There is another, even more modern ghost plane story, this time from January 2004 when two witnesses saw a mystery plane at Barnoldswick, Lancashire. This was backed by the *Craven Herald* of 23 January, which reported, 'Couple Tell of Ghost Plane Mystery' after a visitor to Barnoldswick had an alleged sighting of a large, grey plane which emerged out of 'the mist near the Rolls-Royce factory', before vanishing.

According to the stunned witness the plane was on course to hit the car she was travelling in with her partner but it disappeared in a blink of an eye. The newspaper stated that the witness, a retired policewoman named Moira Thwaites, and her partner Malcolm Spensley, were driving toward Barnoldswick along the Skipton Road at 11.20 a.m. when they saw the huge plane in the vicinity of the Rolls-Royce Bankfield Factory. The plane looked, according to the witnesses, like a Lancaster bomber with four propellers. The plane seemed to emerge from the mist to their right-hand side. Incredibly the plane not only managed to avoid the car but also the houses nearby; there was no sign of a crash.

THE HAUNTED BOMBER

There are literally hundreds of aviation-related ghost stories, and space limits mentioning a majority of them here. However, no chapter on phantom airmen and ghostly aircraft is complete without coverage of the haunted Second World War Lincoln bomber situated at the RAF Museum Cosford, in Shifnal, Shropshire. RAF Cosford houses one of the UK's largest aviation collections, but in 1980 local newspapers were more interested in the wierd happenings reported by those who had worked at the museum.

Strangely, the rumours of a ghost in relation to the RF398 bomber were started for a bit of fun during the late 1970s, by an engineering team who didn't want to see the plane transferred to a new museum in Manchester. One of the engineers came up with a plan to invent a ghost who would be named 'Pete the poltergeist'. The engineers hoped that the legend would bring in the tourists, but little did they realise how their fictional ghost would become reality. After finding out that the bomber wouldn't be moved from Cosford, the newspapers started to get involved with the ghost story. Without realising it was an invention, in 1991 researcher Ivan Spenceley began looking into reports of strange noises that had been heard within the bomber. One night, he left a tape recorder running in the deserted hangar. Strange clicking noises could be heard on the tape, but Ivan had to be sure there was no natural explanation or human intervention and so sealed off the doors of the hangar.

The strange noises continued and so Ivan invited Radio 4 producer Gwyn Richards to an all-night vigil. With all as quiet as a mouse, at 12.30 a.m. both men suddenly saw a tiny pinprick of light appear within the cockpit of the bomber. 'Can you see what I see?' one asked the other. The clicking noises and odd rushing sounds, as well as the pinprick of light, were all verified as being the actions required to start the plane up during wartime. In darkness the light was used by the pilot to view his dashboard and controls. These were verified by a visiting man who was an ex-member of the Lincoln crew. It was alleged that a pilot named Hiller, who'd flown the RF398 on its last journey in 1963, told colleagues that when he died he would come back to haunt the Lincoln. He died flying a Dove aircraft, not long after the Lincoln's last flight. Coincidentally, part of the crashed aircraft was said to be housed at Cosford Museum.

During the late 1970s and early '80s many inexplicable events were recorded by staff and visitors alike. A Mr Small, an ex-engineer, claimed to have seen the ghost of an airman in battledress in 1979, then a psychic from Bedford claimed that the hangar ghost was in fact an AC1 instrument fitter named Ronald, who had died at Cosford Hospital. He collapsed on the Lincoln after suffering a ruptured appendix. A mechanic was aided one night whilst working on the Lincoln alone. He'd dropped his spanner and in the darkness couldn't find his tool when suddenly a spanner was pushed into his hand. Another witness claimed that he'd seen a figure move in the aircraft but when he switched the lights on there was no one there. When the lights were switched back off he saw a cloudy wraith.

More recently, as reported on the BBC Shropshire website, a secretary at the museum was pinning something on a notice board in relation to the Lincoln bomber when suddenly someone called her name. There was no one around when she investigated. One of the more classic stories concerning the plane relates to a mechanic who fell backwards from the wing, some 15ft onto the hard floor, but felt nothing whatsoever. The man, who'd previously injured his spine in a similar fall from a plane, believed that some type of invisible force had aided him.

Things that go bump at Biggin Hill

Biggin Hill – the most famous of airfields – is situated just 12 miles short of the heart of London. From 1917 to 1992 the Biggin Hill Royal Air Force Station was situated there. The site of the old Biggin Hill Aerodrome is considered to be one of the most haunted locations in England. In his superb book, *The Ghosts of Biggin Hill*, author Bob Ogley looked into the history of the place and devotes a chapter to the spooks of the site, as well as looking at some of the heroic service men and women who served there. St George's Chapel, on Main Road, serves to remember those who died for the cause, although it appears that many of those brave souls still linger in the area.

A phantom Spitfire has been seen and heard in the vicinity of the area. In 1994 the *Kent Messenger* reported on the ghost stating, 'People living near the famous Battle of Britain airfield at Biggin Hill, Kent, have often reported the sound of a wartime Spitfire returning home from a sortie.' According to local legend the plane is seen screaming towards the landing strip then performs a victory roll before vanishing into thin air.

In his 1985 book *Ghosts of Kent*, supernatural investigator Peter Underwood wrote, 'In 1982 a couple of former RAF officers became interested in such reports and discovered a surprising amount of good evidence for apparently paranormal activity on and around airfields and they even succeeded in recording sounds, of aircraft and of people, that they were satisfied had no rational explanation.' In reference to Biggin Hill, Underwood adds that many people who reside close to the airfield have experienced the screaming sound the Spitfire makes. Underwood was told that the date of 19 January is significant to the ghost plane and that the long-dead pilot likes to signal his return with a victory roll before the plane vanishes from view. The sound of glasses being clinked together in celebratory manner have also been recorded along with the voices of men.

Bob Ogley mentions that 'ghosts of airmen have certainly been seen inside the Chapel of St George's which is situated on the main road opposite the old mess and slightly to the south of the guardroom'.

One of the strangest ghost stories Ogley mentions concerns retired Wing Commander David Duval, who had a strange experience one afternoon whilst working in the vestry. The spring-loaded door opened and Mr Duval went to investigate the visitor. It turned out to be a rather scruffy man who enquired to the whereabouts of Wing Commander Slater on the reredos (a board in the chapel, which records the names of aircrew killed in battle). Mr Duval pointed to the board and decided to leave the unkempt man to it but when he returned to the visitor there was no sign of him, even though he had not left the building. The same scruffy man had been seen on a couple more occasions by staff who reported that after the man had vanished there was a cold air about the place. Bizarrely, Mr Duval discovered that on the reredos there had been an error – Wing Commander Slater had in fact been left out. As soon as this omission was rectified the spectre never returned.

An ex-policeman and former security guard at the airfield reported an airman had haunted the airfield for many years. A friend's wife saw the ghost at Hayes Common one evening whilst she was cycling home. The apparition was dressed in RAF uniform and seemed to be floating. A few years ago the *Kentish Times* reported on a road ghost within the vicinity of Biggin Hill, as experienced by a John Levy, an ex-soldier. Mr Levy was delivering newspapers in his van at 3.00 a.m. one morning when he was startled to see a man dressed in full airman regalia, standing by the side of the road into Tatsfield. As John pulled over the man completely vanished. Thinking he would be ridiculed Mr Levy told only a few of his encounter, which was confirmed when a local policeman commented that the spook was that of a pilot who died when his plane crashed into a hill. Another road spectre was seen, in 1958, by a Les Lyne. He'd gone to the Farnborough Air Show with a friend but whilst coming home late at night saw a figure of a man walk across the road.

It's likely no one will ever find out exactly how many ghosts haunt Biggin Hill Airfield, but one thing is for sure, it is certainly one of the most haunted. Bob Ogley, again in his *Ghosts of Biggin Hill* book, has attempted to piece together some parts of the ghostly jigsaw, but there will always be an element of mystery to the place. For example, a Barbara Robbins reported her ghost story to a group of par-

A phantom Spitfire haunts the skies of Biggin Hill. (Image created by Neil Arnold)

ents who'd organised a ghost story evening in the lounge bar of the Biggin Hill Squash Club. She mentioned that one day, whilst walking her two dogs down the Polesteeple Hill area, she was enveloped by a coldness, which had spooked her dogs. She heard a voice say, 'Don't be afraid', and believes that the present spectre could have been one of several airmen who crashed at the site of The Grove.

Bob Ogley mentioned another ghost story, pertaining to a Suzanne Harrison who in 1972 purchased a bungalow in Hawthorn Avenue with her husband Gerald. The property backed on to the airfield. On one occasion Suzanne clearly saw the ghost of an airman, as well as experiencing several voices and a succession of thuds. She eventually found out that the room was once used by pilots when they played darts. Another woman, a Roberta Single, had also resided at a property at Hawthorn Avenue and on one occasion had smelled tobacco coming from one of the rooms.

Ghosts of the WAAF (Women's Auxiliary Air Force) also haunt Biggin Hill. One case involved a couple who lived at Vincent Square during the early 1980s. These houses were once used by the WAAF and many people reported feeling a strange presence in the rooms, as one would expect from any property said to be haunted. However, on one occasion a group of women belonging to the NAAFI (Navy, Army and Air Force Institute) reported that one evening whilst standing chatting in the car park they clearly saw some WAAFs, who appeared only from the waist up! Gradually the phantom women faded from view.

A majority of the ghosts who reside around Biggin Hill appear to be recorded spirits: a Spitfire plane coming in to land, ghostly airmen continuing their game of darts and women from the Auxiliary Force gathering to gossip. Again and again these images are replayed to those fortunate enough to see them. Some researchers believe that ghosts are merely energy from the past that eventually fades, but in the case of the Biggin Hill spirits, they don't seem keen to move on.

More Kentish ghosts

Hawkinge Airfield, situated in east Kent, was a Battle of Britain fighter aircraft station. It was active from 1915 until 1958 and the pilot of a Spitfire is said to haunt the site. He is usually seen approaching the cemetery, although ghost hunter Andrew Green claims he has also been seen coming from the area of the fiendishly named Killing Wood. Dressed in full airman regalia, the airman once completely vanished before the eyes of a couple taking an evening walk. As recently as 1998, activity has been reported. In the March of that year a woman residing at one of the properties situated on the site of the old aerodrome went into the Kent Battle of Britain museum. She reported that for thirty seconds water had gushed from her roof and then suddenly ceased. There had been no rain or any other explanation but what she did discover was that many years ago a Spitfire had crashed into an engine shed, at the exact spot where the water had come from.

Lydd Air, situated at Lydd, was once known as Sky-Trek Airport. It was established in 1997. The marshy area of Lydd has long been littered with tales of ghostly smugglers, but the ghost at Lydd Air may have a less sinister explanation. During the late 1950s, according to Andrew Green, '... a small private airfield was built for Silver City between the smuggling village of Lydd and Greatstone-on-Sea. It is now owned by Jonathan Gordon who established Sky Trek airlines …' During the late 1950s a man working as a loader suddenly came over ill and was taken into the cabin, where he dropped dead. Within the next few months strange things began to happen such as the flushing of toilets, doors opening and closing by themselves, and items disappearing then reappearing.

From 1916 to 1984 Lympne Airport was in operation, just 10 miles north-east of Lydd. RFC Lympne began life as an acceptance point for aircraft and then in 1919 became a civil airfield. In July 1980 a Pauline Kane had a weird but wonderful experience in the sky over the old airfield. As she was about to participate in a parachute jump with a group of friends, piloted by a Captain Alex Black, Pauline saw a vision of her father in the clouds who warned her not to jump. Pauline then decided not to take the leap. Andrew Green takes up the story, 'On Wednesday July 2 an EP9 Prospector aircraft, piloted by Alex, left with the group of five parachutists for a routine flight and combined jump, but only minutes after take off, the plane crashed in a field, a few yards from Llydd, and all the occupants were killed.'

RAF West Malling was in use from 1917–18, and then from 1930–69. The airfield was often used as a back-up for Biggin Hill during the Battle of Britain period. The ghost here is said to be of a handsome young pilot and his black-and-white dog. Another airman has also been seen around the area. These ghosts were confirmed during the late 1980s when a television crew were filming parts for a British television drama named *We'll Meet Again*. The director asked if the three actors dressed as airmen and a member of the WAAF could be moved out of shot; the trio were looking into the engine of a jeep which was being used by the television company. When the cameraman approached them, the three people vanished before his eyes! West Malling harbours another eerie story. One such spirit is said to hurl bricks at vehicles. Could this ghost be that of a pilot who crashed in his Spitfire on the airfield after hitting a low brick wall, and was killed instantly by a brick which flew into the cockpit?

Quite recently a ghost plane was heard by Corriene Vickers and her daughter Evelyn 'Missy' Lindley at Maidstone. On Thursday 7 June 2011, around the time of 1.30 a.m. in Perry Street, Corriene went to call her cat in and was alerted to a strange noise overhead. Her cat, Elvis, rushed indoors, ears flat, as if spooked by the sound, which Corriene described as a 'loud plane engine'. The craft, which she could not see, sounded as if it was right above her. Whatever was roaring overhead was lower than the clouds but displayed no lights. Corriene called Missy who came rushing to her side and she suggested the noise may have been coming from the local air ambulance. However, Corriene pointed out that the ambulance did not fly after dusk and if it had been a helicopter they would have heard the blades.

After a short while Missy remarked that what they were listening to sounded like an old bomber. The next day Corriene noticed that on the internet someone had asked if anyone else had heard the deafening sound, but this time over Sittingbourne. According to the two witnesses, they described the sound of a plane engine which was so low that they waited for it to crash, but it never did. Corriene was so intrigued by the sound she looked into it more and discovered that during the Second World War a German fighter plane had been shot down

Missy, and her mum Corriene, saw a ghost plane over their home at Maidstone in Kent. (Photograph courtesy of Missy Lindley)

in the area whilst on a bombing raid – the date? 7 June. The time? Around 1.30 a.m.! Strangely, this wasn't the first time Corriene and Missy experienced a phantom plane. Corriene stated:

> We had previously seen a plane flying very low towards our house during the early hours a few years ago. I was sitting opposite the window of our living room and saw a huge light heading toward us. On each occasion the plane we've heard and observed flew on a completely different flight path to the planes of today and it was so low we could see underneath it. It seemed to narrowly miss the rooftops of the house opposite. It looked like an old bomber and we couldn't work out why it would be flying at night.

Norfolk strangeness

Situated in the county of Norfolk, Bircham Newton Airfield was used in the First World War. In 1966 it closed as an airfield and became the home of the Construction Industry Training Board. Many of the original buildings still remain, and so do some of the pilots!

One fascinating story concerns two men who, one afternoon, were playing squash in the grounds of the hotel. Both men were startled to see a man dressed in RAF uniform looking down from the spectators' walkway. The figure strode along the walkway and out of sight. Both men were so intrigued by the visitor that they decided to leave a tape recorder at the court overnight. The next day they played the tape back and were spooked by the sound of footsteps walking along the corridor. The men also recorded the sounds of an active airfield. The busy atmosphere left the men agog as they heard the voices of men and women and the groans of machinery. On one occasion an aircraft could be heard. So amazed were the men by what the tape had picked up they asked for a BBC engineer to analyse it. He concluded the sounds may have come from outside the building, which seemed highly unlikely, especially as no planes had been in the air that night. According to authors John and Anne Spencer, an investigation into the haunting was conducted by BBC's *Nationwide* programme. A brave reporter spent the night inside the court, armed only with a tape recorder. At 12.30 a.m. the tape recorder stopped and a strange, cold feeling enveloped the woman. When a medium was asked to visit the squash court she stated that an Anson aircraft had crashed in the area, killing the crew of three – Pat Sullivan, Gerry Arnold and Dusty Miller. The medium believed that the airmen were still around.

On another occasion it was reported that a jeep full of airmen laughing and joking was seen heading toward the base. This ghostly re-enactment fades at the spot where there was a terrible accident involving a jeep which killed every-one on board. One of the strangest ghost stories related to Norfolk and airmen, however, concerns the startling vision experienced by Flight Lieutenant Ronald Jacoby who in September 1916 was stationed at Pulham. At 5.00 p.m. one evening he was flying over the Norfolk Broads in the region of Barton Road. 'As I looked down from my cockpit,' he recalled, 'I saw the face of a beautiful girl mirrored as it were in the water beneath. Could scarcely believe my eyes, especially as the face turned in my direction as I passed over it.' The next day Jacoby asked his squadron leader to take to the air with him in the hope of another glimpse, but nothing untoward occurred. Yet Jacoby did find out that other pilots had seen the ethereal face and that they believed the ghost to be of a girl murdered in the lake many years ago.

Lincolnshire phantoms

In her 1997 book *Ghost Encounters*, author Cassandra Eason speaks of a lady named Sheila who reported a ghostly incident pertaining to a spectral pilot and plane. 'During the late 1960s, when I was 17, I had just bought a motor scooter and my father was teaching me to ride it', wrote Sheila. 'We decided to go to a disused Second World War airfield at Barkston in Lincolnshire, near where we lived.'

When they arrived at the airfield it was deserted and Sheila rode up a grass bank and was surprised to see a small plane and two pilots on the airfield. Sheila stated that the two men wore Second World War caps and greatcoats and they were look-ing and pointing over in the direction of Sheila and her father.

One of the men shouted to Sheila not to cross the line and so she turned to call to her father. However, when Sheila turned back the plane and its occupants had disappeared. A few years later Sheila heard a story on the local radio of several sight-ings of ghostly airmen said to have been seen around Barkston Heath Aerodrome.

On the night of 30 March 1944 Christopher Panton, an RAF pilot from East Kirkby in Lincolnshire, was killed in his Lancaster bomber after being hit over Nuremberg in Germany. More than fifty years later Christopher's two brothers,

Harold and Fred, decided that the best way to pay homage to their brother – who was buried at Durnbach Military Cemetery, Bayern – would be to purchase the site that housed East Kirkby Airfield, which adjoined their existing land, and transform it into a shrine devoted to their brother. The building was gradually restored and now exists as the Lincolnshire Aviation Heritage Centre. In 1983 the Panton brothers purchased a NX 611 bomber to sit proudly at the museum.

On 26 April 1994 consulting civil engineer and ghost hunter Eddie Burks, accompanied by freelance writer and editor Gillian Cribbs, investigated a series of strange goings-on at the Lincolnshire Aviation Heritage Centre. They were greeted by Fred Panton. It was at this point that Eddie Burks liaised with the spirit of Fred's brother, Christopher. Eddie stated that the young man had come forward to say that he'd been watching over the centre and guiding his brothers all the way through their project. Eddie and Gillian were then taken through the museum, amazed by how the building now resembled the days of old as models of staff and crew members loitered about the place. From the lamps to the wallpaper, the Panton's had done a remarkable job of re-enacting the 1940s airfield.

In his book *Ghosthunter* (co-authored with Gillian Cribbs) Eddie Burks mentions several communications with spirits from the old airfield at East Kirkby. Not all of these ghosts were settled entities; some displayed mild aggression to Burks. Fred Panton mentioned that visitors to the centre had experienced several strange things, mainly in the control room area. Fred told Eddie that one Sunday afternoon he'd been repainting the old steps in the control room and as darkness fell on the evening he became to feel a little uneasy. A voice in Fred's head told him to leave the room, but he refused, thinking it would be silly to do so, and so he continued to apply the second coat to the steps but for some reason could not get it right. Fred added, 'As I lowered the cushion to the final step, a shiver went down my spine. The step was already wet; someone had painted it. I picked up my paint brushes and ran.'

Fred also described how on one occasion his son David had seen a figure walk from the hangar to the control tower. David had initially thought the figure was a trespasser and so informed Fred, but upon inspection of the area found no one there. Fred later reported seeing the same apparition. David also mentioned how one night he'd observed strange balls of light dancing in the vicinity of the hangar. In the book Cribbs writes, 'Eddie believes the Second World War has left such a tragic legacy of ghosts because, perhaps more than even during the First World War, so many victims were young men bursting with a passion for life which was savagely denied.'

So many tragedies of war appear to have embedded themselves into the framework of buildings. Whilst a majority may be just recorded spirits, or events somehow being played back to those susceptible to observing them, other ghosts are clearly able to communicate with those of today. Some spirits, such as Fred's deceased brother Christopher, may be at ease with their situation in the afterlife and able to view and help their loved ones in the material world, but some spirits are clearly in some distress and seem to appear in some type of limbo.

Another ghost story from the county comes from RAF Metheringham, once situated between Metheringham and Martin. It was built in 1943 and decommissioned three years later. On the RAF Lincolnshire website forum there is mention of an intriguing ghost from someone called 'Jack_Dante', who writes, 'A young girl dressed in an old WW2 RAF uniform has been known to stop passing motorists, cyclists, and even pedestrians to ask for help, saying that her boyfriend has been injured in a motorbike crash down the road.' Those who go and investigate the accident find that there is no trace of boyfriend, motorbike or girl. The female is said to be one Catherine Bystock from Horncastle who, according to legend, was engaged to a young flight sergeant but one dark night whilst she was on the back of his bike, they crashed. It is said that the driver of the bike survived but the young woman died.

Sadly, like many stories pertaining to 'road ghosts', or 'phantom hitchhikers', they have become something akin to Chinese whispers, passed down through generations, only to become distorted over time. Some people report that when the girl vanishes a strong smell of lavender permeates the air. A more ghastly version of the tales states that when the girl fades away the air is filled with a stench of decomposition.

On the Lincolnshire/Leicestershire border, RAF Bottesford, which operated from 1942 until 1948, is said to be haunted by a phantom aircraft. As recently as 4 October 2009 the whir of a Manchester bomber engine has been heard, especially as dusk settles upon the old airfield. The Manchester bombers were replaced by Lancasters during the Second World War as they suffered more losses through crashes than by the actions of the enemy. The old control tower is also said to be haunted – peculiar dancing lights appear just after the sound of the phantom plane.

One of Lincolnshire's most intriguing ghost stories concerns a photograph taken in 1919 at RAF Cranwell. The photo, showing an assembly of servicemen, also includes the partly obscured face of one Freddy Jackson in the back row. Strangely, Freddy Jackson died three days previously after he fell into the propeller blades of a plane. Another fascinating story comes from Lincoln's RAF Scampton. On 7 December 1918 Lieutenant David McConnel left the airfield with Tadcaster as his destination. Sadly, he hit a wall of thick fog and his Sopwith Camel crashed. His watch showed the time 3.25 p.m. At exactly the same time, back at Scampton, Lieutenant Larkin was relaxing when the door opened and in stepped McConnel. Larkin was rather surprised McConnel had come back so early, but McConnel told his fellow lieutenant that it had been a good trip. He then turned around and left the room. Later that night Larkin heard the news that McConnel had died in a crash.

This story echoes another incident, which took place during the 1990s at Glasgow International Airport. A chap named 'Captain Bob' was walking across the foyer of the airport when he had a strange experience, which he spoke of on the Discovery Channel programme *Ghost Hunters*. 'On the way I slightly deviated from my route, instead of going to the boss, and as I deviated I saw this friend of mine, in the door, come in to the airport.'

'Bob' stopped and turned round and the men held a brief conversation. 'Bob' noticed, however, that the man – who he'd known for almost ten years – seemed very gaunt and thin, and refused to shake hands. According to 'Bob' the man then said, suddenly, 'I've got to go' and left. Thinking nothing much of it 'Bob' left too and the next day went to meet a friend in a pub in the town. Whilst having a pint 'Bob's' friend said 'just a minute' and went to fetch a copy of *The Scotsman* newspaper from the rack. When the man returned to his chair he asked 'Bob' if he knew the man mentioned in the article, to which 'Bob' replied 'Yes' – in fact by coincidence it had been the friend he'd spoken to the previous day. However, 'Bob' soon got the shock of his life when his pub mate told him that the article was an obituary and that the man 'Bob' had spoken to the previous day had in fact died a few days earlier!

'I just couldn't believe it. It was not possible', 'Bob' told the programme.

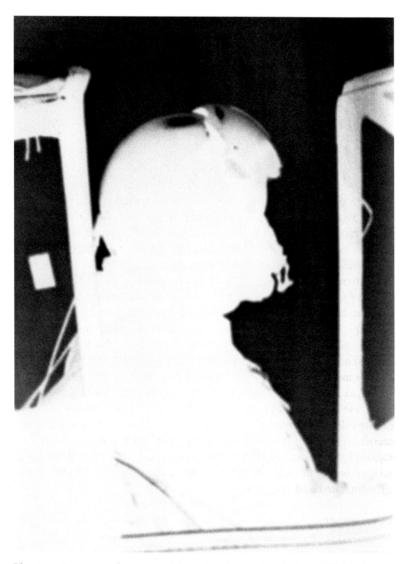

Phantom airmen are often reported from sites that used to harbour airfields. (Image created by Neil Arnold)

Lincoln's RAF Scampton has several more ghosts. In 1943 the 617 Squadron were stationed at the base. They were led by Wing Commander Guy Gibson. During one bombing raid a Lietenant Henry Maudsley, whilst in his Lancaster, was said to have bounced a bomb too late. This resulted in his aircraft exploding. As Gibson radioed through to ask if Maudsley was okay, little did the wing commander realise that the plane was in pieces on the ground. However, this didn't stop the spectre of Maudsley replying, 'I think so – stand by'. Gibson's black Labrador is also said to appear at the base. The dog perished in a road accident and is buried at Scampton.

In 1972 a phantom plane almost melted into UFO folklore. The *Scunthorpe Evening Telegraph* of 2 May reported, 'Search For Mystery Aircraft In North Lincolnshire', after a strange object appeared on radar at RAF Coningsby, not far from Woodhall Spa. As quick as it had appeared, the object suddenly disappeared from the screen. Although police were dispatched to the area the search proved fruitless. The big question on everyone's lips of course was what on earth were the authorities looking for?

Middlesex mystery

The Castle of Spirits website mentions a ghost story (undated) from Middlesex, submitted by a lady named Alison Wilkinson who commented that her friends Susie and Jay reside in the RAF Quarters in Middlesex and the 'experiences belong mostly to them'. According to Alison, a while back she and Susie were at the house and chatting about ghosts when Susie mentioned the sudden appearance of handprints in the house. With that she took Alison upstairs and there, clear as day, above the bed, were the handprints on the wall. Apparently Susie had done everything in her power to remove the prints which had appeared and then disappeared, and then reappeared for more than three years. They only seemed to disappear when Susie fell pregnant but reappeared just after the birth.

The couple reported that a candle on their television had often slid along the top, nappies and other items had been thrown around the room when there was no one present, and on one occasion Alison reported seeing a shadowy figure walk through a glass door into the kitchen.

In 1943 an airman was accused of murdering a woman and a child at a house in Ealing. He was hanged for the crime. However, a few years later a photographer rented the hall which adjoined the house and reported many strange bouts of paranormal activity: ghostly footsteps, swinging lights and eerie whispers. The photographer was keen to find out who was haunting the property and so, with several members of his staff, arranged a séance. They were contacted by the ghostly airman who stated he'd been hung for a crime he did not commit.

Berkshire activity

In her book *The Haunted South*, Joan Forman investigated a haunting at the site of Grove Airfield, which was closed down in 1946. She writes of a Mr Halliday who worked for the Atomic Energy Authority stating, 'The entire plant was housed in an old aircraft hangar and except for breakdowns was run night and day.'

According to Joan, one evening in the summer of 1969 at about 9.00 p.m. John Halliday was working in the office next to the plant, when he heard what seemed to be the loud murmur of voices outside the office door.

John thought that there was a small group of people in conversation and so went to investigate but when he stepped inside the hangar he found the building completely empty. Mr Halliday then decided to check some of the machines to make sure they weren't on and making strange noises, but they were all switched off.

Mr Halliday headed back to his office and telephoned security. The chap on duty at the gate house stated that apart from Mr Halliday, himself and the boiler man, there was no one else on site. Over the next few days Mr Halliday, although still intrigued by what he'd experienced, put the incident to the back of his mind. However, a month later, on his usual 2.00–10.00 p.m. shift, Mr Halliday had another weird experience. It was an eerily still night as one of the machines had broken down and he again heard voices, although a thorough search revealed nothing. A few weeks later Mr Halliday was approached by another operator who stated that he'd also heard the strange voices in the hangar. Forman concluded that, 'Later my correspondent learned that during the last war an American serviceman had hanged himself in the same hangar'.

Shadows at Suffolk

RAF Bury St Edmunds was constructed in 1941. In 1944 the 94th Bomb Group were stationed at the airfield with their giant B17 Flying Fotresses. One such Fortress was 42-30112, nicknamed *Lil' Butch*. On 5 January 1944 all available planes raided Germany, but only four returned. Among the missing was *Lil' Butch*. The next day another Fortress, 42-97253, emblazoned with 'Morgan's Raiders', was taken in by the RAF. The chap whose job it was to maintain such craft was 'Pappy' Cordes. One afternoon Pappy was at the airbase checking on a few of the bombers. He was driving in his jeep when suddenly he came round a bend and there before him stood *Lil' Butch*. Pappy stared at the battered bomber in amazement then drove closer to inspect. He could hear the distinct sound of the engine cooling off, suggesting it hadn't been at the airfield for very long, but surely he'd have heard the bomber land?

There was no sign of the crew and the big square letter 'A', which was painted on the tail, was also gone. Pappy jumped from his jeep and walked to the door of the plane, but it was then that an overwhelming feeling of unease consumed him. He felt as if someone was in the plane staring straight at him. Something was not right about the whole scenario so he decided to get into the cockpit to inspect the logbook. When Pappy opened the door he immediately came face to face with a menacing looking fellow who had his hand on a pistol, which rested in a leather holster. In a deep voice the man asked what the hell he wanted. Pappy fled, leaping into his jeep and driving off to report the intruder. When he reached his senior officer and told his tale he was of course scoffed at. Even more frustratingly, when he drove his superior to the site of the plane *Lil' Butch* was nowhere to be found.

RAF Woodbridge is also situated in Suffolk. It was been in use from 1943–48 and 1952–93, and was originally constructed as one of three airfields to aid bombers that were damaged or short of fuel. In 1997 medium John Cochrane visited RAF Woodbridge with his wife. They were due to spend a weekend at the station with relations. Whilst relaxing one evening the ex-bar manager mentioned that strange things had taken place in the club and bar. John mentioned that he'd become rather sensitive to an old woman with long white hair who was standing perfectly still in the corner of the room. The figure then nodded and a grey figure walked across the room and vanished.

During the late hours of Saturday night, when the club was closed, the group made their way to an area which used to serve as a chapel, but which now existed as a function room. John crept into the room with the group close behind and once inside he told them to sit down quietly. John and a few others could see that the room was full of men and women, all dressed in RAF uniforms and having a wonderful time. However, the mood of the room soon changed and as the party faded the spirit of an RAF flying officer came into view. He was standing on the balcony staring at John. Although John tried to talk to the figure the officer was not interested and appeared quite upset by the intruders. John and the group decided to leave.

A ghost named Old Roger is said to keep a watchful eye over RAF Mildenhall, which is still in operation since its construction in 1934. This bizarre entity is not a ghostly pilot but instead wears a long coat and plays a flute! The ghost was said to be responsible for the sandstorms which deterred German bombers during the Battle of Britain. His flute playing seemed to muster the elements and drive the enemy away.

Another ghost story comes from RAF Waldingfield, which was used by both British and American aircraft. During the 1980s a house built on the site of the old airfield was plagued by supernatural occurrences; a shadowy figure, bumps in the night, rattling doors. Homeowner Angela Richardson, who lived in the house with her husband Richard, explained that there was rumour that a plane had crashed on the site after returning from a raid over Germany. Witnesses who crossed the area often reported getting eerie feelings and many locals avoided the location. Angela concluded that, 'Some of them were very surprised when the airfield was developed after the war. In the end we decided to sell up and leave. It was not a happy time for us – and probably not for that tormented ghost either.'

Curiosity at Cambridgeshire

Two interesting ghost stories are of note here. RAF Wittering, which is one of the RAF's oldest stations and situated in Peterborough, is still in use. During the Second World War a bomber attempted to make an emergency landing but crashed into the control tower. Legend has it that the bomber can still be seen as it silently drifts toward the runway. The control tower is said to be haunted by a phantom airman, too – not too surprising considering several people died when the bomber crashed into it.

Eeriness at Essex

RAF Ridgewell is a former Second World War airfield in Essex, once occupied by the USAAF. The airfield operated from 1942 until 1957. Very little remains of the

The marshes of Canvey Island, Essex, are said to be haunted by spectral aircraft. (Photograph by Neil Arnold)

airfield but strange lights have been seen to dance across the area and the voices of spectral airmen have been heard. RAF Ridgewell appears to occasionally replay back some of the busiest times as the sounds of revved-up engines and returning, war-torn planes have also been heard.

RAF Fairlop, which is now an open space of two lakes and a golf course, also has a ghost story. John Stoker, writing for *Paranormal* magazine in October 2010, stated that one November night in 1942, 603 Squadron – based at RAF Fairlop – were alerted by the prospect that a German bomber was nearby and its aim was to destroy the base and the Spitfire planes. Bizarrely, as the searchlights raked the sky they picked out a Sopwith Camel – an aircraft which, according to Mr Stoker, '…had not been operational for twenty-five years.' Sopwith Camels had certainly been stationed at the airbase during the First World War, and such a plane was useful in destroying German Zeppelins.

North Weald Airfield in Essex, which was established in 1916, is still very active. In 1968 the airfield was used for the film *Battle of Britain* – starring Michael Caine and Laurence Olivier, among others. When the crew were filming a sequence for the movie involving six Spitfires they all stood agog as they observed a seventh plane come into shot. Bizarrely, when the film was rushed to the lab only six Spitfires appeared. The incident was reported on 16 March 1968 in the *Daily Express* under the headline, 'Film Set Haunted by Ghost Aircraft'.

Quite recently Gary Foulger, an aviation archaeologist who conducts lectures on the Second World War, felt urged to commemorate the American airmen who'd perished on the marshes of Canvey Island. Gary's aim was to create a memorial of some kind to acknowledge the war heroes, as his family had a military background and he wanted to show an appreciation of the services of the American airmen. Gary felt that there were many obstacles in his way, but one afternoon a woman named Sandy Phips sat in on a lecture he was conducting at a school. She didn't realise at the time that Gary's dream was to have a plaque of some kind erected in honour of the airmen but two days later whilst sitting at home she had a strange vision, that she had been visited by the ghost of an airman. He told her to pass the message on to Gary that his dream would be realised and to keep on with his work. When the woman told Gary of this vision he was spurred on with his work and eventually a plaque was put up to commemorate the dead airmen.

Even more recently, in 2003, it was reported that a ghostly Spitfire flew over a cemetery in Chingford. Some have connected it, albeit obscurely, to the resting place of the Kray twins Ronnie and Reggie. A magazine called *The Spectator* recorded the unlikely legend that every year at around 11.30 p.m. on the anniversary of the twins' birth, a gang of villains visit the far corner of Chingford cemetery. At approximately 11.40., it is said that a Spitfire takes off from Old Warden in Kent, heads north-west across the marshes of Essex, and then arrives 300ft above the grave. The men are said to listen to the sound of the Merlin engines and then head off to a nearby Italian restaurant for a meal and chat about old times.

Author Peter Haining spotted inconsistencies with this ghost story, however, stating in his *True Hauntings* book, 'The problem with this story is that no Spitfire has flown from Old Warden in many years. The airfield is actually in Bedfordshire not Kent and by flying northwest from there an aircraft would fly over Leicester not Essex.'

Another mystery that defies explanation was mentioned in the *Express & Star* of 3 August 1973. Police carried out a thorough search of Hockley Woods, near Southend, after receiving a call from a distressed person who stated quite categorically that they'd heard a plane crash followed by screams for help. Yet no planes were reported missing from anywhere!

Surrey strangeness

Researcher John Stoker recorded that, whilst filming for the James Bond movie *Casino Royale*, crew saw a ghostly woman walking up the aisle of the 747 that was stationed at Dunsfold Aerodrome in Cranleigh. Apparently a few years earlier a woman had died on the plane.

In 1978 the Society for Psychical Research was contacted by a couple who believed that their house was haunted. The property sat on the site of the old Croydon Airfield and on many occasions they had seen the spectre – a man dressed in RAF attire. Coincidentally, the male occupant of the house was an avid collector of military items and some of these souvenirs had been thrown about the place by the helmeted apparition. Another ghost story concerns a German pilot who was said to have died during the Second World War when he bailed out of his craft in the Addington area. A Dutch pilot also haunts the area of Croydon Airport. His ghost dates back to the 1930s when his plane crashed due to dense fog. Meanwhile, in 1947 twelve people died in a plane crash during a snowstorm. The ghost of three nuns, who died in the plane crash, are said to haunt Croydon.

The Montrose phantom

According to the website for RAF Montrose, 'Britain's first military airfield was set up in Montrose [situated on the east coast of Scotland] by the Royal Flying Corps in 1913'. A heritage centre now exists as a monument to the early days of aviation. The website isn't afraid to speak of the resident ghost either! On 27 May 1913 a Desmond Arthur, who was stationed at Montrose as a member of No. 2 Squadron, was killed when the wing of his biplane crumpled. At the time the Royal Aero Club stated that the crash was caused by an inept repair of the wing. According to the website, another theory was also put forward that the crash was caused by stunt flying. However, since the fatal crash several people have come forward to report a spectral figure at the airfield. In the commander's room and the mess hall there have also been sightings of a phantom airman.

The website states that a Major Foggin has several genuine accounts of ghostly phenomena, adding, 'Shortly after a report published just before Christmas of 1916 exonerating Lt. Arthur, another appearance was recorded and then everything seemed to go quiet until the onset of the Second World War.'

However, when war broke out lots of strange incidents were said to occur at Montrose – mainly concerning sightings of a phantom biplane even though such a plane was not stationed at the base. Phantom airmen had also been observed at Montrose as well as the ghost of a black Labrador often said to follow people who visit and work at the museum.

According to author Bruce Barrymore Halfpenny, airmen on guard at the base in the past were not cautioned for leaving their post, for it was understood that all the men had been suddenly spooked by the appearance of the ghostly pilot.

Isle of Wight weirdness

The Isle of Wight is situated in the English Channel, off the south coast of Hampshire. In his book *Into the Blue*, Alexander McKee gives several ghostly accounts from the island. One story came from a family who reported they had seen a ghostly airman in their house on several occasions. The sightings began in the mid-1970s and would always be preceded by the sound of a bomber buzzing overhead. This would be followed by the appearance of a figure adorned in a bomber jacket. Further investigations revealed that the ghost could well have been a neighbour's son, who died whilst serving in the RAF.

In 1980 two young boys, a David Saunders and his friend Robert Hendry, had been playing near a stream at Ryde when they saw a white figure drifting from the direction of the common. In the same area two Hurricanes had crashed previously. One pilot had received a message to turn back and did so, the other pilot failed to get his message and so his craft collided with the other. One pilot parachuted to safety, the other died in his cockpit.

Some phantom aircraft have been heard to crash, but upon investigation no wreckage has been found. (Photograph by Neil Arnold)

Hampshire also has a ghostly pilot, according to author Ian Fox. His book, *The Haunted Places of Hampshire*, describes a spectral airman at Farnborough. Fox comments, 'The town accommodates the Aerospace Division of the Defence Research Agency, previously known for years as the Royal Aircraft Establishment, to where the remains of a light aircraft were taken in 1964 for examination by air accident investigators. With it, some say, came the ghost of its pilot.' Nancy Spain, a journalist, was covering the Grand National for the *Daily Express* when her plane crashed and it is claimed that her spirit still roams the car park area nearby.

A phantom helicopter is also said to haunt Hampshire, particularly in the region of Brockenhurst, which is a village in the New Forest. On 9 April 1975 the *Southern Evening Echo* reported that rescue services rushed to Rhinefield House after staff had reported hearing the engine of a helicopter, which suddenly cut out. At the time the weather was bad and the area was suffering from a blizzard. Smoke was reported as rising from the woods and police, fire and ambulance staff investigated the area. No wreckage was found.

Wiltshire woes

According to John Brooks' *The Good Ghost Guide*, in the vicinity of the stones at Stonehenge there is a monument to a 'Captain B. Lorraine and Staff Sergeant R. Wilson who died here in 1912 when their aircraft crashed.'

The two pilots belonged to the Royal Flying Corps and were the first members to lose their lives. Sir Michael Bruce was driving past Stonehenge with several companions before D-Day when they all clearly saw a plane crash into a thicket. When the men searched the area all they found was the eerie memorial. Coincidentally, the aviation pioneer Colonel F.S. Cody also died after crashing close by so several phantom planes could haunt the area.

Lost souls at Staffordshire

According to author Harry Ludlam, an airfield at Lichfield in Staffordshire was so haunted that security guards used to dread patrolling certain areas. Some of the experiences recorded by the staff were flickering lights, guard dogs refusing to enter the hangar and certain rooms, and the appearance of a headless flying officer. Some claim the spectre is the pilot of a Wellington bomber who crashed and was decapitated. Another theory is that the ghoul was once a tail gunner who killed himself by walking into the spinning propellers of a Lancaster bomber.

Yorkshire echoes

At Leeming in North Yorkshire, the airfield was used as a bomber station during the Second World War. Several ghostly airmen have since been seen in the more remote area of the field; some believe that this phantom crew all died aboard the same plane, which crashed and has since been swallowed by the soil.

Lancashire's headless airman

Burtonwood Airfield was used by the United States Air Force during the Second World War and the Cold War. On Christmas Eve in 1946 two non-commissioned officers were heading back to their living quarters after a celebratory night at the Rose Hotel, when they encountered a weird column of mist on the road. Suddenly, the mist transformed into a figure of a man who resembled an airman, but one without a head. A few sightings of this headless wraith have taken place and some believe it may well be the tormented spirit of a pilot who, in 1944, crashed at the base. His head was decapitated when by mistake he pressed his ejector button and his head was sliced off in the half-open turret.

Darkness at Dorset

Blandford Camp at Dorset is a military base and the current home of the Royal Signals ... and a few spooks. In the past the camp has been used by the Royal Air Force, the Royal Navy and the army. The ghost said to haunt the camp is more unusual in that it is a nurse known as the 'lady with the lamp'. In his book *Ghosts Among Us*, Harry Ludlam reported that on the orders of the commanding officer, the sergeant major kept watch over the barrack room at night because the young soldiers were too afraid to venture there. The ghostly nurse failed to materialise and a few weeks later the activity has ceased. Ludlam concludes that, 'It almost seemed the ghost was aware of the forbidding nature of sergeant majors.'

A daunting haunting in Devon

There are a couple of ghost stories of note from north Devon, both of which are mentioned in Peter Underwood's *Ghosts of North Devon*. The first comes from Cullompton and its beautiful pub The King's Head. A spectral airman haunts the public house and it is believed that many years ago tempers flared one night between British and American airmen and an American pilot was stabbed. Customers and staff alike have reported that for a very brief time the airman still appears on the exact spot where he met his death.

A house in the area of Tiverton is said to be haunted by a phantom plane, which was experienced by two children of the Penn household. The low-flying craft was heard a few years ago as it crashed, but there was no sign of the wreckage. The family, who had experienced several bouts of paranormal activity, researched the history of the building and found that it used to be a hospital during the First World War and a rest home for American servicemen during the Second World War. Legend has it that those who were discharged from the hospital would often fly over the house – but on one occasion a pilot flew too low and hit the tops of the trees and crashed.

A spook in Sussex

A ghost of an airman was seen at Tangmere's RAF Museum in 1984. The phantom pilot was blamed for the moving about of objects. No one seemed to get a good glimpse of the spectre, who was only ever reported as a fleeting shadow, but in the past the sound of a low-flying aircraft has been heard. Some believe a pilot crashed after being shot down, but details are vague. Issue 25 of the *Fortean Times* (spring 1975) make a brief mention of a phantom plane crash at Bognor Regis, in West Sussex. The snippet states that a mystery light, believed at the time to be a plane crashing into the sea, was recorded – but others argue it may have been a shooting star!

West Midlands madness

According to the *Sunday Mercury* of 7 October 1984, RAF and American bases in the Midlands were alerted to a low-flying military plane which had been reported to them from the Selly Oak area. Yet both bases denied having any aircraft in the area at the time! Ghost plane or covert project? In Coventry the sound of piston-engine bombers has also been heard above the ruins of the medieval cathedral.'

The Cheshire chopper

In Issue 3 (March 1974) of *The News* there is mention of an intriguing but alternative mode of spectral transport, a phantom helicopter, said to have buzzed areas of Manchester, Derbyshire and Cheshire. The mystery chopper caught the attention of *The Daily Mirror* who, from 15–18 January 1974, ran stories of the spook chopper and its daring exploits – such as flying below 55ft level under the cover of darkness, without any clearance and evading police pursuit. The phantom 'copter was

A phantom helicopter was rumoured to haunt Manchester, Cheshire and Derbyshire. (Image created by Neil Arnold)

also said to land in fields and its red and green lights were clearly on display, but as Special Branch closed in to nab the phantom flyer, there was no sign.

'Whoever he is, this pilot is no fool', stated a controller, 'but he must have plenty of nerve. How he can see baffles me. One theory is that the chopper has an accomplice on the ground, somebody who lights up a makeshift flare path. Maybe, too, he refuels the chopper.'

According to a police spokesman, although the helicopter appeared to be no danger to planes in the areas, its flight paths had been tracked for more than six months. On most occasions the chopper would take to the air after midnight and buzz around the skies until about 3.00 a.m. but then suddenly vanish. 'We are literally lying in wait for him,' another police spokesman added, but every time officers searched an area where the helicopter was thought to have landed, there was no sign.

Opinion was divided as to where the chopper came from but most agreed that whoever was flying the thing lived not far away and probably knew the areas it frequented. Another officer commented that, 'It uses so much fuel when it veers off straight flight and starts hovering and changing direction that its range becomes limited.'

The article concluded that sightings had taken place at Goostrey, Cheshire, before dawn on the 14th then on the 16th at Arclid. As unmarked police cars sped towards the chopper it took off. Although some researchers theorised that the chopper had a ground-dwelling accomplice but this was never proven and the phantom chopper melted into local folklore, never to be seen again.

A Welsh wonder

In Issue 5 (July 1974) of *The News*, there is an interesting snippet in reference to the South Stack cliffs area of Holyhead, Anglesey, with mention of 'Mystery Object Washed Up On Beach'. The story came about after a Mr Philip Ledger had been investigating the discovery of a strange 'plane-like object rumoured to have been washed ashore on the night of 4 February 1974'. The unusual object was said to have a wingspan of 5ft and a length of 9ft and have a black, aluminium body. The article also mentioned that, 'It bore obvious traces of being carried in and out on the tide for a few days – obvious, that is, to the police spokesman.'

Although the craft, in description, sounded like a model plane that had gone astray, serious investigations were underway to find its source, with the RAF and the Aberporth Range Establishment both stating that it is not one of theirs. If the 'plane' had simply been a heavyweight model then it doesn't explain why the bomb disposal unit were drafted in and a description of the object was sent to Portsmouth's underwater naval research base. According to the *North Wales Chronicle* of 7 February 1974, 'Holyhead coastguards were reported to 'have been instructed not to comment'.

A coastguard at the time added that 'Several plugholes and discs on the outside point to the fact that it is full of instruments.' Sadly, many people had flocked to the scene and taken parts of the mystery object as souvenirs.

Phantoms of the north

In his excellent book *Grisly Trails and Ghostly Tales*, author Alan Robson writes of several air-related hauntings at Wearside, in the north-east of England. He states: 'Nissan's gigantic factory was constructed on the old site of Washington airport, used by pilots during World War II and long afterwards.' A Canadian pilot named George Hamilton is said to haunt the building but no one is sure how he died. According to Robson he may have either perished whilst standing on top of the hangar and suffered a fall, or crashed as his aircraft took off from the airport. The wraith is said to most often be seen in the vicinity of the old Lamella hangar. One anonymous witness reported to Mr Robson that they'd seen the spectral pilot on three occasions but most people will not come forward to talk of their sightings for fear of ridicule. The pilot is said to stand around 6ft in height, has blue eyes, brown hair and a small moustache. Witnesses often describe the figure as wearing an air mask around his waist.

The spook has also been seen by a local fireman, who one night was locking up the hangar and saw a pilot hovering a foot above the ground.

Teeside, which includes Middlesbrough, Redcar, Billingham and Stockton-on-Tees, is said to have a haunted airport. Durham Tees Valley Airport isn't haunted by a phantom pilot; instead something more sinister seems to be resident, particularly in the vicinity of St George Hotel. One Barney Concannon, a senior captain, was asleep one night in the hotel when a cold presence made itself known in the room and seemed to spread across his head and shoulders. Putting it down to a draught, Mr Concannon stirred but then felt something on his legs. Barney flinched and cursed at the non-specific presence and the pressure and coldness subsided.

Many airline crews, whilst staying at the hotel, have experienced paranormal activity too: the slamming of doors, personal items disappearing then reappearing, banging noises in the dead of night and an alleged case of a bed lifting up from the floor of its own accord. Even so, hotels can be quite noisy places even of a night, as staff and customers move around the place. According to Alan Robson, in 1951 an RAF pilot died when his plane crashed near the site of the hotel. Could the ghost of the pilot be responsible for the occasional bouts of high strangeness? Probably not, but something is!

London – the man on the runway and others

Airport runways are probably the last place you'd expect to be haunted. One day in 1970 a police car was radioed by staff at Heathrow Airport to investigate a man who had appeared on the runway. According to the airport ground operations team the gentleman was on runway No.1. The police arrived on the scene quickly but could find no trace of the man. An hour later the police were notified for a second time that the man was in the area but, again, their search proved fruitless. Later that evening the control tower stated that a slow-moving object had appeared on the runway and was probably human, and immediately three squad cars raced to the scene. Again, there no sign. By this time the wild goose chase had become extremely frustrating for all involved. Later that night the radar picked up the man and the three cars, accompanied by a fire engine equipped with searchlight, approached the runway. Bizarrely, when they reached the area the control tower radar showed that the mystery man was still there, just 25yds away, but the police could find no one. At one point a police vehicle ran over the object that had showed on the radar, but still the police witnesses saw nothing. Suddenly, the control tower radioed that the figure was now walking away from the runway – the police followed but could see nothing at all.

No one ever found out who the mystery man was, but some believed the apparition to be of a man who, in 1948, was aboard Sabena Belgian Airlines' DC3 Dakota, which crashed after a bout of heavy fog – all aboard were killed. Staff at Heathrow had to pick their way through the wreckage on runway No.1 in hope of finding survivors, but some members of staff reported seeing a man in a suit and bowler hat who asked each witness, 'Excuse me, have you seen my briefcase?' Could this be the same spirit who eluded police in 1970?

On 22 October 1974 the *Evening News* reported on another Heathrow phantom under the heading, 'Jumbo the Jet Age Ghost' after several witnesses, mainly cleaners at the airport, had come forward to report sightings. The cleaners stated that they were too afraid to work alone on some planes due to an evil presence that attempted to pick them up and throw them. Other witnesses claimed they were paralysed by an invisible presence. The night foreman for the cleaning company, a

The murky marshes of outer London are the haunt of ghost planes and spectral pilots. (Photograph by Neil Arnold)

Mr Parson Lal Palmer, stated, 'It all started when we opened the doors one day and there was a strange smell. It went away but came back again later.'

Mr Palmer also reported that on one occasion he'd sat down in a chair and was horrified when he could not get up again. He explained that his eyes shut fast and he could not open them. 'It was as if someone was holding me down by the shoulders. It was four or five minutes before I was able to move.'

On 6 July 1980 a 'ghost in a light grey suit' was reported by the *Sunday People*, who commented that a pale wraith had been seen in the VIP Suite at Heathrow's Terminal One.

Erith Marshes, situated in the London Borough of Bexley, are said to be haunted by two military ghosts. A German ghost plane has been seen in the past crashing into the marsh, whilst some folk who reside near the marsh claim that their property is haunted by a British airman who died when his Spitfire crashed. Interestingly, at Thamesmead, which is in close proximity of Erith, there is another spook tale in reference to aviation ghosts. The *Kentish Independent* of 11 December 1975 reported that during excavations for the 'new town' of Thamesmead, a Second World War fighter plane was discovered on the murky marsh. The plane was bereft of pilot. Maybe it's the pilot's ghost who loiters near Tavy Bridge? At the time it was reported that a butcher's shop, which was built on the site of the plane crash, was haunted by a spectral pilot. The chap who used to own the shop said he had conversed with the wraith. Author Eric Maple attests that local residents had on several occasions heard the sound of a plane in distress over the area. Oddly, however, the

Kentish Times of 18 December ran a different version of the tale, and stated that when the plane was found, intact, on the marsh, the pilot was still in the cockpit. Still, other sources claimed that no plane had ever been found on the marshes! Weirdly, a council spokesman mentioned that the only story he'd heard concerned a First World War plane crashing somewhere locally ...

A Gloucestershire ghoul

In east Gloucestershire sits the market town of Cirencester. On 28 June 1999 *The Times* reported on the 'US Airman's Ghost – Spooky sightings at Cirencester Park, the stately pad of Lady Sarah Apsley'. According to the newspaper the ex-beauty queen was taking a stroll with her dogs when she came upon a young man dressed in airman attire. He was leaning against Queen Anne's Column. Lady Sarah told the newspaper, 'The clouds were just breaking up and I glanced at the sky and said, "It looks as if it's going to brighten up". When I looked back he had vanished.'

According to local folklore the spectre of an airman has also haunted the park since the First World War.

An Oxfordshire oddity

RAF Upper Heyford, situated in Oxfordshire, has one of the weirdest ghost stories. Forget tales of phantom aircraft and ghostly airmen, but instead consider the tale from 1996 concerning a security guard at RAF Upper Heyford. One night, whilst on patrol, he heard the sound of horse's hooves coming towards him. When his gaze met the owner of the hooves, however, he was shocked to have come face to face with a centaur – a mythological creature said to be half-man and half-horse!

Black clouds over Bodmin

During the early part of the twentieth century a Royal Navy pilot flying to Plymouth had a spooky encounter whilst over the rolling moors of Bodmin. The pilot saw a mass of dark cloud up ahead and, rather unnerved, he contacted the control tower who advised that he seek another runway. The pilot was rather reticent to find another airport, but eventually decided on this option when suddenly from the cloud just 200m ahead came a Tiger Moth plane. The pilot in the Tiger Moth, in goggles and leather helmet, gave the bemused pilot a thumbs-up and then pointed down, suggesting that the unnerved pilot follow him. Concerned still about seeking another route, the Royal Navy man decided to follow the Tiger Moth; they slipped through the dense cloud and suddenly, to the relief of the Royal Navy pilot, he could clearly see the runway a short distance away. Bizarrely, there was no sign of the Tiger Moth. When he finally landed he was scolded for not obeying orders to seek another runway, and was also told that there was no Tiger Moth in the sky that day. In fact no Tiger Moth had operated in the area since the Second World War!

What you have just read is by no means an exhaustive catalogue of phantom airmen and ghostly planes, but hopefully it does show that the realm of the paranormal is diverse in what it displays to the susceptible mind. If you're still not convinced, or at the very least interested, the next batch of oddities will hopefully stir your imagination.

BATTLES IN THE SKY – MYSTERIOUS BOOMS, PHANTOM EXPLOSIONS AND IRRITANT HUMS

Charles Fort, the original collector of unusual data, recorded in his book *New Lands* a host of peculiar incidents in relation to unexplained aerial phenomena. Some of these, of course, included phantom lights and other odd aerial forms, but consider the cases of armies in the sky and spectral sounds of sky-based wars! For example, he writes of an occurrence said to have taken place on 8 October 1812 involving 'phantom soldiers' at Havarah Park, near Ripley. At the time meteorologists tried to explain such visions as the aurora borealis (a natural light display – sometimes known as the Northern Lights – caused by the collision of charged particles).

Writing in *Ghosts and Legends of the Lake District* in 1988, J.A. Brooks confirms Fort's notes, stating that there have been a few reports of phantom armies – one said to have presaged the battle at Culloden, another at Souther Fell, and a third witnessed at Helvellyn on the eve of the Battle of Marston Moor. Brooks also mentions that '…in *Lark Rise to Candleford* Flora Thompson told of a ghostly army that had been seen in Oxfordshire'

A regiment of phantom soldiers had been allegedly observed marching through the sky accompanied by drum and fife band. Strangely, it had been confirmed that around 6 miles away a real regiment had been in the vicinity of Bicester and theorised that the ghostly image had been some sort of freak reflection!

At Castle an Dinas, an Iron Age hill fort situated near St Columb Major in Cornwall, there is a strange legend about a sighting of a ghostly army in the sky which was recorded by eighteenth-century historian Samuel Drew. Castle an Dinas is a mystical place indeed, for it was from here that King Arthur reportedly rode off to participate in the Tregoss Moor hunt. In Sussex, particularly in the Ditchling region, it has been recorded that a phantom army crosses the sky, often leaving a pungent stench in its wake. This bizarre trail of soldiers is said to take to the sky between 24–26 May every year.

Samuel Clarke's seventeenth-century chronicle, *Mirror or Looking Glass*, also mentions a spectral sky army, stating: 'A little before Marques Hambleton came with his army into England, two armies were seen in Yorkshire, in the air, discharging and shooting one against the other; and after a long fight, the army which rose out of the North, vanished.' This epic ghost battle would have taken place during the late 1640s. Maybe such an apparition of marching sky soldiers was simply a bizarre reflection; the same type of weird natural phenomenon which we apply to other inexplicable manifestations such as roads, cities and ships in the sky. Of course, if there are spectral armies in the sky then wouldn't we hear their menacing artillery?

Fort, once again from his *New Lands* work, tells us of the *London Times* of 9 November 1858, which recorded the following: '… in Cardiganshire, Wales, in the autumn of 1855… sounds like the discharges of heavy artillery, two or three reports rapidly, and then an interval of perhaps twenty minutes, also with long intervals, sometimes of days and sometimes of weeks, continuing, throughout the winter of 1855–56.'The sound was mentioned as being heard again on 3 November 1858, even louder, then confirmed by another report at Dolgelly (north-west Wales).The sounds of heavy artillery were last heard at Swansea. 'Merely a boom of thunder,' I hear you cry with a scoff. Maybe. Maybe not.

Fort tries to explain such fancies as quarry-blasting, only to find that such operations were not in effect at the time of the sounds. Such ghostly rumblings then melt into the mystery of British earthquakes and phantom explosions, until, from the *London Times* of 20 January 1860, 'several correspondents write as to a sound "resembling the discharge of a gun high in the air" that was heard near Reading, Berkshire.' Some would argue that a meteor may have passed over – because in 1860 we couldn't blame the sound on the roar of a phantom Lancaster bomber! Fort also mentions handfuls of other similar cases, as if spectral armies have taken to the sky and discharged their ammunition into the clouds. Maybe it always rains because there are holes in the floor of heaven caused by phantom, trigger-happy soldiers!

From the Border Counties there is a fascinating legend about a spectral 'boom' in the sky, which resulted in what can be considered only as a Martian army! In 1592 the residents of Castlecraig were as panic-stricken as their flocks when a ground-shaking booming noise emanated from the heavens. A mighty shadow blotted out the sun and a long object of mystery loomed over the village before zooming off with another ear-bursting boom. It must have been some exhaust pipe! However, there does seem to be an uncanny relation between so many of the phenomena already reported in this book. It's as if they are all part of a mystifying puzzle and each part has the frustrating ability to melt into one another. They can at a turn become remote, unique and almost laughable, but they do occur.

Sixty years after the Castlecraig incident a group of shepherds were said to have heard in the sky over Warwickshire the sound of distant, beating drums and the cacophony of marching soldiers. Suddenly, an army of men and horses came into view from the zenith and a battle raged amongst the clouds. On 23 October 1642 the Battle of Edgehill had taken place in Warwickshire, and maybe this had somehow been re-enacted in the sky as some type of celestial reflection. Since the seventeenth century reports of armies in the sky have become scarce. Is this simply because we know more today about the natural phenomena this planet conjures up so as to understand any unusual formations, which centuries ago may have been perceived as phantom armies or messages from the stars? Even so, modern reports do exist. In Issue 89 (August 1996) of *Fortean Times* a Brian P. James of Didcot, Oxfordshire, wrote a fascinating letter with regards to phantom booms, stating that he'd been interested in the mystery of 'unidentified aerial booms for twenty years since the phenomenon plagued southern England in 1976 and 1977.'

Mr James commented that his village was plagued by a phantom boom regularly since 12 December 1976, taking place usually on a Monday night at around

Ghostly soldiers and phantom battles have been observed in the skies of Britain. (Image created by Alan Friswell)

9.20 p.m. The distant boom would be heard from a specific point in the night sky and yet according to Mr James, 'homes less than one kilometre away had doors, windows, and loose objects rattling. Also the boom was inaudible in the next village, only two kilometres away.'

Mr James also mentioned that ITV's *News At Ten* covered some of the mysterious booms but with no resolution especially as at the time the Warminster region of England was experiencing high levels of strangeness and UFO activity. Some 'experts' at the time investigating the phenomena tried to explain the sounds as coming from 'English and French Concorde's heading out over the Atlantic', but, as Mr James commented, 'that suggestion ignores the basic fact that the nocturnal aerial booms heard here were a single, sharp report, not a double boom.'

Some of the witnesses who experienced the booms were so hysterical that 'personnel at nearby RAF Benson went on full alert after a boom sparked an IRA bomb scare.'

Mr James eventually set up a tape recorder to record the sounds as the booms were becoming so regular but during the ninth week the mysterious noises stopped and over the next five or so months they occurred sporadically, eventually ceasing for good in the April of 1977. However, the mystery deepened. Whilst on holiday at Weymouth in Dorset, on 1 June 1977, Mr James, whilst taking a stroll, heard the same familiar noise. Upon looking up he saw an arrow-headed object which left a thick, white vapour trail as well as a strange blue cloud. He stated, 'I cannot be sure that the obviously manufactured craft was not an advanced military aircraft, but the way it seemed to defy our laws of physics and aerodynamics, possibly gaining virtual instant supersonic speed, suggested that it was a UFO of alien manufacture.'

By this point he was convinced that there was some connection between the sonic booms and UFOs. However, and rather oddly, it seems that whilst some people experience these booms, others close by could on occasion seem to be completely unaware of such a sound!

Whilst Mr James may be all too quick to jump to the conclusion that strange booming sounds in the sky are caused by giant UFOs, what his letter does show is how once again these varying mysteries melt into one another.

On 16 November 1895 a phantom explosion occurred at Fenchurch Street in London. There was no trace of any explosive and no debris could be found either. However, an hour or so later, in the vicinity of Mansion House, another explosion took place – this one even more violent than the first. People scurried from buildings but once again, all investigations and searches for a source proved fruitless.

Another intriguing and recurring aerial mystery was mentioned in the *Daily Mirror* of 10 June 2011 concerning 'Humthing in the air...' after many villagers in the region of Woodland, County Durham, began to experience a peculiar and irritating hum that had started some two months previous. The strange noise often started at around midnight and carried on until about 4.00 a.m. – the sound had scientists baffled. One villager, a Marylin Grech, told the newspaper she'd suffered several sleepless nights, commenting, 'It vibrates right through the house. It's definitely coming from outside – it's in the air.'

Strangely, just like with Brian P. James's mystery boom, only certain people seem to be able to hear the irritating hum. During the 1970s a mystery hum was experienced in the North Wales village of Minffordd. In the January 2009 issue of *Paranormal* it was stated that the hum had returned. Minffordd resident Nan Griffiths commented, 'The situation is made worse because there is no way to predict when it will start. It's not there all the time, and then it'll wake you up at three in the morning.'

Mrs Griffiths thought the hum was down to a condition known as tinnitus until the mystery sound was confirmed by her neighbours. Rhian Williams, a neighbour of Mrs Griffiths, claimed that the noise was so bad that to drown it out she would have to turn the radio up. The report, which was mentioned by the BBC website, stated that the sound was described as something akin to a generator or diesel engine. Could a phantom bomber have been plaguing the vicinity? Was there a phantom battle taking place in the sky?

In 1769 Gilbert White, in his *Natural History of Selborne*, commented:

Humming in the air. There is a natural occurrence to be met upon the highest part of our downs in hot summer days ... a loud humming as of bees in the air, though not one insect is to be seen. The sound is distinctly to be heard the whole common through. Any person would suppose that a large swarm of bees was in motion and playing about his head.

The mystery hum has been experienced all over Britain, including Norfolk, Cornwall and Yorkshire. If such a hum had been heard over Derbyshire's Peak District, would it be perceived as the sound of a phantom bomber? Certainly, should such a hum or boom plague an individual, then maybe we could blame a medical condition: Low Frequency Noise sufferers are driven dizzy by hearing problems, which can be blamed on industrial sources or even the buzz of a pylon. In today's mobile phone-filled environment there are occasional panics in which some users of phones claim that their modern tool, although being a necessary evil, can cause damage to the human body.

During the 1980s and early '90s parts of Ayrshire in Scotland were annoyed by a pulsating throb, which worsened as night drew in. In Issue 56 (February 2011) of *Paranormal*, a Mike Covell wrote in to speak of his experience with the 'Hull hum', commenting that one night, 'I had left the heating on until late so when we retired to bed, the bedroom was like an oven. I made the unusual decision of opening the front bedroom window as Susan and I were really hot.'

Shortly after 2.00 a.m. on the Thursday morning of 28 October something roared through the sky over East Hull, and headed towards Humberside Airport. Mike had grown accustomed to hearing all sorts of planes passing overhead at night but this was extremely unusual, and the strange aspect of this sound was confirmed when Mike checked the departure and arrivals timetable of the airport to discover there was no flight activity at that time. 'The noise was reported on Facebook and Twitter… and a number of residents across Hull have come forward with their own experiences,' Mike added.

One witness came forward to say she had heard the roar over the Avenues area of Hull, and that it was so loud it awoke her from slumber. The sound she heard was something akin to a First World War bomber passing overhead, whilst others commented that whatever it was must have been flying incredibly low to give off such a noise. Houses were reported to vibrate when the sound occurred, and so Mike contacted the Civil Aviation Authority, Humberside Police and Humberside Airport, and local newspapers were also alerted to the phantom noise, but all investigations drew a blank. The Ministry of Defence stated that there had been no known military aircraft in the area and neither had the police helicopter been in the vicinity. So what was it?

On 18 March 1980 the *Victorian Advocate* was one of several newspapers who covered the story of a mystery aerial hum in Bristol, stating, 'Environmentalists will conduct an all night stalk next month seeking the source of the "Bristol Hum", after the mysterious noise 'had puzzled and infuriated residents of this southwest England port for two years and defeated those trying to track it down.'

John Day, a Bristol-based television reporter told the paper that what he'd heard was a 'low, droning noise like a hiss'.

High-tech equipment, 'costing the city more than $60,000' would be used by a group of experts, fronted by Donald Barnett, the chief environmental officer, to solve the riddle after many local residents came forward to say they'd been suffering headaches because of it.

Twenty years previous, the *Saskatoon Star-Phoenix* of 25 April 1960 reported 'Strange Hum Jangles Kentish Nerves' as residents in the 'garden of England' had

Were phantom bombers responsible for the irritating drone heard over Hull? (Image created by Neil Arnold)

reported a peculiar and irritating noise. The noise, said to be experienced only by those able to pick up the low-frequency range, has become so annoying that according to the paper, 'Electricity and telephone men have checked all the wires strung across the countryside and say they emit no drone.'

Bizarrely, the government at the time 'disavowed all knowledge of the matter' – but the nuisance was soon picked up on by William Deedes, Conservative MP for the market town of Ashford, who stated that 'the hum is something to do with defence warning apparatus' and planned to bring the matter up in Parliament. Before Mr Deedes had begun to take the sound seriously – a sound, by the way, that he could not hear – over 100 residents had complained about it only to be told it was all in their mind. A woman named Mrs Hyams, who resided with her novelist husband near Canterbury, wrote to the local newspaper of the hum but was advised to consult a doctor. However, just when Mrs Hyams was about to give up all hope in her quest of finding another drone sufferer, a friend who hadn't been in the country for many years came to her house and asked her, 'My dear, what is that awful humming noise? Can't you turn it off?'

Like many of the mystery booms, and hums reported in this chapter, however, the puzzle remains unsolved.

SOMETHING MORE SINISTER?

Nine years later another Kent resident, Antony Verney, and his wife, Doreen, purchased a cottage in Biddenden. The couple only lived in their rural abode on occasion as they also had a property in Bloomsbury, London, and saw their Biddenden house as a holiday residence. In 1983 when Antony retired from a textile company the couple moved to Biddenden full time, hoping to enjoy the rural pleasures of countryside strolls and scenic views. However, on 1 October 1983 something very strange began to happen. For four consecutive days a weird humming noise seemed to emanate from the sky. The couple were not overly put off by this at first, as they were due to go on holiday and return on 25 October. When the Verneys returned they were greeted by an even louder humming noise. At night this would turn into a deep throbbing sound and the woodland around their cottage would become illuminated by pink and yellow lights.

During the November of 1983 the noise became even worse and Mr Verney believed the noise was making his wife ill. One night the couple became so concerned about the noise they took to the woods in search of its source. Whilst out they came across two policemen who were in their vehicle. The officers told the Verneys that the noise may have been coming from an area known as Shorts Wood and that they would note the report and look into it. On 26 November Mr Verney visited Tenterden Police Station only to find that the matter of the humming noise had not been logged and so Antony decided to make a formal complaint to the sergeant. However, Mr Verney became extremely frustrated when he was told by the policeman that the matter was not for the police to deal with but was in fact the responsibility of environmental health. Two days later Mr Verney phoned the environmental health department situated within Ashford Council and was told they would call him back, but they didn't.

On 1 December the Verneys went on a well-earned break from the hum, but when they returned their investigations and phone calls to the council drew a blank. Why had no one returned their calls? During the weekend of 17 December the Verney household experienced several electrical problems and engineers came out to investigate. New power lines were installed in the woods but the vibration continued to cause Antony and Doreen distress. A firm of acoustic engineers were then called out and an environmental health officer phoned Mr Verney to say he would be back in touch before Christmas. He broke his promise.

By this time the Verneys were under a great deal of stress; not only were they being plagued by a throbbing sound but they were becoming increasingly frustrated at the lack of effort and communication on the part of the authorities, who seemingly failed to realise the serious nature of the noise. The Verneys visited a firm in London who thought that maybe the Ministry of Defence were to blame for the hum. Throughout Christmas the couple were plagued by the worsening vibration, and things got weirder when Mr Verney observed a peculiar horseshoe-shaped object in the sky. By this point the Verneys decided it was time to look for a new residence. They went on holiday to Sussex, put in an offer for a property and returned to Biddenden. Then, on 5 January, Mr Verney and his wife had a terrifying experience. They claim to have been 'zapped' (blasted by an invisible force) after being subjected to twenty-four hours of vibrating noises. The following day they were zapped again, but an environmental officer seemed reluctant to look into the mystery.

On 18 January a scientist came to investigate the area but, whether by some strange coincidence or not, when the Verneys took the man to a pub for a meal their car was broken into and their cheque book and a bank statement stolen. The problems for the couple were mounting up and the soundtrack to their hellish life was the continuous vibrating hum. When they took the scientist back to their droning home they were met by an environmental officer and the hum was recorded by the scientist, who said he would be back in touch. Of course, the investigations never eased the hum and every night, deep into the early hours, the Verneys were tormented beyond belief.

On 21 March the house was put on the market and it was sold on 2 April. This sale wouldn't be completed until 24 May and so the Verneys tried to stay away from the house for as long as possible. However, whilst away in London the house was broken into. Bizarrely, all that was stolen were some financial papers belonging to Mr Verney and a bar of chocolate. According to the book *Unexplained Kent* (edited by Trevor Sturgess) Mr Verney's diary entry for 20 May (his last record while at Biddenden) read as follows: 'About 1:30 am, all hell was let loose. The noise at the highest level ever was heard, vibrations tearing through the ground of the woods towards the house at a frightening velocity. The zapper was depleted once again. The whole operation went on non-stop until 7 am.'

The following week the Verneys escaped from their nightmare when they moved to a house in Sussex. In February 1996 Doreen Verney died following a stroke. Previous to 1983, before they moved to Biddenden, Doreen had been given a clean bill of health, but Antony believed that the stresses, strains, zaps and noises at Biddenden had caused her death. In the summer of 1984 Doreen was diagnosed as suffering from lymphatic leukaemia but managed to pull through, whilst Antony lost most of his hair, his teeth fell out and X-rays revealed damage to his spine. The nightmare scenario experienced by the Verneys may sound like something from a Science Fiction novel, but it happened… Of course, when Mr Verney claimed that his phone was tapped and he'd been harassed by police officers, his allegations were denied by officials from the Ministry of Defence and police.

Were the Verneys guinea pigs in a bizarre, covert experiment conducted by mystery assailants? Was the hum a natural phenomenon beyond the investigations of environmental health or was the lack of investigation down to some cover up? Were UFOs using the woods at the back of the cottage? Or was the whole nightmare nothing more than the wild imaginations of a paranoid couple?

When one considers how many mystery hums have plagued parts of Britain, and the rest of the world, it does make one wonder just how severely a cacophony can affect those able to hear it. The scary part, of course, is that whilst some phantom drones could well be blamed on industrial mechanics, or even spectral aircraft, there are cases, such as that involving the Verneys, which once again prove that there are sinister forces at work.

The sky is a very strange place indeed.

6

MONSTERS FROM THE SKY

Monsters have plagued the nightmares of man and his folklore since the beginning of time. They exist beyond the realm of the imagination, and they instil an innate sense of dread whether we believe in them or not. We know of science, and science teaches us what can or cannot be, and yet some have experiences which contradict science's laws.

From mythology we have learned of the harpy, the unicorn, the dragon, the vampire, the mermaid, the werewolf and the cyclops. Especially in the modern era, we have confined these fantastic beasts to the realms of fiction; the fantasy of film, television and literature. Occasionally, however, the monsters of tribal folklore and ancient belief are investigated in case they might be exaggerated versions of possible unknown species as yet to be classified by science. When we fail to find them we relegate them back to folklore. When we do discover them, we claim them as our own. Although the deepest steaming jungles and the inky depths of the oceans have not yet yielded every beast they hide, there are still some monsters which cannot exist scientifically, biologically or zoologically – and yet people claim to have seen them.

In 1992 researcher Jonathan Downes gave these elusive, nightmarish creatures a category – zooform phenomena. Whilst unsure whether such critters were the product of imagination, ghostly manifestations or demonic entities, one thing seemed apparent to him: that every culture of this mysterious world harboured a surreal Ark of contentious entities. Phantom bogeymen, winged humanoids, paranormal manimals, ghostly animals – dubious they may well be, but every year someone across the world reports seeing one, and history suggests they are more than just fable.

The hardest part of Downes' research was investigating creatures which simply couldn't exist. Whilst cryptozoology is the study of hidden animals (extinct species awaiting discovery, newly discovered species) the realm of zooform phenomena is literally akin to one chasing shadows. It is similar in many ways to UFO or ghost reports: they are popular in culture but evidence for their existence is scarce. And when these three subjects collide, it creates a cauldron of impossibilities and vague manifestations. The following accounts are what could be deemed as impossible animals. Others may regard them as true monsters, or spectral entities bestowed with animal characteristics ...

THE OWLMAN COMETH

On 17 April 1976 twelve-year-old June Melling and her sister Vicky (nine) were on holiday with their parents near Truro, in Cornwall. The sisters decided they wanted to explore the local area and so after stopping for a family picnic in the woods of Falmouth, Vicky and June took a look at Mawnan Old Church. As Mr and Mrs Melling enjoyed their snack they were suddenly startled to hear their daughters scream and for them to come dashing from the woods. The children demanded to leave the area and their parents obliged, taking them back to the safety of their campsite where Vicky and June told their astonishing story. The girls described hearing a 'funny noise' and were then horrified to see a large, feathery creature hovering over the tower of the church. The creature was no ordinary bird; it resembled an owl crossed with a man, but was far bigger and had red, glowing eyes. At the

time such a report seemed far-fetched, until of course more people came forward to report their sightings in the vicinity of the old church.

Two fourteen-year-old girls had also been camping in the woods by the church, at around 10.00 p.m., when they heard a peculiar hissing noise and then saw the creature about 20yds away. One of the girls, named Sally, reported:

It was like a big owl with pointed ears, as big as a man. The eyes were red and glowing. At first I thought it was someone dressed up, playing a joke,

Owlman of Cornwall.
(Illustration by Mark North)

Owlman as sketched by B. Perry, 4 July 1976. (Image courtesy of Jonathan Downes)

trying to scare us. I laughed at it. We both did. Then it went up in the air and we both screamed. When it went up you could see its feet were like pincers.

Sally's friend, Barbara, added, 'It was horrible, a nasty owl-face with big ears and big red eyes. It was covered in grey feathers. The claws on its feet were black. It just flew up and disappeared in the trees.'

Bizarrely at the same time Sally and Barbara reported their sighting of the monster, two further girls also saw the beast. In a letter to the *Falmouth Packet* newspaper, they wrote:

It was in the trees standing like a full grown man, but the legs were bent backwards like a bird's. It saw us and quickly jumped up and rose straight up through the trees. My sister and I saw it very closely before it rose up. It had red slanting eyes and a very large mouth. The feathers are silvery grey and so are his body and legs. The feet are like a big, black crab's claws. We were frightened at the time. It was so strange, like something out of a horror film. After the thing went up, there were crackling sounds in the tree-tops for ages. Our mother thinks we made it all up just because we read about these things, but that is not true, we really saw the bird-man though it could have been someone playing a trick in a very good costume and make up. But how could it rise up like that? If we imagined it then we both imagined it at the same time.

There's no question that 1976 was a strange year for Cornwall. The feathery monster, which would become known as Owlman, would put in several more appearances. At the same time, sea monsters were observed in the bay at Falmouth, odd lights were seen in the skies and all manner of unusual activity was recorded. These sightings led researcher Jonathan Downes to write his brilliant book *The Owlman and Others*.

One of the most intriguing aspects of the Owlman case was that all the witnesses appeared to be young girls, suggesting that either someone had perpetrated a very elaborate hoax, in the hope that only young, teenage girls would experience it, or maybe there was a more obscure reason – that this manifestation was the unintentional product of the human psyche, perhaps. Such a theory may sound bizarre, but as in similar cases, especially with regards to poltergeist activity, it is often recorded how witnesses tend to be teenage girls. Jon Downes' book delves deeper into the mystery but does make one wonder just what type of apparition could have been lurking around Cornwall in 1976. A sceptic could quite easily dismiss the reports as the product of an over-active imagination, and that would seem fair enough, but in 1995 a man named Gavin came forward to report that he'd visited Mawnan woods as a twelve year old. He had been accompanied by his thirteen-year-old girlfriend and they both saw the dreaded Owlman. They said the monster, which stood approximately 4ft high, was perched on a thick branch of a conifer tree. The beast was grey/brown in colour and had glowing eyes. When the Owlman saw them it lifted its wings and jumped backwards. They were terrified by the apparition and were positive it was no owl, but in fact a humanoid with owl characteristics.

One of the most well-known winged humanoid spates took place in 1967 in an area known as Point Pleasant in West Virginia, USA. This red-eyed winged fiend was known as the Mothman and, once again, the activity was accompanied by other strange phenomena such as weird lights in the sky. Eerily, the winged creature was seen near the Silver Bridge which, after the sightings reached a peak, collapsed and killed forty-seven people. Some researchers at the time, and since then, believe the Mothman entity was some type of bad omen. The high strangeness that affected West Virginia was eventually used for the basis of a film in 2002, *The Mothman Prophecies*, starring Richard Gere. The fiction of the movie was nowhere near as strange as the facts.

In his 1925 work *Fairies At Work And At Play*, Geoffrey Hudson spoke of a winged entity which he'd observed in the Lake District, stating:

Was the dreaded Owlman simply an owl, or something more sinister? (Photograph by Neil Arnold)

My first impression was of a huge, brilliant crimson bat-like thing, which fixed a pair of burning eyes upon me. The form was not concentrated into the true human shape, but was somehow spread out into the shape of a bat with a human face and eyes, and with wings outstretched over the mountain-side. As soon as it felt itself to be observed, it flashed into a proper shape, as if to confront us, fixed its piercing eyes upon us, and then sank into the hillside and disappeared.

KENTISH CREATURES

What are we to make of such winged beasts? Well, four years before the 1967 Mothman drama of West Virginia, the county of Kent was visited by a similar monster. On the night of 16 November 1963 four youths were walking along a country road in Hythe. The area, known as Sandling Park, was dark but not the sort of place one would expect to encounter a monster. John Flaxton, aged seventeen, was accompanied by three friends, including eighteen-year-old Mervyn Hutchinson, and they'd all been to a dance. As they strolled along the lane they became aware of a bright object overhead, which they at first took to be a star. The teenagers were spooked by the object as they watched it hover and then drop out of sight behind some trees. The boys decided to leave the area with haste but the light came into view again. It hovered around 10ft from the ground, 200ft away from the youths, then once again went out of sight.

'It was a bright and gold oval,' one of the boys reported. 'And when we moved, it moved. When we stopped, it stopped.' Suddenly, the boys heard the snapping of a twig from a nearby thicket and from the wooded area shuffled a terrifying creature. 'It was the size of a human,' reported Mervyn Hutchinson, 'But it didn't seem to have any head. There were wings on its back... like bat wings.'

The boys were extremely scared by what they saw and although the monster wasn't seen again, reporters and amateur investigators scoured the woods for

The location of the 1963 winged entity sighting at Hythe, Kent. (Photograph by Nick Ames)

clues. Five nights after the sighting a seventeen year old named Keith Croucher saw a strange object floating across the football field near the Sandling Estate. Two nights later John McGoldrick and a friend were investigating the area when they claimed to have found strange indentations in the soil, as if some type of aerial craft had landed. Large footprints were also found in the area. They were said to have measured 2ft in length and were 9in across. On 11 December McGoldrick and a newspaper reporter claimed they saw a peculiar light over the woods.

Since this brief spate of reports nothing untoward has plagued Hythe. The case, despite being mentioned in many reports concerning the West Virginia Mothman, died a quick death and since then many authors have regurgitated the information author John Keel originally covered in his book *Strange Creatures from Time and Space*.

Whether the Hythe entity was from outer or inner space we'll never know; too much time has passed since the incident. However, zoologist Karl Shuker, who has investigated reports of strange creatures for many years, wrote of another winged anomaly in his 2008 book, *Dr Shuker's Casebook*: 'The following winged wonder only became known to me in mid-October 2007, when Jan Patience, acting editor of the erstwhile British monthly magazine *Beyond* for which I contributed a major cryptozoological article each issue, brought to my attention a truly extraordinary email that she had just received from a reader.' The reader was a woman named Jacki who resided at Tunbridge Wells in Kent. She had sighted a strange creature on three occasions.

The first sighting took place when Jacki was just four years old, back in the year 1969. She was in her parents' vehicle coming back from her auntie's residence in London. Her father had been driving for half an hour or so when Jacki was startled by an awful screaming noise. Jacki's parents seemed oblivious to the scream as they were busy chatting but when Jacki looked out the vehicle window she saw something she could only describe as a 'monster'. In the twilight Jacki realised that the scream had come from a creature that had red eyes and leathery bat-like wings which it unfolded from its body and then retracted. The beast – which stood around 3ft tall – resembled a monkey in its facial features but seemed to have the beak of a parrot. To Jacki's innocent mind it was the stuff of nightmares and it plagued her dreams for several weeks afterwards. She found it difficult comparing the creature to any known animal and so gave it the name, 'The Bat-Winged Monkey Bird'. Bizarrely, seven years later Jacki saw the monster again, when she peered out of the back window of her parents' car as they travelled back from Hastings. Jacki also had a recent encounter; at 4.30 one morning in her own home, she was awoken by a terrible scream, 'as if someone was being murdered', and so she hopped out of bed and looked out of the window and saw the tail end of the creature as it flew by the window. She told the magazine, 'I knew immediately what it was... the same horrible monster thing I had seen all those years ago. The Bat-Winged Monkey Bird was back.'

Karl Shuker was intrigued by the extraordinary encounter and contacted Jacki asking for further information. She emailed back with extra details and her own sketch of the critter. My own opinion on such sightings is that such monsters are manifestations connected to the human psyche. I have no explanation as to why

The bat-winged monkey bird. (Illustration by Simon Wyatt)

the young Jacki saw such a creature but, as in the case of the Owlman and the Hythe entity, I do believe these sightings require a certain mind-set in order to be perceived. Whether this is based on some type of emotional level I am unable to say, but such experiences bring to mind something that happened to me when I was young.

I'm guessing I must have been around eleven or twelve at the time and I was playing with a friend outside my parents' house in Chatham, Kent. It was a warm summer's night and it wasn't until 10.00 p.m. that darkness had begun to creep in. We were throwing a tennis ball to one another; there was a distance of about 50yds between us. I was standing near to my parents' front door, and my friend near the shadows of an oak tree. I recall throwing the ball and my friend must have lost the flight of it in the dusk, for as he clasped his hands to catch it the ball hit him in the face. I rushed over to see if he was okay and as I reached him we heard, from the high branches of the tree, something leap and hit the ground running. We were so terrified that all I recall is us both looking at each other and sprinting back to my parents' front door, where we stood, huddled in the gloom, expecting to see some type of winged monster pursuing us. There was nothing. I believe there is a possibility that what we experienced was some type of emotional apparition. It was not a deliberate entity and I believe it had somehow fed on our subconscious. Many times I have walked under that old oak tree and whilst it still gives me a feeling of dread, I never again experienced the phantom leaper.

RETURN OF OWLMAN?

Winged monsters are not strictly confined to the possible imaginings of youngsters. In 2010 I was contacted by a man named Mark who had a terrifying encounter to speak of. His email read as follows:

> Okay, before I report this I want you to know that I'm in no way over the top, crazy or mad … but one night while driving home from Exeter to Torquay on the A38 a couple of years ago (during November) I saw a large winged creature. I had just got to the top of Haldon Hill and as I came to the top of the hill something swooped down and flew up and over my car so close to my windscreen you could have fit a Rizla paper between it! The only way I can explain how these wings looked was the same as how bat wings are but much bigger! The wingspan was wider than my Honda Civic 1.5, I'd say each wing was about 2.5 metres across.
>
> I hadn't heard of anyone else who had reported this until now so I felt I should share with you what I saw. The area I saw this has a lot of thick dense woods … and I mean miles of woods.

When I interviewed the witness about his sighting he stated categorically that it was neither a bird nor a bat. He commented, 'On that drive I was stressing out about how I was going to raise money for presents. When I saw it I reacted with fear and put my foot down and got to the nearest town, which is Newton Abbot. I was the only car on the A38.' I pushed the witness for a better description of the monster, to which he replied:

> I know this sounds dumb but the only way I can describe what I saw is like the monster from the movie *Jeepers Creepers*. The wings were more like a bat, too wide for an owl. I didn't see the head as it was too fast but the wings reminded me of a pterodactyl. It literally swooped over my car and the car shook, similar to when a lorry goes by on the motorway. I was doing about 65 mph and I wish I'd stopped but at the time my heart was pump-

ing. This thing was more reptile-like in its skin texture and the colour was a beige-brown.

I had no doubt that the witness was genuine, but wondered just what surreal menagerie existed in the nether world we so rarely stumble across. Owlman, Mothman and the Bat-Winged Monkey Bird may sound like villains from a comic book, but I strongly believe that such entities exist in the ethereal sense and can be made stronger if they are believed in enough. The press most certainly, albeit perhaps unintentionally, created a sinister aura with the names of the Mothman and the Owlman. I look upon such cases as something akin to the snowball effect and believe that these beasts are thought forms, or tulpas, if you wish.

The tulpa is something which can be created by sheer willpower alone, and can gain strength or weaken depending on the devotion of thought applied to it. Some thought forms are created unintentionally and said to be caused by stress and other emotions – maybe this is why such manifestations can appear in such odd guises. The other theory is that such beings are demonic, or even angelic. One of the original Mothman reports described a naked human with large wings, which contradicts a majority of the reports which described a black, leather-winged entity with burning red eyes. However, no one described a humanoid resembling a moth! During the 1990s a creature resembling a winged humanoid was seen over Edingburgh, in Scotland. On 6 May 1981 two schoolgirls were spooked by a flying humanoid adorned in a black cape in the vicinity of Keston Ponds, Bromley. The figure also wore a black pointed hat and a belt that glowed.

Despite the fact these manifestations have appeared in the last few decades, in folklore such beasts, such as the harpy, have existed for centuries. Of course, there are those who believe that such encounters involve merely birds. For instance, the *Cornish Echo* of 4 June 1926 reported: 'Boys Attacked By Strange Bird – Unpleasant Experience Near Porthtowan' after two youths, whilst travelling between Mount Hawke and Porthtowan, were drawn towards a strange, fluttering thing situated on top of a mine burrow. The boys, out of curiosity, approached the object and found what appeared to be a large, dead bird but as one of the witnesses examined it he was attacked. He fled the scene and the other managed to throw his jacket over the creature but the winged thing escaped from the coat and began to attack the older boy. After a short struggle the boy managed to kill the creature by beating it with a stick. When properly examined the bird was said to have measured, '6ft 3 inches from tip of one wing to the other, and was 3ft in length.'

The bird had a very powerful pointed beak measuring 6in in length, and its short legs short ended with full webbed feet, which were striped with green and yellow, and it had a duck-shaped body. The plumage of the unusual bird was of a cream colour, tinged with brown on the beak, 'and also on the upper wing-coverts, the tips of the wings being black.'

It seems that when the boys approached the creature it had been suffering from a severe wound to an area under the right wing which had no doubt, according to the newspaper, 'caused it much pain, and must have infuriated it.' Although many villagers were said to have observed the specimen before it was buried, no one had the expertise to identify what exactly it was.

In Issue 22 of *Dead of Night* magazine, editor Lee Walker wrote of a strange 'thing' seen in the Lake District in 1987, which had echoes of the winged creature described in Geoffrey Hudson's 1925 work and also Jacki's Kentish sighting. Lee states:

> The witness, Chris S., then aged 5, was sitting in the backseat of his family's car as they drove to their holiday destination in Cumbria. The actual details are a little sketchy, given the passage of time. He remembers it was dark, sometime between 11–11:30pm, when he happened to glance out of the rear window of the car. Chris was amazed to see what he could only describe as 'two large, bright glowing red eyes, hovering about six feet above the surface of the road'. He couldn't discern the shape of the body, as it was too dark, and he could only surmise that it appeared as though the owner of those glowing red eyes was following the car at 40-odd mph. Chris turned to his parents, anxious to alert them to the presence of the thing, but when they all turned to look the creature had disappeared. He never saw it again.

In the June of 1998 Mr Simon Clabby, accompanied by a few friends, was on a biology field trip at Marlow's Sands in Wales. They were keen to research the rocky shores of the location and came across a truly monstrous bird-like creature which Mr Clabby wrote to *Fortean Times* about – his letter featuring in Issue 119. Mr Clabby stated that whilst walking along the cliff tops with friends they observed a tall figure standing further along the path which at first they took to be another friend who had requested to stay behind. However, as they approached they realised it was a 'man-bird' resembling a raven but 'about human size with a fairly wide wingspan.' The creature then flew off the edge of the cliff and out of sight.

BIG BIRDS?

With an alarming number of sightings being reported across the British Isles, could witnesses simply be seeing enormous, possibly escaped, birds? Ravens certainly do not grow to the size of a man, but large birds, especially birds of prey, do escape from zoo parks. Could they all be responsible for the winged monsters reported by so many witnesses? One could argue yes, and that, in the case of the Owlman or the Bat-Winged Monkey Bird, the witnesses were too young to be able to identify any large, known species of bird.

On 20 June 1986 the *Portsmouth News* reported that a 6lb Siamese cat named Blackie had been plucked from the garden of its owner, Jackie Greenwood, in Droxford, Hampshire. Jackie reported to the newspaper: 'The bird's wingspan was so large it completely covered Blackie. As it swooped down on him I shouted and waved my arms, but it took the cat in its talons and carried him up to the top of the fence.' A representative for the Royal Society for the Protection of Birds commented that the bird had possibly been a buzzard. Fortunately for Jackie, and Blackie, the bird dropped the cat. Then during the 1990s a large bird attacked a

Can alleged sightings of huge, winged monsters be explained by large birds? (Photograph by Neil Arnold)

woman who was riding her horse at Minster-on-Sea, Sheerness. The lady was thrown from her horse and despite noting its incredibly large wingspan she could not identify the mystery creature.

In 2001 and 2002 there were several reports over the United Kingdom of birds looking very much like vultures. Such birds, which are not native to Britain, are extremely large. During the summer of 2001 a griffon vulture with an 8ft wingspan escaped from Banham Zoo and was on the loose in skies over Norfolk. In Bedfordshire a white-backed vulture named Sydney escaped from the English School of Falconry and turned up a week later in Essex. On 21 February it was reported that a huge golden eagle was on the loose over Buckinghamshire – the bird had been seen to pluck a lamb from a field and also attempted to snatch a Jack Russell. During the same year a bald eagle escaped from Windsor Safari Park after strong winds had blown it off course during a training exercise. Large birds were also reported from Humberside and Northumberland.

Whilst there are hundreds of cases on record of large birds escaping from zoo parks and menagerie collections – from Sandhill cranes to Squacco herons, and from golden eagles to eagle owls – none of these avian predators match the monsters described earlier on. If man-sized birds are being seen in the woods of the United Kingdom then one thing is for sure, they do not live in the actual woods, but instead exist on some spiritual plateau. There can be no other explanation for such manifestations.

In 1733 a beast called a cockatrice was said to have terrorised the church at Renwick in Cumbria. The church that now sits at Renwick is not the original; that particular building was demolished in, rather coincidentally, the same year as the appearance of the monster. There is a record of the appearance of a strange creature in the church documents, which state:

> The inhabitants of the village are called Renwick Bats because they fled from a Cockatrice (Crack a Christ) monster flying out at them from the foundations of the old church they were rebuilding in 1733. All fled except John Tallantine who armed with a Rowantree slew the monster. For this act his estate was enfranchised to him and his heirs forever.

In mythology the cockatrice is a winged beast resembling a dragon, although it has the characteristics of a cockerel.

There is also a cockatrice legend from Scotland. Three miles north-west of Lerwick, in the Shetland Islands, there is a legend that a dragon left an egg at Dale. A woman found the egg one day and put it under one of her hens, but when the creature hatched it killed the hen. The monster that grew became a hellish beast that made its home near the farm until it was eventually set alight. Also from the Scottish Highlands was a winged creature known as the Skree, said to have been sighted in 1746 on the eve of the Battle of Culloden. As Karl Shuker explains, 'the Duke of Cumberland's troops amassed against the Jacobite rebels, who were fighting to restore the Stuart lineage to the British throne.' Before the battle exploded into life, Lord General Murray saw a bizarre creature with black leathery wings that flew over a group of soldiers, who scattered in fear. The monster screamed into the sky and many considered such a form an omen of doom.

There were two more sightings of the winged horror, one from 22 May 1915 when more than 500 Royal Scots were waiting to catch a train at Larbert station when the monster showed up. The petrified soldiers did not want to board the train but were forced to do so at gunpoint. Tragically, the train crashed later that day killing 227 and injuring 246. The skree's last visitation to this planet allegedly took place in 1993 when two hill walkers had become lost in the treacherous mists of Glencoe. One of the ramblers observed the enormous critter as it perched on some rocks shortly before it disappeared.

During the September of 1968 two men were fishing off the Mersey estuary. It was approximately 11.30 p.m. when, suddenly, a giant bird with a 12ft wingspan swooped out of the sky and headed straight toward them. The bird, even from a distance, gave off a pungent odour and the men were horrified by its red eyes. The bird perched on a large barge, rocking it under its weight. One of the men, who'd been out hunting rabbits previously, still had his rifle with him and took aim at the winged menace – but in the blink of an eye it vanished!

ATTACK OF THE GRIFFINS

London is probably the last place you'd expect to see a winged monster. London's most famous aerial monster made itself known in 1984 in Brentford – a suburban

In 1984 a griffin was said to have been observed over north London. (Illustration by Simon Wyatt)

town in west London. It was a warm summer's day when Kevin Chippendale was strolling along Braemer Road. His attention suddenly became drawn to an object soaring in the sky towards, rather coincidentally, the Green Dragon building. This wasn't a bird, a plane, or even Superman, because what Kevin described was something akin to a griffin – a mythological creature often confined to adventure films such as *Sinbad*. The following February was a bitterly cold month but it didn't stop the winged creature appearing to Kevin Chippendale again. This time he was able to get a better look, describing the monster as being dog-like in form but having wings. The beast had a dog-like muzzle, too. Shortly afterwards, a friend of Kevin's named Angela Keyhoe also spied the monster as it was perched on the Waterman Art Centre. Then, a psychologist named John Olsen, who was jogging near the Thames, saw the beast.

The flurry of sightings attracted the attention of the national press and the legend of the Brentford griffin was born. Some suspected a hoax perpetrated by several individuals, but a hotline was still set up in case anyone had seen the creature. Sadly, the sightings of the griffin subsided all too quickly, but this wasn't the first time a griffin-like monster was seen in Britain. For example, in his excellent *Dangerous Ghosts* volume O'Donnell, under the segment 'Homicidal Ghosts', mentions a story concerning a Mr John Luck. O'Donnell takes the story from two old works, being *A Strange and True Relation of One Mr John Luck* and *Legends & Traditions of Huntingdonshire*, both, I assume, by W.H.B. Saunders in 1662. O'Donnell goes on to mention the following:

> [Mr John Luck] a farmer from Raveley, set out on horseback one morning to the annual fair at Whittlesea. On the way he met a friend, with whom he had a drink at a wayside inn. After drinking somewhat heavily Mr Luck became very merry, and perceiving that his friend was getting restless and desirous of continuing on his way to the fair, he said, 'Let the devil take him who goeth out of this house today'.
>
> The more he drank, the merrier he grew. Forgetful of his rash saying, he called for his horse and set out for the fair. The fresh air seemed to have a sobering effect, for he had not travelled very far before he remembered what he had said. He was naturally superstitious and became so perturbed that he lost his bearings. He was endeavouring to find the way home – it was getting dusk and far too late to go to the fair – when he espied 'two grim creatures before him in the likeness of griffins'.
>
> They handled him roughly, took him up in the air, stripped him, and then dropped him, a sad spectacle, all gory, in a farm yard just outside the town of Doddington. There he was found lying upon some harrows. He was picked up and carried to a house, which belonged to a neighbouring gentleman. When he had recovered sufficiently to talk, he related what had happened to him. Before long he 'grew into a frenzy', so desperate that the inmates of the house were afraid to stay in the room with him. Convinced that Luck was under evil influences, they sent for the clergyman of the town. No sooner had the clergyman entered the house than Luck, howling like a demon, rushed at him and would have torn him to pieces, had not the servants of the house come to his rescue. They succeeded with great difficulty in overcoming Luck and tying him to the bed. No one was allowed to enter his room, the door of which was locked.

O'Donnell goes on to describe that the next morning Mr Luck was found dead in his bed. His body a crooked, broken mess; black with bruises, neck snapped and tongue hanging from his chasm of a mouth. His face wore an expression of utmost dread. Many believed that the griffin monsters were sent by Satan and had succeeded in their quest.

WINGED SNAKES OVER LONDON

During the eighteenth century *The Gentleman's Magazine* reported a strange account of a serpent over London:

> In the beginning of the month of August, 1776, a phenomenon was seen in a parish a few miles west of London, which much excited the curiosity of the few persons that were so fortunate to behold it. The strange object was of the serpent kind; its size that of the largest common snake and as well as could be discovered from so transient a view of it, resembled by its grey, mottled skin. The head of this extraordinary animal appeared about the same size as a small woman's hand. It had a pair of short wings very forward on the body, near its head; and the length of the whole body was about two feet. Its flight was very gentle; it seemed too heavy to fly either fast or high, and its manner of flying was not in a horizontal attitude, but with its head considerably higher than the tail, so that it seemed continually labouring to ascend without ever being able to raise itself much higher than seven or eight feet from the ground.

Then, in 1797, another flying monster was seen, this time between Hammersmith and Hyde Park Corner. The witness, a 'J.R.', recalled he'd seen the serpent on 15 June at 10.00 p.m. and wrote to *The Gentleman's Magazine* that 'the body was

London's Hyde Park Corner was subject to a visit from a flying serpent in 1797. (Photograph by Neil Arnold)

of a dark colour, and about the thickness of the lower part of a man's arm, about two-feet long … the wings were very short and placed near the head. The head was raised above the body. It was not seven or eight-feet above the ground.'

The witness, however, was quick to note that the creature appeared the day before a tremendous storm, as if to suggest it was a most unnatural phenomenon.

THE WINGED WOTSIT OF WEST DRAYTON

A spectral bird is mentioned in Revd F.G. Lee's 1885 work *Glimpses in the Twilight*. Since this case of the flapping horror, many more recent versions of the tale have painted the winged creature as a bat-like monster – although judging by what was originally written it seems that the following account concerned nothing more than a bird such as a raven … albeit a ghostly one! Lee wrote:

> In the middle of the last century, circa 1749, owing to several remarkable circumstances which had then recently occurred, a conviction became almost universal among the inhabitants of the village, that the vaults under the church of West Drayton, near Uxbridge, were haunted.
>
> Strange noises were heard in and about the sacred building, and the sexton of that day, a person utterly devoid of superstition, was on inquiry and examination compelled to admit that certain unaccountable occurrences in regard to the vault had taken place … Others maintained that three persons from an adjacent mansion-house in company had gone to look through a grating in the side of the foundation of the church – for the ventilation of the vault, and from which screams and noises were heard constantly, and had there seen a very large black raven perched on one of the coffins. This strange bird was seen more than once by the then parish clerk pecking from within at the grating, and furiously fluttering about within the enclosed vault. On another occasion it was seen by other people in the body of the church itself. The wife of the parish clerk and her daughter often saw it.
>
> The local bell-ringers, who all professed to deny its existence and appearance, one evening, however, came together to ring a peal, when they were told by a youth that the big raven was flying about inside the chancel. Coming together into the church with sticks and stones and a lantern, four men and two boys found it fluttering about amongst the rafters. They gave chase to it, flinging at it, shouting at and endeavouring to catch it. Driven hither and thither for some time, and twice or thrice beaten with a stick, so that one of its wings seemed to have been thus broken and made to droop, the bird fell down wounded with expanded wings, screaming and fluttering into the eastern part of the chancel, when two of the men on rushing towards it to secure it, and driving it into a corner, vaulted over the communion-rails, and violently proceeded to seize it. As the account stands, it at once sank wounded and exhausted on to the floor, and as they believed in their certain grasp, but all of a moment – vanished!

The wife of ex-vicar R.L. Burgh penned a letter to Revd Lee in reference to the anomaly, stating on 16 July 1883:

> It was many years ago; and I had quite forgotten it until I got your note. I can remember feeling persuaded that a bird must have got into the family vault, and in going outside to look into it through the iron bars to try if anything could be seen there, the sounds were then always in the chancel in the same place.

A record of the strange bird also exists from 1869 when two sisters claimed to have seen an enormous black bird whilst visiting the church, which they believed would have looked more at home in the Zoological Gardens.

On a less sinister note, at Great Russell Street in the Borough of Camden a spectral magpie was once said to materialise every morning between the hours of 2.00 and 3.00 a.m. The fluttering menace often taps on the window of a particular house, before materialising inside the property. The bird then appears on a floating twig, possibly a ghostly branch, before vanishing into thin air.

OMENS OF DOOM

The appearance of a spectral bird has long been considered a bad omen in the British Isles. In Lancashire the 'Seven Whistlers' are said to be birds heard at night. According to T.F. Thiselton Dyer: '[they] are supposed to contain the souls of those Jews who assisted at the Crucifixion, and in consequence of their wickedness were doomed to float forever in the air.' Numerous stories have been told, from time to time, of the appearance of the 'Seven Whistlers', and of their being heard before some terrible catastrophe such as a colliery explosion. A correspondent of *Notes and Queries* relates what happened during a thunderstorm, which passed over Kettering, Yorkshire, on the evening of 6 September 1871: 'on which occasion the lightning was very vivid, an unusual spectacle was witnessed. Immense flocks of birds were flying about, uttering doleful affrighted cries as they passed over the locality, and for hours they kept up a continual whistling like that made by sea-birds.'

Wordsworth wrote of the 'Seven Whistlers' in connection with the spectral hounds of the wild huntsman, poetically stating:

> *He the seven birds hath seen that never part –*
> *Seen the seven whistlers on their nightly rounds,*
> *And counted them. And oftentimes will start,*
> *For overheard are sweeping Gabriel's hounds,*
> *Doomed, with their impious lord, the flying hart,*
> *To chase for ever on aerial grounds.*

In Yorkshire a phantom goose was said to haunt a place called Berry Well. However, this spectral bird is not as sinister as the white bird reputed to haunt Arundel Castle in Sussex. In 1917 the white bird was said to have appeared outside the window

Ghostly birds are considered omens of doom. (Illustration by Simon Wyatt)

of the Duke of Norfolk before his death. Another doom-laden bird from Sussex is known as the Puck Bird. Charlotte Latham wrote of the spectre in 1868, stating that this was a devilish manifestation which swooped from the sky and preyed on cattle. The Puck Bird was also said to inflict a terrible disease upon cattle. Another legend in relation to the Puck Bird mentions how, especially in the Fittleworth area of Sussex, should such a bird appear on the path before you then never overtake it; should one do so they will be cursed. In his book *Sussex Ghosts and Legends*, Tony Wales writes of a Fittleworth servant who was sent upon an errand but returned very late. However, she had a good reason for the delay; she had seen a Puck Bird fly in front of her and refused to walk by it. Only when the bird had left did she dare continue her venture.

Sussex has another aerial anomaly which originates from Partridge Green. The old Jolesfield windmill was a much-feared property, for it was once said to be haunted by a miller who was murdered many years ago. However, one night a local man in the area reported seeing a strange, white misty object flying over and around the mill. Of course, there is a possibility that the 'ghostly flyer' was nothing more than a pair of barn owls, which, of a night can be quite an eerie sight to behold as they take to the darkness.

In Lincolnshire there is a legend of a death bird from Boston. In his *Mysterious Lincolnshire* Daniel Codd writes of a 'gloomy portent' that was said to have perched on the Boston Stump in the September of 1860. The creature was a 'big, black cormorant'. Many people at the time knew this bird was an unlucky omen associated with maritime misfortune and many sailors mentioned that should such a bird be observed at sea then disaster will occur. Another legend paints the cormorant as an unclean bird, and Codd mentions that a Charles Ingamells, in the *Stamford Mercury*, records seeing such a feathery fright on a Saturday 8 September, where the large bird remained still on top of the tower and was still there when he looked the next morning. With many locals panicking about the presence of the bird the church caretaker according to Codd, 'took matters into his own hands and shot it on the following Monday morning.' According to reports the cormorant measured 4ft 6in from wing tip to wing tip. The Boston folk knew that some type of disaster was around the corner; then received news that the passenger steamer *Lady Elgin* had sunk on Lake Michigan. Legend has it that the cormorant was stuffed by a taxidermist, but no one knows where the body is now. Interestingly, the Liver Birds of Liverpool are said to be based on cormorants and legend has it that should they ever face each other they will mate, and the young fly off, bringing bad luck to the city.

Daniel Codd also writes of several other phantom birds seen around Lincolnshire, which only appeared when someone was about to die or a disaster was about to take place. At the Grange at Linwood, rooks are said to desert their nest when someone is about to commit suicide. In 1893 it is recorded that two unusual birds flew around a house at Caistor before the owner died. The white birds of Salisbury Plain in Wiltshire also appear when a death is imminent. The birds, according to author Kathleen Wiltshire, are '… large … like albatrosses, with dazzlingly white

Death birds can take on varying forms, but those who see them are sure to die. (Image created by Neil Arnold)

wings which do not move as they fly'. In 1885 a Miss Moberly saw the birds just before her father, the bishop, died. The phantoms were also observed on 15 August 1911 when a Miss Edith Oliver had taken the choirboys of Wilton on an annual jaunt. As they were travelling back on a wagonette they saw two white birds flying over Hurdcott meadow. The birds appeared to float and not once did they flap their wings. Miss Oliver had not previously heard of the ghostly legend, but when she returned home she discovered that the bishop (Wordsworth) had suddenly died.

In Wales there exists a 'corpse bird', also known as *Derwyn Corph*. This particular creature sits on the windowsill of those who are about to die. Usually the bird will tap on the window. This brings to mind a rather creepy incident which happened to me a couple of years ago. On Thursday 9 July 2007 I was awoken around 7.00 a.m. by a squawking noise. At the time I lived in an historic apartment, top floor, overlooking a castle. I sat bolt upright and saw on the window ledge a large, black crow. Suddenly, the bird turned to look at me and then tapped four times on the window and then flew off. I'm pretty sure there's nothing sinister about this but it was rather odd at the time, especially as I was fully aware of birds as omens of death.

Kathleen Wiltshire mentions several other accounts of the ghostly birds, stating, 'Bishop Hallom of Salisbury, died in Constance during the Council of Constance in 1414' and whilst 'lying-in-state in the great hall of the town', there is legend that a great flock of birds perched upon the roof of the hall, 'where they stayed all night, making harsh, discordant cries.' By the next morning the birds had left.

Wiltshire also states that, 'The Reverend W. W. Fowler, a canon of Lincoln, retired to a rectory in Wiltshire to write a book on ornithology. On the day he died, all the owls in the neighbourhood seemed to have gathered around his house…' Before his death these great birds perched on gateposts, pinnacles, rooftops and anywhere else they could hook their talons, and there they stayed till he had passed on, and then they left. Interestingly, the day the Revd Fowler was buried a large, white owl glided through the churchyard close to the coffin and perched itself in one of the big yew trees. Was it a mere coincidence that the crest of the Fowler family had been an owl?

Another case of a spectral white bird is recorded from Market Lavington and was told to a Mrs Gye by her aunt. A great white bird was recorded as flying from the ground around midnight in the vicinity of Clyffe Hall Hill. Mrs Gye's great-grandmother, who was born in 1827, was travelling home late one night from Trowbridge when the horse began to shy. Suddenly, from the road ahead emerged a huge white bird.

Wiltshire further records that in Blunsdon the Devil was once said to have taken the form of a crow. The village of Alfrick, 8 miles south-west of Worcester, is haunted by a spectral crow.

At Skene, in the Grampians of Scotland, author John Brooks records a legend pertaining to a famous warlock named Alexander Skene who was 'laird here and died in 1724'. Folklore claims that the warlock 'had lost his shadow in escaping from the Devil.' Skene, like some witches, was said to have had four familiars; these took on the form of a jackdaw, hawk, magpie and crow, and these sat beside him when he took to the unlit roads in his coach drawn by headless black horses. The most bizarre story that author Daniel Codd speaks of concerns a strange tree in Lincolnshire which is said to produce geese! But my favourite bird-related anomaly comes from Charles Fort's 1931 work *Lo!* in which he writes of a luminous owl. According to Fort the *Eastern Daily Press* (Norwich) from 7 February 1908 reported that on 5 February a Mr E.S. Cannell, a Lower Hellesdon resident, had come across a shining object on the ground that seemed to flutter toward him. The witness, although startled, realised that the creature was a luminous owl and so he picked it up and took it home but unfortunately it died, 'still luminous'!

Fort argues that the bird may have suffered from feather fungi, but even so, such a bird would have been quite a sight on a dark and stormy night!

Phantom birds are said to guard the burial place of two kings at Carburrow Tor, in Cornwall. The bodies are housed in golden coffins and legend claims that should any thief attempt to unearth the treasures buried beneath the coffins, then they will be set upon by the ferocious fluttering phantoms. In parts of Northumberland it is said that should you hear the flapping of birds' wings of a night then someone close to you will suffer misfortune. At Wallington Hall in Northumberland there is a rumour that in the past, beating wings have been heard against some of the windows.

Closeburn Castle is an extremely old tower house situated in Scotland. The ghostly bird legend here concerns two red-breasted swans which used to appear on the loch. These beautiful swans were once considered omens of good luck until one was shot with an arrow. From that moment on it was said that every time a swan appeared in the area, a member of the Kirkpatrick family would die. Nowadays the legend lacks effect because the loch has been drained; some say that the water was emptied in order to prevent the spectral swans from returning.

BLACK WINGS OVER BRISTOL

During October 2005 a friend of mine named Vic Harris, who has a keen interest in cryptozoology, sent me a letter regarding something very unusual he'd seen in the summer of the previous year in Bristol. We'd been discussing, via email, strange creature sightings, when he recalled a bizarre event. His letter read as follows:

> I'll make it brief, in August 2004 (a Tuesday or a Wednesday) I was at the local park with my daughter, teaching her to ride her bike, it was about 6:00 pm. The park is quite high and gives a great view across the city, we had just finished and decided to head for home and I looked out over the city and saw a very large black shape moving slowing across the sky, so I said to my wife, '… look at that,' and she rolled her eyes and said, '… it's just a black bag caught in the wind.'
>
> 'Ok,' I said, '… but there's no wind today and that is moving very slowly and purposefully and if it's a black refuse sack it's enormous and it appears to be flapping, as in wings flapping.' She had to grudgingly agree.
>
> We stopped and watched it for approx 5 minutes as it passed across the city and eventually out of sight, I thought about it all night, I knew I'd seen something out of the ordinary.

The next evening my daughter wanted to resume her bike lessons and also one of my sons wanted to come along as well, so we set off and arrived at the park about the same time. I kept glancing up at the sky, but was sure I wouldn't see a repeat of the day before. So I couldn't believe it when at near enough the same time there it was again! This time my wife had to admit that this was something odd, it was just too much of a coincidence for two black bags to go across the skyline at exactly the same time on two consecutive days. Well, I was too excited to carry on with the bike lessons and we headed for home with me keeping my eye on the object as we walked home; I hoped I would be able to keep it in sight until I was able to get back and watch it through my binoculars. I kept it in sight and as we walked I became more convinced that this was something very unusual. As we walked down the street we came across quite a few people just stood staring up at the sky watching the black object. As we approached my house it went out of sight behind the house, I rushed in and got my binoculars and went into my back garden and sighted it again and I was not the only one, several other gardens were occupied with people watching and pointing up at it.

I watched it for approx. one minute through the binoculars – it was hovering over a water tower which is approximately fifteen minutes' walk from my house. It was jet black and very matt, it did not reflect the sun which was still bright in a very clear sky, it almost seemed to be absorbing the light it was so black, it was triangular in shape and seemed to be slowly flapping what appeared to be the rear two points of the triangle, which lead me to believe that the other point was in some way it's head or the front of what ever it was. It appeared to be flat with no details that were evident. The size amazed me, using the water tower and buildings around to estimate it's size, I would have said it was at least 35 to 50 feet across from point to point.

After approx one minute I heard a helicopter and quickly moved my head slightly to the right where I could hear it coming from, it was the police helicopter that we regularly get over our area after joy riders, it was heading straight for the black thing. I returned my view to the black object to see what would happen and it was gone! It must've taken a couple of seconds to move my head to look at the helicopter and back to the black thing. There was no way it could have moved fast enough to disappear from my field of vision in two seconds, the sky was clear and I could see for miles.

After seeing the police helicopter I was convinced that something would be on the local news, TV, radio or papers, but nothing was ever said about it. From just estimating the people in my street that I saw watching it at least fifteen other people saw it and the occupants of the police helicopter obviously saw it as they were making straight for it. Not sure what it was, but it wasn't a bird, it had no natural looking features at all, I'm pretty certain it wasn't an aeroplane and I'm fairly convinced it wasn't an alien craft, it appeared to be completely flat with nowhere for any occupants to travel in it. It definitely left me feeling rather uneasy, whatever it was it definitely had a negative feel to it. The thing that really struck me was the total blackness of the thing, usually even the blackest objects seem to have some areas of shade or light reflection, but this had none whatsoever.

Across the British Isles, and Europe for that matter, there have been numerous reports of what people call black triangles. Some researchers believe these are covert stealth craft operated by the military, or constructed by extra-terrestrials. However, the sighting made by Mr Harris suggested a living object that had no room to fit occupants in it. Was this a remote-controlled object or an unknown monster?

THE HORROR OF HERTFORDSHIRE

More than a century ago a curious incident took place in the neighbourhood of Hoddesdon in Hertfordshire. Mr Boreham was a well-respected man who lived in the area with his wife and three daughters. One evening as the family sat around a crackling fire talking to a neighbour, their tranquillity was shattered by a knocking sound followed by several screams and shouts. The neighbour, a Mrs Hummerstone, who was closest to the door, ran out towards the kitchen and saw the servant girl, called Elizabeth Harris, trying to defend herself from a knife-wielding maniac named Tom Simmonds. The eighteen-year-old Simmonds, who was employed by Mr Boreham, had been dismissed after being found to be more than unsuitable for

The 'horror of Hertfordshire' was described as a winged entity. (Photograph by Neil Arnold)

the job. Simmonds had also been dating Elizabeth Harris, but was overcome with a murderous rage after Mr Boreham advised the servant girl against continuing to see him.

Simmonds rushed out of the house and then smashed a window with a chair and climbed through, stabbing Mrs Hummerstone in the throat on the way. Simmonds then brutally attacked Mr Boreham's oldest daughter, stabbing her to death before slashing at Mrs Boreham and Elizabeth Harris. But then, whilst in the throes of his murderous mission, Tom Simmonds suddenly ceased with his actions, dropped his knife, screamed and fled from the building.

A few hours later Simmonds was tracked down by police to an old barn where he was found shivering and staring wild-eyed into blackness. Simmonds was to be executed, but before his death he told a very strange story to the chaplain. He commented that as he was about to slash Miss Harris with the knife something cold tapped him on the shoulder. When Simmonds turned he was confronted by a huge, dark-coloured creature, which had large wings. Although its face was human-like, it frowned heavily at him. Many would have perceived Simmonds' rambling as the words of a madman, were it not for the other witnesses who came forward to speak of their own personal encounters with the winged monster. One local man, after hearing about the story, came forward to say that after a bout of heavy depression he decided to commit suicide. Suddenly a winged humanoid appeared and its appearance alone forced the man to reconsider his actions.

Hertfordshire has an even weirder monster bird story, one so strange that it simply defies logic. In 1980 a nine-year-old boy named Alex Driscoll was walking to school along Gammons Lane, in Watford, when he was confronted by a monstrous bird-like creature. Originally, Alex thought that the being was someone dressed-up in a bizarre costume because it stood over 6ft in height, had a huge orange and yellow beak and enormous webbed feet. Most of the body of the beast was obscured by a gate but Alex could see that the bird had no feathers and thick black fur on its head. So unnerved was he by the strange being that he fled, leaving the creature to its own weird devices.

FLYING HORSES AND DOGS ...

One very obscure story pertaining to a flying, spectral horse is mentioned in Michael Hervey's book *They Walk By Night*. In it he mentions a fascinating account of a Canterbury (in Kent) woman named Miss Dorothy Ramsay, who, whilst driving her sports car along Littlebourne Road, got the shock of her life when a 'horse seemed to fly up from the road like a great shadow'. The beast then came down upon the sports car, smashing the roof and the windshield before vanishing. At the time police investigated the story, and an officer commented, 'We don't want to start a ghost horse scare, but we have searched for the animal without success.' This also reminds me of an account I heard as a child, growing up in Chatham in Kent. A relative of mine named Joe Chester mentioned how local police had been called out to investigate a stretch of hill apparently haunted by a horseman. Legend has it

Ghostly winged horses, although rarely sighted, have been seen at Sussex, York and Kent. (Image created by Neil Arnold)

that the Royal Engineers attempted to shoot at the wraith but their bullets glided through it.

Another flying ghost horse, known as the 'thunder horse', was said to have haunted York in 1065. The *Chronicon de Melrose*, a tome compiled by the monks of the Cistercian Abbey of Melrose, recorded:

> Great tempest and thunders at York, when the old enemy was also seen by many in that horrid tempest, mounted on a black horse. The monster was of very large size and preceded the storm. He was always flying towards the sea to tread it underfoot, and was followed by the blast of thunder and the flash of lightning, with horrid cracklings. Indeed, the tracks of this horse, aforesaid, were seen, of enormous size, imprinted on a mountain at the city of Scandeburch [Scarborough], whence he leapt into the sea. Here, on the top of several ditches, men found, stamped in the earth, prints made by the monster, where he had violently stamped with his feet.

The sound of horses' hooves in the sky, accompanied by the baying of airborne hounds, has been experienced in the region of Ditchling Beacon hill fort in Sussex. In 1933 a wild hunt was seen traversing the sky. Legend has it that shepherds would often describe how their dogs, of a night, would cower in the fields and stare up at the stars. The dogs would then flee as 'witch-hounds' flew overhead.

In folklore the Black Dog, or 'hellhound', is a ferocious spectral canid said to roam remote moors and lonely roads of a night. They are described as shaggy, red-eyed, calf-sized monsters that accompany weary travellers. Although these ghost hounds do not attack people, they are often said to appear when a death is about to occur. Of all the hellhounds said to roam the British Isles, only a handful are rumoured to take to the sky. Todmorden, in West Yorkshire, is haunted by Gabriel's Hounds, which are said to fly through the Cliviger Gorge. This spectral 'wild hunt' is considered a bad omen and usually takes flight around Halloween.

DASTARDLY DRAGONS ...

The dragon is considered very much a monster of myth and British folklore is littered with tales of such beasts as if they were once inhabitants of our dense forests. There are so many stories pertaining to knights slaying leather-winged beasties, and hillsides said to hide the skeletons of such fabled beasts. Not many British folktales mention winged dragons flying over villages, however, in fact a majority of old yarns seem to suggest that such monsters were nothing more than large snakes or reptiles. Even so, chronicler Charles Igglesden, in his 1906 volume of *A Saunter Through Kent With Pen & Pencil*, writes of a Kentish airborne dragon at Cranbrook, stating:

> The magnificent wooded park of a hundred and fifty acres is richly watered by a huge lake, made in 1812, and a smaller one within the garden grounds, while further west is an old mill that rejoices in a curious legend. It is an old one, and the subject of it must be very ancient indeed, and as rare as it is horrible. Nothing less than a flying dragon is said to haunt the pond, but on certain or uncertain nights of the year it wings its flight over the park and pays a visit to the big lake yonder. But he always returns to the mill pond and it is said to pay special attention of a vicious kind to young men and women who have jilted their lovers. A legend with a moral is this. But a winged dragon! A dragon of the ordinary kind is bad enough, but a flying dragon! Augh! It is Mr Tomlins' opinion that there is stronger evidence of the existence of this dragon than of most of his kind, and of his fires having gone out in the closing years of the last century. Nothing short of this monsters malign influence could account for the curious fact that, till the coming of Mr Tomlins' eldest daughter, no child has been born at Angley for upwards of a hundred years.

Henham in Essex was also the subject of a dragon. Chronicled in 1669, a pamphlet entitled *The Flying Serpent, or Strange News Out of Essex* records:

> The place of his abode and where he hath been oftentimes seen, is called Henham, but most commonly Henham on the Mount, the town standing upon a hill, having many fair farms and granges belonging to it, in one of which named The Lodge, near to a wood called Birch-wood, by reason of the many birches growing there, in a pasture-ground close by the same, hath this

monstrous serpent been often seen as he hath lain upon the sides of a bank, beaking and stretching himself out upon the same, at such time as Sol did parch the earth with his resulgent beams.

The first time that he was seen was about the 27 or 28 of May last, a gentleman's way lying by the place where this serpent keeps his station, as he rid carefully on, expecting to receive no hurt as he intended none, on a sudden this Serpent assailed his horse, affrighting the rider so much with his monstrous proportion and bold courage to give such an onset, that all in a maze he spurred his horse, who almost as much afraid as his master, with winged speed hafted away, glad that they had escaped such an eminent danger.

Being come home he acquaints his friends and neighbours with what he had seen of this monstrous serpent, especially makes it known to a neighbour in whose grounds this serpent doth lurk, wishing him to beware of his cattle, and to use his best indeavour for destroying it, least by protraction of time it might do much mischief when had I wist would be but small comfort to him for the losses he might sustain.

Not long after two men of the same parish walking that way, espied this serpent as he lay on a hillock beaking himself again in the sun, where they beheld his full proportion, being as near as they could guess 8 or 9 foot long, the smallest part of him about the bigness of a man's leg, on the middle as big as a man's thigh, his eyes were very large and piercing, about the bigness of a sheep's eye, in his mouth he had two row of teeth which appeared to their sight very white and sharp, and on his back he had two wings indifferent large, but not proportionable to the rest of his body, they judging them not to be above two handfuls long, and when spread, not to extend from the top of one wing to the utmost end of the other above two foot at the moll, and therefore altogether too weak to carry such an unwieldy body. These men though armed with clubs and staves, yet durst not approach to strike this serpent, neither it seems was the serpent afraid of them, for railing himself upon his breast about the height of two foot, he stood looking on them as daring them to the encounter.

Wales has many dragon legends; in fact such a beast adorns the national flag. In his highly recommended book *Dragons: More Than a Myth?* Richard Freeman speaks of many dragons from the Welsh hills and valleys. Such winged serpents are also mentioned in Marie Trevelyan's *Folk and Folk Stories of Wales*, in which she states that the wooded areas around Penllyne Castle once had a devilish reputation for being haunted by leather-winged beasts. The monsters became the stuff of folkloric tales passed down through generations and to terrify the young and old alike. Legend has it that one former resident of the area, an old man who passed away a few years ago, spoke of 'beautiful' serpents in the region which 'looked as if they were covered with jewels of all sorts. Some of them had crests sparkling with all the colours of the rainbow.'

If these creatures were ever disturbed from their slumber then they would glide away, all the while 'sparkling all over' before reaching a new hiding place. When angry, these serpents 'flew over people's heads with outspread wings bright, and

Dragons: terror of the skies that have embedded themselves in world folklore. Here, the author gets attacked by such a beast! (Illustration by Adam Smith)

sometimes with eyes too, like the feathers of a peacock's tail'. The old man also claimed that this legend was 'no old story invented to frighten children,' but a real fact. According to Trevelyan's source, his father and uncle had killed some of them for they were 'as bad as foxes for poultry'. His source attributed the extinction of the winged serpents to the fact that they were 'terrors in farmyards and coverts'.

One has to wonder just what type of creature these folktales are describing. Whilst seemingly snake-like in form, many of these tales clearly describe a winged, flying serpent form that fits into no known species of the British Isles. Richard

Freeman also mentions winged serpents in Glamorgan, particularly from the area of Penmark Place where such dragons were feared in the local neighbourhood. The woods around Bewper were said to be riddled with such beasts. There is also mention of how two men sought out one such feathered critter and shot it, but like a wounded tiger it attacked the men, beating them with its strong wings. The men eventually succeeded in slaying the serpent.

Whilst a majority of dragon sightings are confined to the murky past, there is mention of a flying monster from 1982, when one allegedly appeared over the Aire Valley in West Yorkshire. On 12 September a flying creature was observed in a wooded area. It flew erratically and low to the ground and the witness claimed that the creature resembled a pterodactyl. Several more sightings followed, all describing the same bat-winged creature. Astonishingly, the beast was tracked down by Mike Priestly, features editor on *The Telegraph & Argus*. He managed to photograph a strange flying creature in the skies of Bradford but his 300mm telescopic lens was unable to get a clear enough snap. Richard Freeman argued that the object in the photo was a bird, something akin to a buzzard.

In 1999 another airborne serpent was reported, this time on the other side of the Pennines. A grey-skinned creature with a massive wingspan was observed by several witnesses at Everson, and three witnesses claimed to have seen a winged monster in the Scottish Highlands, too. During a night-time trek, Damien Smith and his two uncles reached the remote region of Sutherland when they heard a flapping sound. Their torches highlighted an enormous creature with a wingspan of around 20ft. This echoed a 1996 encounter involving one Neil Mitchelson, who was camping in the Lake District with a few friends when they observed a huge winged creature shaped like a manta ray. All the witnesses agreed that the grey monster had a wingspan of over 30ft.

One of the most popular British dragon legends originates from Sussex, but there appears to be some confusion and the legend seems to describe a snake-like creature and certainly not a winged monster. *Ethelward's Chronicle* of AD 770 mentions 'monstrous serpents', but the eighth-century *Anglo Saxon Chronicle* records them as 'wondrous adders that were to be seen in the land of the South Saxons'. Another Sussex dragon account originates from Fittleworth from the 1860s. The monster was said to inhabit a lair near a pathway; those who attempted to travel by it would be confronted by the hissing creature. Again, this is suggestive of a snake rather than a formidable winged dragon. Some of these tales were said to have been made up by local smugglers, knowing that their nightmarish creations would deter local folk from venturing into places where they could stash their goods.

Sally Jones, in her book *Legends of Somerset*, recalls a dragon legend from the village of Norton Fitzwarren. After a bloody battle a vile beast was said to have risen from the gory pile of corpses. This seemingly supernatural monster took to the sky and plucked children from the village, leaving their parents screaming. Legend has it that a man named Fulke Fitzwarren speared the beast and decapitated it, ridding the village of this terrible menace. Another Somerset leviathan was once recorded from the foggy marshes of Carhampton. At the time, during King Arthur's reign, it was said that an evangelist named St Carantoc had ventured to the Carhampton wilds. One afternoon King Arthur was on horseback travelling through the fens after he'd

True and Wonderfull.

A Difcourfe relating a ftrange and mon-
ftrous Serpent (or Dragon) lately difcouered, and yet
liuing, to the great annoyance and diuers flaughters
both of Men and Cattell, by his ftrong
and violent poyfon,

Jn Suffex *two miles from* Horfam, *in a woode*
called S. Leonards Forreft, and thirtie miles from
London, *this prefent month of Auguft.* 1614.
With the true Generation of Serpents.

Printed at London by *Iohn Trundle.*

The fearsome dragons of Sussex folklore were probably nothing more than snakes or other escaped reptiles.

heard from villagers that a great flying serpent had been torching crops and carrying off people in its mighty jaws. The beast, however, was eventually tamed and
waddled timidly to St Carantoc's side; rendered powerless by his holiness. When
the monster was eventually released back to the marshes it no longer chose human
flesh but instead became a vegetarian! Villagers grew to adore the creature (clearly
forgetting the slaughter and damage it had caused previously!) and began to use it
for chores – its fiery breath only put to use for lighting fires in the rain.

The village of Aller was terrorised by a far more bad-tempered flying dragon,
which took great pleasure in scorching the landscape with its fiery breath and
leaving villagers choking on its fumes. The Aller beast had a penchant for milk, as
well as human flesh. Such was the devastation caused by the leathery monstrosity that a knight named John Aller went in pursuit of it. He adorned himself in a
thick mask to avoid being poisoned by the fumes of the dragon and set off, armed
with a spear. He came upon the dragon sleeping in its lair. When the beast awoke,
it attempted to blast the brave knight, but he was too agile and eluded its spray of
fire which scorched the hills all around. After a long game of cat-and-mouse, John
Aller finally slipped within the guard of the creature and speared it through the
heart. With the dragon still, Aller crept into the cave where the dragon had been
sleeping and was shocked to discover a trio of baby dragons. Aller quickly fled the
nest but returned shortly after with an army of local men and together they sealed
up the hole of the cave and eventually the dragons died of starvation. Of course,
like all good monster stories, there is an alternative version. Another tale claims
that although Aller killed the dragon, he was eventually poisoned by the strong
fumes from the dragon's breath.

In their book *Mysteries of the Mersey Valley*, Peter Hough and Jenny Randles speak
of a fearsome dragon, too, said to roam the once-forested areas of Runcorn – long
before people had settled. The beast was said to have measured more than 50ft in
length and had a stinking lair close to the river. When hungry the dragon would
take to the skies and carry off sheep and cattle.

Of course, despite many locals also being slain by the jaws of the beast, eventually a hero came along to conquer the creature; his name was Robert Byrch, a
blacksmith. He believed that because all of his livestock had remained untouched
during the dragon's spate of killing, it was possibly afraid of forge-fire. However,
one afternoon Byrch saw the mighty beast swoop down from the sky and take one
of his cows and so, angry at this act of predation, Byrch built himself a special suit
of armour in the disguise of the skin of a cow. Byrch, armed with a sharp sword,
patrolled the fields on all fours, hoping that the dragon, soaring overhead, would
spot him and attempt to swoop down. Byrch knew he would only have one chance
to spear the dragon beneath its wing, the only area bereft of tough scales. When the
encounter finally came about, Byrch almost made a fatal error. The beast loomed
out of the sky and grasped the blacksmith at great speed. Soon, Byrch was in the
sky, over the River Mersey. He stabbed the beast under its wing, but prayed that the
monster would not drop him or come down with him into the water, because in
such a heavy suit he would be sure to drown. Byrch devised a quick plan to stem
the bleeding of the wound, and the great winged critter finally landed weakly on
the banks, where Byrch then finished off the job. According to the legend, Byrch

became known as 'Robert the Bold' and was granted as much land by the king as the dragon skin could cover.

Of course, many may mock at such a tale and deem it as nothing more than myth, but Hough and Randles point out that, should you venture to the aptly named Griffin Inn situated on the Warrington Road, then you'll be at the site which once boasted a strange painting said to have depicted the great battle between Robert Byrch and the monster. The painting was said to have been hung over the kitchen fireplace but was destroyed when refurbishment was carried out.

Randles and Hough also speak of another legend, one which claims that a mysterious sample of skin used to hang over the Bold family pew in Farnworth, near Widnes. This piece of skin, which was said to have fallen to the floor of the building in 1870, was rumoured to have belonged to a cow but further examination of the hide revealed great claw marks as if some ferocious beast had slashed at it. Perhaps this had been the untanned hide of a cow that long ago fell victim to the winged dragon...

TROOPING OF THE FAIRIES ...

Not all fairies are confined to the bottom of the garden. Despite being one of folklore's most dominant figures, the fairy has long since been discounted as a possible real being. Instead, these winged entities have become the stuff of fantasy. Alleged real reports of such figures are scarce, and those concerning airborne fairies even rarer still. In 1917 a photograph of 'fairies' was taken in Cottingley near Bradford, but later was exposed as a hoax. Then, on 8 September 2009, the *Daily Mail* reported, 'Croydon Tinker Bell ... are there fairies at the bottom of the garden?', after fifty-five-year-old Phyllis Bacon photographed what initially looked to be a fairy in full flight in her garden. The photograph, taken in 2007 of her back garden, shows a small object that appears to have two wings, two legs and two arms, and resembles the archetypal fairy.

Experts who analysed the photo said there had been no tampering but believe the image more than likely showed a moth.

... AND ANGELS

Angels; winged messengers and protectors from the heavens. Mankind has spoken of such beings for more than 4,000 years. Are such sky people holy beings? Are they, like other creatures in this book, variations of surreal, unexplained humanoids moulded by society? In an article for the January 1997 issue of *Encounters* magazine, Nick Farrell states, 'The term "angel" comes from the ancient Greek "angelos" and can be translated as messenger, or someone sent.'

David Goddard, in his book *The Sacred Magic of the Angels*, claims that angels are ambassadors from a divine centre of the universe. He writes, 'It would do no good if the person to whom the message was delivered was too freaked out by the experience, so the messengers choose to appear in forms that people can relate to. This is why most people see them as young, tall humans, with large wings.' Goddard also notes that the appearance of such beings is moulded by the cultures they are a part of. This is something I've always been intrigued by and wonder if how such beings appear, whatever they are, simply depends on those who see them.

Angel encounters are not rare but, like dragons, they have embedded themselves into folklore as archetype images. St Mary's church at Udimore in Sussex has an angelic legend. Author Tony Wales, in his *Sussex Ghosts & Legends*, records that construction of the church originally began on one side of a stretch of water, but often the work and materials would vanish completely. He adds, 'Some of the villagers sat up and watched and listened, and afterwards described how the air was full of the rushing of wings of angels, who were carrying the building materials across the water, chanting "Over the Mere, Over the Mere".' Eventually, those who were constructing the church decided the building should go where the angels wished.

Charles Fort records a remarkable angel encounter in his book *New Lands*. He writes of an old pamphlet called *Wonderful Phenomena* by a Curtis Eli, which speaks of a weird case investigated by a spiritualist named Addison A. Sawin. The pamphlet goes on to speak of 3 October 1843 and a witness named Charles Cooper who heard a strange rumbling sound in the sky and observed a cloud which appeared to have three human, 'perfectly white' forms floating beneath it. The cloud sailed through the air just above the tree-tops. The beings were reported as being 'angels' – all male – and as they drifted through the sky belts were noticed around their waists. It was as if the angels had been dropped down by the object above (which brings to mind some of the Biblical angels and also those connected to UFOs). Charles Cooper called out to a group of men working in a nearby field and although they saw the strange cloud they could not see the angels. A local boy claimed that he'd seen the beings 'side by side' but making a 'mournful noise', which seemed to contradict Cooper's account. Another witness who lived 6 miles away said he saw the cloud, the people and heard the noise and Mr Sawin had quoted others who had seen 'a remarkable cloud' and heard the noise but seen no figures!

One of the most enigmatic legends in reference to the appearance of angels concerns the 'Angel of Mons' in Belgium. British troops battled the Germans on 22 and 23 August 1914 in the Battle of Mons. It was claimed that angelic forces intervened, although accounts vary regarding what was actually seen by the British troops. Some described a strange cloud formation, others silvery flights of arrows which aided them in their quest to push back the enemy, whilst some soldiers allegedly saw phantom cavalrymen. This story has become legendary, but is dismissed by many as nothing more than legend alone. Despite the fact that soldiers, nurses and others on duty described seeing figures in the sky, the story has often been considered a hoax. Yet my great-grandmother, Lily Lydia Arnold, recalled to my grandfather many years ago how she had seen the figure of an angel appear in the sky over her house in Chatham, just days before the war ended.

On 8 September 1944 the *South London Times* reported, 'Angel seen in Peckham raid' after numerous witnesses had come forward to say they'd seen the winged wonder during a bombing raid. The apparition lasted for more than twenty minutes and was seen in several areas over southern England and was said to resemble the 'Angel of Mons' which was observed in the previous war. A Mrs E. Halsey, of Horby Road, told a reporter, 'I have never seen anything so wonderful, I believe it was the Angel of Peace. It appeared quite plainly in the sky. The figure was perfect, with large outstretched wings, as if guarding something.'

Others described the angel as holding its arms out and looking down over the region. According to the newspaper, 'Mrs Halsey was asleep when her husband, who was "spotting", called her to see the figure.'

'I was rather annoyed at being awakened at 6.00 a.m. for I had had very little sleep,' she remarked. 'Afterwards I was glad I did not miss it. It shook us all up and made us think.'

Another witness to the extraordinary event was a Mr D.L. Phillips. 'It was early in the morning so no one could say I was not sober. There was a large cloud of dust rising where a bomb had fallen and the figure seemed to turn its head and look in that direction.' Other people also say they are sure it was the figure of an angel.

Peter Haining, however, writing in his *True Hauntings* book, gave an alternative explanation for some of the early angel sightings. His belief was that the apparition was some type of projection or holographic image, cast onto the clouds by German Intelligence to fool British troops. According to Haining, in the February of 1930 a former member of the German Intelligence Service named Colonel Friedrich Herzenwirth had told the *New York Mirror* that the figures were 'motion pictures' projected onto 'screens of foggy white cloudbanks' over Flanders.

These startling effects were created by 'cinematographic machines' with powerful Zeiss lenses mounted on German aeroplanes hovering above the British lines.'

Herzenwirth's statement – which was accompanied by an explanatory diagram mentioned how German Intelligence believed such visions would 'create superstitious terror in the Allied ranks'.

Clearly, this plan backfired and if anything drove the British troops on. Colonel Herzenwirth also claimed that the 'trick' had worked to full effect when applied on the Russian front in 1915, when an image of the Virgin Mary had allegedly been projected onto clouds.

A more recent, so-called angel mystery comes from London and has become known locally as the 'Thames angel' – it even has a website devoted to it. In 2006 several witnesses came forward to report they'd not only seen but photographed and filmed a shimmering apparition. Sceptics argue that the object bears no resemblance whatsoever to an angel, and could be some type of atmospheric phenomena, or reflection. Even so, the legend of the angel seems to originate from 1667, a year after the Great Fire of London. Since then there have been more than thirty sightings. A legend from the sixth century claims that a group of fishermen rowing near the south bank of the River Thames encountered a monk-like apparition who asked them to take him across the river. After the journey the newly built church, dedicated to St Peter, became illuminated and many angels were said to have appeared in the sky overhead.

In 1865 an etching showing a winged humanoid seemed to echo numerous sight-ings at the time of a similar airborne being, said to have appeared near Embankment. In 1914 a photograph taken at Southwark Docks was said to show an angel, and four years later another photograph taken was said to show the same figure. To many, the photographs show nothing more than a faint blur, but to some this whitish image is indeed an angel and belief is strong enough that the legend lives on.

In 2007 reporter Richard Porritt wrote of several Thames angel sightings includ-ing one made by a sixteen-year-old student named Jemima Waterhouse, from Sheen, who stated she'd seen the angel in the May whilst on her way to meet a friend. As she walked down the South Bank she felt 'a sense of calm spreading over me. It was comforting and familiar – a kind of peace that lasted for a while after. It is really hard to put into words, but I guess you could describe it as peace of mind.'

Jemima quickly took a photograph of an apparition which she said was floating in the vicinity of the *Queen Mary*. However, the photograph on her phone was too poor in quality to determine what exactly she'd taken a photo of. In fact a majority, if not all, of the photographs which claim to have snapped an angel are inconclu-sive, although Jemima added, 'My friend remained unconvinced until we got the photo onto a computer that evening – when the image became clearer and the outline of what could only be described as an angel became distinct.'

In many cases people seem to be seeing, and at times photographing a whitish, mist-like object on the stretch of river, but according to Porritt's article, 'South London Press chief photographer Leah Desborough thinks there might be a more scientific explanation.' Desborough stated that the 'angel' image could be attributed to several factors such as boat fumes creating some type of mirage on the water. For how long the angel of the Thames legend lasts we'll have to wait and see but Leah Desborough was happy to point to the fact that in most of the photographs, the image captured does seem to have the outline of what we'd term a winged angel.

In August 2009 *The Telegraph* ran the headline, 'Angel sightings should not be dismissed'. This came in response to a study conducted by Dr Kate Adams, a senior lecturer at the Anglican Bishop Grosseteste University College in Lincoln. She stated that too many children were afraid to speak of their encounters with angelic-type beings for fear of ridicule.

Since the earliest history of mankind there have been reported encounters with angels. (Photograph by Neil Arnold)

FLYING MONSTERS THAT NEVER WERE …

As a bit of fun I end this monstrous chapter with three hilarious accounts of flying monsters which were nothing more than misinterpretation. Enjoy!

On 18 June 1829 *The Times* ran this bizarre story after a weird happening over the capital:

A New Flying Fish

A very strong sensation was excited a few days ago in the vicinity of Wandsworth, by the appearance of an extraordinary animal, which was observed floating slowly through the air nearly over the village. Its appearance, which was that of a fish of about 20 feet in length, and proportionate bulk, excited alarm amongst many, and astonishment amongst all, who beheld it. What is was? And how it came there? were questions very eagerly and very naturally asked, but not so easily answered. Conjectures were hazarded, without number, and without result. Nobody could give a satisfactory explanation of the phenomenon, though every body made the attempt. It was a fish – it was a sea serpent – it was 'very like a whale', and there were not a few who thought that it was none of these, but something supernatural, portentous of strange and awful events; one or two of the more shrewd looked upon it as one of the visitations with which the country had been threatened in consequence of the passing of the Catholic Bill.

But whatever it was, it seemed to be the general wish that it should if possible be removed from the neighbourhood. But then came the question – how? To take a monster of such dimensions alive, was an attempt which might be attended with much danger. It was therefore considered prudent to kill it first, if it could be killed. For this purpose some of the best shots in the neighbourhood were put in requisition. Several fowling-pieces were discharged at it, without any other effect than that of adding to the terror of many of the spectators. At last a gentleman brought out a long strand-piece, loaded with duck-shot, and took his aim: he was successful. Some of the shot pierced the animal's side, when, to the terror of the crowds who looked on, it changed its form and sunk to the earth, a shrunken and misshapen mass. For a time no person was hardy enough to approach it; but at last, not seeing it move, the gentleman who brought it down advanced, and to his surprise, and the great relief of many present from their alarms, found that it consisted of a quantity of silk made in the shape of a fish and inflated with gas. The phenomenon was now explained.

Further inquiry lead to the discovery of the place from which it came; and it appeared that it was a 'loose fish' which had escaped from Vauxhall Gardens. The proprietors, it seemed, had prepared the monster intending that it should rise from the waters of the Hydropyric Temple, and float amidst the fireworks over the heads of the spectators. Having been properly inflated, it was slightly fastened to that part of the temple from which it was to ascend; but, in the course of the night, the strings became loosened and the monster escaped.

Where it passed its night is not known but early on the following morning it was seen floating over Wandsworth, as we have described. The truant monster has since been restored to its owners.

Sixteen years later, in 1845, a monster of a different guise floated over the capital, and again *The Times* (12 September) was on hand to cover the story:

A Monster Policeman

On Tuesday evening the inhabitants of Brixton, Walworth, and Peckham, were considerably amused by the aerial gambols of a 'monster' policeman, who was seen floating about the air for some time, and who at length fell upon the roof of a house in Minerva-place, Old Kent-road. It appears that Mr. Bass, a gentleman of fortune residing in Kent-terrace, Lyndhurst-road, Brixton, has been in the habit of letting off small balloons from his pleasure grounds, for the amusement of his friends. Latterly he has caused the construction of a figure of 12 feet in height in glazed paper, wih head, neck, arms, and legs, and painted in colours to represent a perfect facsimile of a 'peeler' with truncheon in hand, and on Tuesday night he (Mr. Bass) had caused this figure to be attached to a pilot balloon, and so arranged it that it should drop from its companion upon the former attaining a certain altitude. The experiment was very successful, and, upon ascending, the figure of the peeler had an exceedingly ludicrous appearance, and seemed as if in the act of being hung. On attaining a certain altitude the figure dropped from the balloon, when its appearance became much more comic and laughable. It had been so constructed as to maintain an erect position, and its various evolutions in the air were truly ludicrous. It gradually descended, until at length it fell on the top of one of the houses in Minerva-place, Old Kent-road, and was secured by police-constable 146 P, who on Wednesday restored it to Mr. Bass. It was fortunate it had not fallen on the ground, for had it done so, no exertions of the police would have prevented the public from seriously damaging the representative of the law.

Then, during April of 1979, the skies of Southampton were plagued by a mysterious creature which had soared to more than 12,000m in the sky. Passengers on an aircraft were startled to see an orange elephant flying through the clouds, according to an agency report. The inflatable beast was a balloon being used to promote a local circus!

After this weird menagerie of winged impossibilities, I leave you with an apt quote from Jesse Saxby's 1932 work, *Shetland Traditional Lore*, '... there's many kinds of life that lives in the air, in the earth and water – forby the clouds above. And we, poor mortals, have no vision to hear or see, or understand the like. We must just leave that to the Powers above.'

It's not Raining Cats and Dogs ... Just Pennies, Fish and Frogs!

More than a century ago it was believed by some that an ocean existed above the clouds. This theory came about due to the amount of strange, unexplainable things that had fallen from the blue sky of the day and the black sky of night. It has been recorded (and quite often, too) that large hailstones the size of golf balls have plummeted from above and rain has descended so hard as to shatter windows. I now present to you a chronology of even weirder falls from the sky that will not only leave you scratching your head in bewilderment, but possibly rouse you to reinforce your umbrella!

EARLY WEIRDNESS

Although brief, and at times lacking in detail, early records of strange phenomena are extremely noteworthy. In the lengthily titled *A General Chronological History of the Air, Weather, Seasons, Meteors, etc, in sundry places and different times; more particularly for the space of 250 years. Together with some of their most remarkable effects on animal (especially human) bodies, and vegetables*, chronicler Thomas Short mentions several weird falls from the heavens, such as:

AD 4 – It rained blood above five hours in London.
89 – It rained blood three days together in England.
324 – It rained blood six hours in Somersetshire.
442 – It rained blood in York.
685 – It rained blood in England.
688 – Rained blood seven days together through all Britain; milk, cheese, and butter, turned to blood.

A sixteenth-century woodcut depicting fish falls.

1176 or 7 – It rained blood on the Isle of Wight two hours.
1178 – It rained blood in England.
1198 – May, it rained blood in England; on St John Baptist's Day fell a dew, like and as sweet as honey.
1274 – It rained blood in Wales.
1459 – A bloody rain in Bedfordshire.
1649 – Feb. Rained blood in Gloucestershire.

1648–53: More blood!

Fortean Times magazine, Issue 51, p.56, looks at strange portents and falls of the seventeenth century as recorded by a Samuel Clarke, who from 1633–45 was a rector of Alcester, Warwickshire. A page of his *Mirror or Looking Glass* looks at 'Examples of Strange Prodigies', listing the following relevant information:

> Presently after the Scottish army came into England, to assist the Parliament, it rained blood, which covered the church and church yard of Bencastle in Cumberland.
>
> In June, Anno Christi 1653, a black cloud was seen over the town of Pool, which a while after, it was dissolved into a shower of blood, that fell warm upon men's hands; some green leaves with those drops of blood upon them, were sent up to London. Attested by eye witnesses.

1656: Wheat from the clouds
Chronicler Thomas Short records that in this year, near Oxford, it rained wheat.

1666: The sea rains!
During the Easter of 1666 in the county of Kent, a shower of sprats, whiting and smelts bombarded roads and houses. Some local people had the business acumen to scoop them up and sell them at Dartford and Maidstone. Another strange fall was mentioned in a letter from a Dr Rob Conny to Dr Or Plot, stating:

> On Wednesday before Easter, Anno 1666, a pasture field at Cranstead near Wrotham in Kent, about two acres, which is far from any part of the sea or branch of it, and a place where are no fish ponds, but a scarcity of water, was all overspread with little fishes, conceived to be rained down, there having been at that time a great tempest of thunder and rain; the fishes were about the length of a man's little finger, and judged by all that saw them to be young whitings, many of them were taken up and shewed to several persons; the field belonged to one Ware a Yeoman, who was at the Easter sessions one of the of the Grand Inquest, and carried some of them to the sessions at Maidstone in Kent, and he showed them, among others, to Mr Lake, a bencher of the Middle Temple, who had one of them and brought it to London, the truth of it was averr'd by many that saw the fishes lye scattered all over the field, and none in other fields thereto adjoining: The quantity of them was estimated to be about a Bushel, being all together. Mr Lake gave the charge at those sessions.

1683: Toads on the road
According to Michell and Rickard's *Phenomena* book, a shower of toads is recorded from 24 October 1683 over Acle in Norfolk. 'They had made a nuisance of themselves invading people's houses, and the Acle publican, unable to endure the smell of them, had thrown them by the shovelful into the fire or out into the yard. Next day they were all gone.'

1686: Seeds of strangeness
An account from this time mentions how something akin to wheat, encased within hail, fell in Wiltshire. The grains were examined and thought to have been seeds of ivy berries.

1686: It's raining clothes ... and weapons!
Michell and Rickard's book *Phenomena* mentions that, 'According to a contemporary record, on Clydeside in the summer of 1686 there were showers of bonnets, hats, guns and swords, which covered the trees and the ground ...'

1695: Utterly butterly!

According to Charles Fort, the *Philosophical Transactions* record that on 15 November 1695 in the counties of Limerick and Tipperary, there had been a fall of a greasy, buttery substance which had a 'very stinking smell.' The substance, also observed in Munster and Leinster, was mentioned in a letter by the Bishop of Cloyne who stated that the substance, which country people called 'butter', was 'soft, clammy and of a dark yellow' and where the stuff lay cattle had begun to feed indifferently. A few people, curious about the butter, collected it in pots for they believed it to have medicinal properties.

1741: Wonder web

Charles Fort states in *All Year Round* that the most peculiar rainfall was recorded on 21 September over Bradly, Selbourne and Alresford. The substance described as 'cobwebs' fell in a flake formation, each being up to 6in long. 'The quantity was great – the shortest side of the triangular space is eight miles long.'

   This type of phenomenon has become known as angel hair. This thread-like material often dissolves when it comes into contact with anything, but according to Fort the webs that landed over the trio of villages was quite heavy and fell with some velocity. In his book *The Natural History and Antiquities of Selborne*, the Revd Gilbert White reported that he'd been walking his dog when, 'I found the stubbles and clover grounds matted all over with a thick coat of cobweb, in the meshes of which a copious amount and heavy dew hung so plentifully that the whole face of the country seemed, as it were, covered with two or three nets drawn one over the other.' White also goes on to report that at 9.00 a.m. later that day:

> An appearance very unusual began to demand our attention, a shower of cobwebs falling from very elevated regions and continuing, without any interruption, till the close of day. These webs were not single filmy threads, floating in the air, but perfect flakes or rags; some near an inch broad, and five or six long, which fell with a degree of velocity that showed they were con-siderably heavier than the atmosphere. On every side as the observer turned his eyes might he behold a continual succession of fresh flakes falling into his sight, and twinkling like stars as they turned their sides towards the sun.

1797: Fall of hay

The Kentish Note Book of 17 December 1892 records as follows:

> Notes: I have in my possession a letter in the hand-writing of Samuel Horsley, LL.D., Bishop of Rochester, written in 1797, at Bromley House, giving an account of a remarkable fall of hay from the clouds as witnessed by him and his family on July 10th of that year. I do not know whether the Bishop's letter ever appeared in print, but I reproduce it here for the benefit of the readers of the K.N.B.:

Copy: Bromley House – July 10th, 1797 – 'Sir – The forenoon of this day [July 10th] was remarkably sultry, with little sunshine, except for about two hours and a half from noon. The greatest heat was about 3 o'clock when the sky was overcast again. At that time the Thermometer already in the shade, at a window on the north side of my house, and so fixed as to face the east, was at 81 degrees. But a little before it was taken to 77 degrees, and the Barometer at the same time, which in the morning had been at 30,08, was sunk at 30,03. Just about this time I observed the cows and Welsh poneys [sic] in my paddock all galloping towards the yard, as if something had frightened them. The sky was overcast with dark lowering clouds, the swallows were flying very low, and from many appearances I apprehended that a heavy thunderstorm was approaching. We had sitten [sic] down to dinner (perhaps about 5 or 10 minutes past four) when a young Lady at table suddenly exclaimed in great surprise, that "the hay was all falling about the garden". Running to the window I saw many little handfuls of hay falling gently and almost perpendicularly through the air upon my lawn. Going to the front door, I saw the same sort of shower descending upon the grass on the contrary side of the house, and found my gardiner (sic) and labourours (sic) gazing at it. I observed a large black cloud coming over the house with a very slow motion from south to north, or nearly in that direction. Fixing my eyes steadily on the middle of that cloud, I saw several of these parcels of hay, one after another, dropping in appearance from the bosom of the cloud, and becoming first visible at a great height in the atmosphere. They descended with a very slow motion, and with a very small deviation from the perpendicular in the direction in which the cloud moved. The atmosphere all this time was remarkably close and still. Not a leaf of the trees moved, not a breath of air was stirring, and my own hay was lying motionless in the field. Towards the evening a light breeze sprang up, which soon died away again; and the whole day has passed off without thunder, rain, or storm of any kind. The specimen of this hay, which I have the honour to send you, is the aggregate of two of the little parcels picked up by myself on opposite sides of the house.

> I have the honour to be, Sir
> With great respect,
> Your most obedient,
> Very Hble Servant, Rochester.

Undated: Frog fall

Nineteenth-century lecturer Thomas Cooper recorded that, as a boy whilst living in Gainsborough, Lincolnshire, he observed a fall of frogs. Such was the fall that people in their homes reported how the amphibians were leaping into the fireplace after tumbling down the chimney.

1837: Snow worms
On 14 April, according to the *London Times*, a shower of black worms fell upon the parish of Bamford Speke. Absurdly, the worms, measuring almost 1in, fell during a snowstorm!

1838: Frog storm
On 30 July of this year a heavy storm battered London, which left hundreds of little frogs strewn about the place as if they'd ascended from the sky.

1841: Fish and ice
A large fish fall was recorded in the *Timb's Year Book*. Parts of Derby were pelted with fish measuring up to 2in. A report in the *London Times* claimed that the fish were sticklebacks and they had tumbled from the sky alongside frogs and ice. Later in the year fish were recorded as falling over Dunfermline.

1849: Black rain
On 14 May black rain fell in Ireland. According to Charles Fort it was recorded in the *Annals of Scientific Discovery* and the *Annual Register*. It was the colour of ink and had a fetid odour. Thick black rain was also recorded at Castlecommon in Ireland on 30 April 1887, and 8 and 9 October 1907 in Ireland. On 1 Marsh 1884 black rain fell on the Clyde Valley, echoing a fall in the same area from 1828. In 1873 black rain fell at Marlsford, England, and there were several more bouts of the black stuff at Slains in Scotland. On 16 July the sound of rumbling wagons was heard in the skies of Northampton. Three days later a strange black rain fell.

1858: Aerolite fall
On 14 June 1858 in a piece for the *Birmingham Daily Post* a meteorologist named Mr C. Mansfield Ingleby stated that, 'During the storm on Saturday (12th) morning, Birmingham was visited by a shower of aerolites. Many hundreds of thousands must have fallen, some of the streets being strewn with them.' It was also reported at the time that some of the falling stones had damaged greenhouses. On 15 June someone else, writing in the *Post*, claimed that after microscopic analysis the stones turned out to be fragments of Rowley ragstone. It appears that it had simply been loosened by the heavy rain and when strewn across Birmingham appeared to have fallen from the sky. However, a Dr Phipson at the time commented that the stones had in fact fallen from the heavens after been swooped up by a whirlwind at Rowley – several miles away from Birmingham.

It's raining fish! (Illustration by Simon Wyatt)

1859: Something fishy
During February, fish, said to measure up to 5in in length, fell over Aberdare, in South Wales. Rooftops were smothered in the fish and children scooped them up in excitement. The British Museum identified the fish as minnows.

1860: Black stones over the Black Country
The *Wolverhampton Advertiser* recorded that in the summer, during a violent storm, a vast amount of little black stones fell from the sky. Strangely, these types of stones had never been recorded anywhere else except in Birmingham, 13 miles away, two years previous.

1868: More black Birmingham stones
English Mechanic, according to Charles Fort, on 31 July reported that stones 'similar' to those previously mentioned had fallen on Birmingham. It was recorded that on 30 May 1868 the stones had fallen for one hour. 'They resembled, in shape, broken pieces of Rowley ragstone ...'

1869: Black stones again
On 25 May 1869, after a severe storm 'a great number of small, black stones had been found in the streets of Wolverhampton ...'.

1871: As the worms turn
The Times of London from 24 April recorded a storm of glutinous drops at Bath. 'Many soon developed into a wormlike chrysalis, about an inch in length.'

1872: Flying haystack!
Author Jacques Vallee records in *Passport to Magonia* that at King's Sutton in Banbury, on 7 December at 1.00 a.m., an 'object resembling a haystack flew on an irregular course. Sometimes high, sometimes very low, it was accompanied by fire and dense smoke. It produced the same effect as a tornado, felling trees and walls. It suddenly vanished.'

During the same year, an area of Bermondsey, London, was bombarded with stones and other missiles which injured children. Despite a strong police presence no one could fathom where the objects had fallen from.

1881: Periwinkle panic
In the book *The World's Greatest UFO Mysteries*, it is mentioned that, 'A terrible thunderstorm swept the English city of Worcester in May.' The storm was so severe that hailstones shredded leaves and a poor donkey was struck dead by lightning. In Cromer Lane it was reported that gardener John Greenhall ran for cover in his shed. As he peered from the doorway he was amazed to see periwinkles falling from

the sky and bouncing off the ground. When the storm had subsided amazed towns-folk collected the molluscs. One man managed to fill two buckets. Another picked up a huge shell and found it occupied by a hermit crab.

The strange incident was described in more detail in the *Worcester Daily Times* of 30 May 1881.

1886: Snail storm
Science Gossip recorded that on 8 July at Redruth in Cornwall, during a heavy thunderstorm, roads and fields were strewn with hundreds of small snails which were picked up by astounded locals.

1887: Any ol' iron
After a violent thunderstorm in Brixton, London, on 17 August, it was recorded that a lump of round iron had fallen from the sky and landed in a back garden. A chemist could not identify the object. Around the same time an 'iron cannon ball' fell from the sky onto a pile of manure in Sussex.

1892: White frogs
Such creatures, and tiny in size, were said to have fallen over Birmingham on 30 June.

1893: Roach on chub
Bearing in mind a chub is the name of a freshwater fish, the following incident proves that surely there is no such thing as coincidence. One autumn evening in 1893 a Mr Chub was walking home from work in the vicinity of Kensington High Street, London, when he received a blow to the head which felled him. Thinking he was under attack, Mr Chub was surprised to see no sign of his assailant, but was aided by a witness who told him that a fish had in fact fallen from the sky and hit him! Mr Chub, brushing the silvery scales from his shoulder, got to his feet and there before him was a roach – a freshwater fish! It was likely that the fish had been dropped by a bird, or maybe it had fallen from the sky!

1894: Jumping jellyfish!
Notes and Queries records a remarkable fall of August 1894 in which thousands of jellyfish, each the size of a shilling, had appeared at Bath. Charles Fort comments, 'I think it is not acceptable that they were jellyfish: but it does look as if this time frog spawn did fall from the sky … at the same time small frogs fell at Wigan.' Twenty-three years earlier, Bath experienced a similar fall.

1902: Wacky West Midlands

In his book *Dr Shuker's Casebook*, Karl Shuker mentions a bizarre fall from the sky, which concerned his grandmother Mrs Gertrude Timmins. One day, when she was around the age of eight, she was walking with her mother and dog across a field in what is now the West Bromwich area, when it suddenly began to rain. Gertrude and her mother were equipped with umbrellas which they soon opened. However, when their brollies began to be hit hard by objects that were clearly bigger than your average raindrop, they began to wonder what was going on. It was then they realised that they were being bombarded by frogs. Gertrude was terrified by the sudden appearance of the frogs but her mother assured her she was safe and they made their way home.

1911: Jelly vision!

On 24 June at Eton, in Buckinghamshire, jelly fell from the sky. The ground was covered with pea-sized blobs, which may have suggested frogspawn, from which larvae were said to have emerged.

1918: Eels like rain!

Charles Fort notes that a correspondent from the Dove Marine Laboratory, Cuttercoats, England, mentioned that on 24 August at Hindon, a suburb within Sunderland, hundreds of small fish 'identified as sand eels', had fallen on an area of '60 by 30 yards'. The eels dropped from the sky after a storm. The fish were dead, stiff and hard.

1920: Hounslow showers

A Mrs Grace Wright reported to *TV Times* that whilst walking along a street in Hounslow, a terrible thunderstorm brought with it a rain of tiny frogs. Mrs Wright's son filled a sweet box full of the frogs.

1944: High strangeness at Hopwas

Mr John Pitman reported that in 1944, close to D-Day, he, his wife Caroline and their two daughters visited Hopwas, Staffordshire, on a bus. As the vehicle passed Whittington Barracks it began to rain frogs. At the time, 10.00 a.m., it was a clear blue sky.

1945: A croaking quirk

On a clear, mild day at Rickmansworth, Hertfordshire, a man named Bill reported to a radio station that he'd seen a shower of frogs pour into a lake. According to *Fortean Times* magazine this is a bizarre role reversal, because one theory put forward to explain strange falls suggests that frogs, fish etc. are scooped up by water spouts.

1954: The day it rained frogs

It's highly unlikely that cats and dogs will rain from the sky, but during the June of 1954 at Sutton Park in Birmingham it did rain tiny, pale frogs. Shoppers were shocked to hear frogs splattering on their umbrellas and women screamed as they scurried into shops to avoid the surreal shower. Whilst many of the falling frogs hopped away to safety, the pavement was still covered with a lot of dead specimens.

1955: The day it rained frogs, again

In a letter to *Fortean Times* magazine a Mrs Mowday of Bodorgan wrote of a series of peculiar events which took place one June in the mid-1950s. At the time she was watching a Royal Naval display with her daughter inside Sutton Park when there was a sudden shower, which brought with it several tiny frogs! Those who had umbrellas up were astounded to see the frogs bouncing around and as Mrs Mowday records, 'we were afraid to walk for fear of treading on them.'

1957: A splash of cash

As we know, money doesn't grow on trees, but wouldn't it be great if it rained money? Oh, it did! On 17 February 1957 it allegedly rained money in the Tyne and Wear town of Gateshead. After a flurry of snow thousands of halfpennies were said to have rained down over the vicinity of Ellison Street. People, despite the excitement, had to run for cover as the pennies hit skulls very hard. Those brave enough to stand the shower, or wait for it to subside, ran into the street and picked up what they could.

1962: Sky rains seashells from the seashore

Alan Robson recorded that in 1962 a rain of seashells had taken place over the Sheriff Hill area of Gateshead. Some theorised that a storm out at sea had somehow sucked up thousands of tiny shells from the seabed and the strong gusts had carried them inland. However, if this was the case then why were there no fish, pebbles, seaweed etc., just small limpet and cockleshells?

One witness, a Moira Thomas, when interviewed in 1989 about the strange fall stated that her car had been scratched by the shells.

1964: A hairy experience

Strange strands, resembling hair, fell over Acton in London during a storm. A Mr Murray scooped up some of the strands.

1966: Summer ice fall

Whilst I've refrained from recording the hundreds of strange falls of ice, one case of note comes from Meadway in Sevenoaks, Kent. In August 1966 a Mrs Jane

Williamson's house was bombarded by huge chunks of ice, which crashed through the roof. Police believed the chunks may have fallen from an aircraft.

1967: Mystery bomb

On 28 October of this year the *Evening News* reported, 'Mystery "bomb" drops on house', after a 'mystery metal object fell from the sky and crashed on to the roof of a house in Bickley, Kent'. The object measured 2ft in length and 2in round, and broke telephone wires before hitting the house of a Mr John Boatwright, of Homemead Road. Bromley police were called to investigate the strange fall and took the item away in a bucket. A neighbour of Mr Boatman heard the object fall with an almighty bang, but ruled out that it had come from a plane as there was no noise from above to suggest an aircraft had passed. Strangely, around the same time unidentified flying objects were seen over London.

1974: Kent soot

Parts of Dartford, Bexley and North Cray were plastered with a strange, black soot-like substance.

1976: Plop from above!

The *Daily Mirror* of 22 March 1976 reported that a Somerset woman, Leslie Skuse, had a revolting experience when her washing and cabbages in her back garden at Bason Bridge were splattered with excrement, which had fallen from the sky. A spokesman from Lulsgate Airport expressed doubt that the faeces had come from a plane. So, where had it come from?

1977: Are you nuts?

One of the quirkiest falls to take place over England took place in the March of 1977 at Bristol. Alfred Wilson Osborne and his wife were on their way home from church one Sunday morning, when hazelnuts began to fall from the cloudless sky. The nuts fell for several minutes, bouncing off cars. According to Mr Osborne, the most amazing thing about the nuts was the fact that they were ripe and fresh, even though such nuts were not in season until the autumn. 'I have thought that it might be a vortex that sucked them up,' he told a local newspaper. 'But I don't know where you suck up hazelnuts in March!'

1978: Star rot

On 23 June a Cambridge woman named Mrs M. Ephgrave noticed that her lawn had been covered by a strange, jelly-like substance. Cambridge had just recovered from a heavy downpour. The following day the stuff had vanished.

A tiny frog that appeared during a downpour in 1979. (Photograph by Vida McWilliam)

1979: Strange shower in Southampton

On 12 February pensioner Rowland Moody sat in his conservatory potting seeds when he noticed it had started to snow. However, the noise on the roof suggested something harder was falling and when he went to investigate he was startled to discover that his and the neighbours' garden, and the surrounding area, were covered in jelly-coated cress seeds! The objects were extremely sticky but two days later things got even weirder when mustard seeds were seen raining from the sky!

1979: Frogs keep falling on my head

A Mrs Vida McWilliam found her garden hopping alive with tiny frogs after a severe downpour one June afternoon.

1980: Grotesque gel

On 3 February 1980 a Hemel Hempstead man named Philip Buller found, to his utter astonishment, a weird, colourless gel deposited on his lawn. The substance was taken for analysis and deemed to be of amphibian origin. Some researchers believed it hadn't fallen from the sky but instead had been regurgitated by a bird.

1982: Pennies from heaven

Parishioners of St Elisabeth's church, Reddish, which is situated between Manchester and Stockport, were astounded on 28 May when a young girl reported that a 50p had fallen 'from nowhere' as she strolled through the churchyard. A few hours later, more coins were found littered across the paving stones. An owner of a local corner shop became suspicious after handfuls of children suddenly bombarded his sweet counter, and so he approached the Revd Graham Marshall to ask if any money had been stolen from the Poor Box. Upon investigation it was revealed that the children had genuinely experienced a fall of coins and that there was no way that someone could have thrown the money as the wall around the church was too high. The Revd Marshall stated that the coins must have fallen from a great height due to the noise they made on the path, because when he tried to throw a handful of coins himself they made a different sound.

1982: Sandy skies
During early September in 1982 a strange substance fell on Mansfield, Nottinghamshire, and was identified as sand. Over the years sand has been reported covering vehicles from all over Britain, and this is often blamed on freak winds distributing the grains from the Sahara. Some researchers find it highly unlikely that any type of wind would simply scoop only a few dunes and allocate them to certain areas of Britain.

1982: A plague of pollen
'Sometime in the first week of November, Mr Christopher Newberry, of Sonning, Berks, stepped outside his front early in the morning and stared in disbelief', so stated *The News*. It seems that during early November the witness had noticed his white house had taken on a yellowish hue, and so had several parked cars, neighbouring houses and roads! It was as though someone had been to work with 'a giant paint sprayer'. Mr Newberry, fearing some type of chemical contamination, hastily phoned his local council who sent over an environmental health officer.

Samples were taken of the sticky primrose-coloured powder, which was later identified as pollen, and sent to Dr Michael Keith-Lucas, of Reading University botany department, who in turn identified the goop as cedar pollen.

1983: Jumping jellybeans
A Mrs Rita Gibson of Topsham, near Exeter, found a scattering of pink beans in her garden. The objects were larger than rice grains.

1984: Roof slappers
During late May 1984 at East Ham in London, Ron Langton was watching some late-night television when he heard a curious slapping noise on the roof of his home. Thinking a storm was brewing, Ron snuggled up and eventually retired to bed. The next morning, however, a local builder named Edward Romell who, with his son, was decorating Mr Langton's property, discovered four dead fish. Two were

found in Mr Langton's yard, another amongst rubble, the other was only viewable from an upstairs window as it was on the roof. Strangely, Ron's wife mentioned that whilst out for a walk the same day as the fall, at Green Street, she'd seen a fish in the gutter. When the story was mentioned on the front page of the *Newham Recorder*, another man come forward to say he'd found around thirty fish in his garden at Canning Town. During the same year a fish fall was recorded from Wigmore, near Rainham in Kent.

Strange balls of sand were then reported falling from the sky over Dorset. On 8 and 9 November residents of East Crescent, Accrington, Lancashire, were baffled by a fall of more than 300 apples. The apples rained for an hour and no plane was heard or observed overhead. However, the weirdest thing to have fallen from the sky in 1984 did so on 23 September at Norfolk Street in Swansea. A black, glassy material, which people began to call 'glass rain', was discovered by a physics teacher named Paul Carter. Was it connected to the volcanic eruption in the Philippines, or were the raindrops really made of glass?!

1985: A hail of snails

A Ms K.J. Kimberly of Dagenham, Essex, reported a peculiar fall to *Fortean Times* magazine from 'when I was a student living in Walthamstow, east London'. It had taken place in the mid-1980s as Ms Kimberley was using a phone-box to call her mother. Whilst in the phone-box it began to rain and but whatever was hammering down on the phone-box clearly wasn't just rain. Ms Kimberley commented that she was on the phone for an hour or so but her conversation was disrupted by constant knockings on the roof. 'As I left the phone-box I saw that it was covered with snails (I think they were common banded snails)'. Despite being a life sciences student, Ms Kimberley was too spooked by the downpour to take a snail away for analysis.

1987: Not just any old frog fall

According to the *Daily Mirror* and the *Daily Star* of 24 October, an elderly lady from Gloucestershire had reported to the GTNC (Gloucestershire Trust for Nature Conservancy) a fall of 'tiny rose-coloured frogs' during a torrential downpour of rain in the Stroud area. Despite hitting the ground quite hard, many of the creatures sprang away into the undergrowth. It is possible the strange colouration of the frogs was due to an albino strain. Pink frogs were also reported as falling from the sky at Cheltenham and Cirencester. Whether by some bizarre coincidence, at the same time a new film had been released called *The Love Child*. The promotional posters for the film portrayed pink frogs falling from the sky.

1988: Warning! Wet paint!

The *Daily Mirror* of 20 October 1988 reported how police were baffled by the fall of white paint on houses in Bournemouth, Dorset.

1989: Pelted by coins

A Mr Albert Williamson of Ramsgate in Kent claimed that for six years, up until 1989, his house had been pelted by occasional showers of coins. Mr Williamson's neighbour, a Kim Moody, stated that she'd been waiting for a bus when she was struck by several coins. 'I kept watch on windows and my friend kept an eye on the sky. More fell, but we couldn't see where they came from,' she said.

1991: A fall of grace

A Nicola Savage wrote to *Fortean Times* magazine in May 1996 after having a very weird experience that had taken place about five years earlier whilst she was visiting her mother in Isleworth, Middlesex. Nicola had travelled on the bus and when she stepped off onto the pavement and began walking something fell from the sky – it was a rosary. 'I looked all around me, but there was no one in sight and the street was completely quiet. I wasn't standing underneath a tree and there were no planes overhead.'

Nicola never considered herself to be a religious person but after the event friends and family told her that what happened must have been some sort of sign.

1991: Strange soot

The *Daily Post* of Liverpool reported that, on 9 September 1991 at 10.00 p.m., parts of Wirral were covered with a fine black dust which resembled soot. Cars, houses and even a dog were sprinkled with the mysterious layer. Local councils failed to identify the dust.

1991: A rain of five fish

On Sunday 22 September five fish fell from the sky into the back garden of a property at Stafford Road, Plaistow, East London. The fish, which were dead, measured 4in. The *Newham Recorder* of 26 September speculated that the fish had probably been scooped up by a freak wind (which is unlikely) or plucked from a pond by a heron and then dropped. Interestingly, the fish were identified as sardines which, according to *Fortean Times*, are 'a marine fish not well known for frequenting British waters and unknown in the Thames. Neither heron nor whirlwind can pluck what is not there.' The other theory was that maybe someone had purchased a pack of sardines from a nearby supermarket and thrown them.

1994: Crayfish craziness

The *Weekend Telegraph* of 19 November reported that a freshwater crayfish had been discovered in a flowerbed at Alexandra Park, Scarborough. Expert opinion was that it had most probably been dropped by a bird rather than rained from the sky.

1994: Pebble-dash!
The *Dorset Evening Echo* of 7 December reported a marvellous fall of dozens of red and blue stones at King's Road, Radipole, near Weymouth. The strange fall came over the weekend of 3 and 4 December and was witnessed by a Steve Clarke.

1995: Now that's what I call a windfall!
On 21 February 1995 the *Western Morning News* reported that hundreds of £10 notes fell over Kidlington, Oxfordshire. Police were at a loss to explain how or why.

1995: John, meet Rod
During March a Mr John MacGregor was counting himself lucky to be alive after a 3in metal rod fell from the sky, zipped through the roof of the Symphony Furniture factory in Leeds and landed inches away from him. The noise of the object crashing onto the floor was enough to give anyone a heart attack, too. An operations manager dismissed the possibility the object had dislodged from an aircraft. He told the *Yorkshire Evening Post* of 8 March, 'All aircraft are checked routinely by their captains and engineers and nothing has been found missing.'

1995: The straw that (could've) broke the camel's back
On 27 July 1995 at 3.00 p.m., a John Knifton of Nottingham was visiting Sheringham in north Norfolk. He was accompanied by his wife and daughter. Whilst in a large car park they witnessed a fall of straw. The bizarre fall seemed to be concentrated on the car park, which was situated between the main A149 coastal road and the railway station. Whilst only a few strands fell on the road, the car park experienced 'good quantities at a more or less uniform rate, rather like the beginning of a decent snow fall'. The straw fell vertically from an almost clear blue sky. Due to the way the straw fell Mr Knifton immediately ruled out the possibility that it had been blown off the back of a lorry. Two days before, a straw fall was also reported from Wiltshire. It lasted five minutes.

1995: Paint the town brown
One of the weirdest, and certainly most revolting, things to fall from the sky has to be excrement. You couldn't make it up, could you? Yet that's what happened in August 1995 during a tennis tournament in Edinburgh. The East of Scotland tournament, which was taking place at Craiglockheart Tennis Club, Colinton, got a big, brown surprise. A John Paterson, commenting in the *Edinburgh Evening News*, said: 'I was sitting on the grass watching the tennis when I heard a loud slap. I looked around and my wife Jane's back and arms were covered in human excrement. Several other people sitting near her were covered too. The smell was unbearable – no one would go near them.'

Whilst this weird fall brings a whole new meaning to phrase, 'when the s**t hits the fan', one can only wonder as to where such a load came from. Originally aircraft were blamed for the accident, but Edinburgh Airport ruled this out. No alternative explanation was forthcoming, leaving some of the victims rather browned off!

1995: Jelly from heaven!

The *Banbury Citizen* of 29 September reported that on 23 September a clear, jelly-like substance had been found in a garden in Horley, Oxfordshire. An anonymous man scraped up the strange substance and said there was enough to fill a kettle. A friend of the witness named Ian Lawson told the newspaper, 'It has obviously come from the sky. Maybe it is some form of refrigeration substance used on aircraft.'

1996: When the sky cried

The *Sheffield Star* of 18 March 1996 reported on the huge, teardrop-shaped lump of ice which fell from the sky at Ecclesfield in Sheffield. A handful of people waiting for a bus got the shock of their life as the object, weighing in at 4lb, crashed onto the grass. Staff at Tankersley fire station put the block of ice in their freezer but later it was dropped!

1996: A slap in the face

Fortean Times magazine of August 1996 reported 'something fishy' going on at Hatfield, in Hertfordshire, because on 17 May 1996 at approximately 6.30 p.m., a lady named Ruth Harnett was unloading shopping from her car when suddenly there was a loud thump on the roof of the vehicle. Lying on the roof was a fish. Ruth looked up, wondering, to the heavens when suddenly another fish fell and slapped onto the bonnet. 'I look around, thinking it was kids mucking about,' said Ruth. 'Then three more fish dropped on my garden and I realised they were falling from the sky.'

Ruth's husband came out of the house just in time to see several fish suddenly bombard Ruth; one specimen struck her on the face. Around twenty fish fell on the garden and these were gathered up by some local children. The fish varied in length from two to five inches and seemed to be rudd, dab and roach. Ruth told *Fortean Times* that although the fish were dead they were still warm. Bizarrely, this experience wasn't unique to Ruth. She added, 'I remember as a child my father telling me that his father was caught in a shower of fishes and frogs near Welwyn Garden City, just seven miles away, about 60 years ago.'

2000: East Anglia gets fishy

During the August of 2000 several newspapers, including the *Daily Telegraph* and the *Daily Mail*, reported a fall of 2in-long fish in Norfolk. Fred Hodgkins of Alderson Road, Great Yarmouth, went to investigate a suspected fall of hail after the sky had turned eerily dark and thunderclaps had begun to reverberate around at 11.00 a.m. 'At first I thought I might have something wrong with my eyes,' he said, 'because the whole of my back yard seemed to be covered in little slivers of silver.' When

'Dave, I don't remember the weatherman forecasting this'.

Fred looked closer he was right, there were lots of tiny fishes strewn about the garden and so he ran to tell his next-door neighbour. According to the newspaper sources the fish may have been sprats or whiting but Fred added, 'I live about half a mile from the sea, so the fish must have been carried some distance.'

The bizarre fall appeared in the October issue of *Fortean Times* too, when a correspondent named Claire Blamey, who resided 2 miles from where the fish fell, reported it was a nice sunny day when the downpour occurred. She added, 'In contradiction to wind direction indicated in the *Daily Mail's* map, there was a moderate wind from the northwest; in other words out to sea.' There had been a severe storm the previous Wednesday with, according to Claire, 'a blue-black cloud trying to put down "funnels".' Ms Blamey thought it would probably develop a spout over the sea.

2004: Terror on the Thames
The penultimate story of a freakish fall comes from the February of 2004. A boat, the *Thames Bubbler*, was in the vicinity of Dagenham when those aboard got the fright of their life: a fish with razor-sharp teeth suddenly fell from the sky. Okay, so maybe the fish had been dropped by a seagull, but the bizarre twist to the story is the fact that the fish was a piranha, a ferocious predator from the Amazon, in South America, and not the sort of fish that could survive in a British pond!

2006: A rotten ending

I end this chapter, and this book, with a tale that would seem better placed in a weird, science fiction novel. In 2006, on a farm in North Devon, a Mr Heywood found a peculiar gel-like substance, which appeared in patches on the grass. This jelly-like goo is known as 'star rot' as it was once thought that after the sighting of a falling star, the ground would appear coated in this strange slime. Karl Shuker, in his book *Dr Shuker's Casebook*, writes, 'Star rot, or *pwdre ser* – names given to weird globules of gelatinous material, sometimes discovered on the ground and elsewhere... and which have even been said by eyewitnesses to pulsate as if alive!' Tests on the 'star rot' identified it as *Fuligo septica*, a slime mould. However, many centuries ago one could imagine the commotion caused if such a jelly had been found in fields across the British Isles.

So, there you have it. Not a comprehensive list of strange falls by any means, but one which chronicles the more bizarre, sinister and quirky 'nature' of that unfathomable ocean of the sky. And remember, the next time you are perched on a hillside scouring the heavens for UFOs or phantom aircraft, be careful not to get hit in the face by a falling frog... or something even worse!

SELECT BIBLIOGRAPHY

Arnold, Neil, *Monster! The A-Z of Zooform Phenomena* (CFZ Press, 2007)

———, *Mystery Animals of the British Isles: Kent* (CFZ Press, 2009)

———, *Paranormal London* (The History Press, 2010)

Berlitz, Charles, *Charles Berlitz's World of Strange Phenomena Vol 2* (Sphere, 1990)

Bord, Janet & Colin, *Modern Mysteries of The World* (Guild, 1989)

Brooks, John, *Ghosts & Legends of the Lake District* (Jarrold, 1988)

———, *Ghosts and Legends of Wales* (Jarrold, 1987)

———, *Good Ghost Guide, The* (Jarrold, 1994)

Burks, Eddie, & Cribbs, Gillian, *Ghosthunter* (Headline, 1995)

Codd, Daniel, *Mysterious Lincolnshire* (Breedon, 2007)

Devereux, Paul & Brookesmith, Peter, *UFOs and Ufology* (Blandford, 1997)

Downes, Jonathan, *Owlman and Others, The* (CFZ Press, 2006)

Eason, Cassandra, *Ghost Encounters* (Blandford, 1997)

Emenegger, Robert, *UFOs Past, Present and Future* (Ballantine, 1974)

Evans, Hilary, *UFOs: The Greatest Mystery* (Albany, 1979)

Forman, Joan, *Haunted South, The* (Jarrold, 1978)

Fort, Charles, *Book of the Damned, The* (Abacus, 1941)

———, *Lo!* (Gollancz, 1931)

———, *New Lands* (Sphere, 1974)

Fortean Times, 1–15: Yesterday's News Tomorrow (Fortean Tomes, 1992)

Fortean Times, 16–25: Diary of a Mad Planet (Fortean Tomes, 1991)

Fortean Times, 31–36: Gateways to Mystery (John Brown Publishing, 1993)

Fortean Times, 42–46: If Pigs Could Fly (John Brown Publishing, 1994)

Fortean Times, 47–51: Fishy Yarns (John Brown Publishing, 1995)

Fox, Ian, *Haunted Places of Hampshire* (Ensign, 1993)

Freeman, Richard, *Dragons: More than a Myth?* (CFZ Press, 2005)

Green, Andrew, *Haunted Kent Today* (S.B. Publications, 1999)

Haining, Peter (ed.), *True Hauntings* (Robinson, 2008)

Hervey, Michael, *They Walk By Night* (Ace, 1968)

Hough, Peter, & Ranles, Jenny, *Mysteries of the Mersey Valley* (Sigma, 1993)

Igglesden, Charles, *A Saunter Through Kent with Pen & Pencil* (Kentish Express, 1906)

Jones, Ivor S. (compiler), Stewart-Jones, Mark (ed.), *Ghosts of the Ghost Club 2001* (The Ghost Club, 2001)

Jones, Sally, *Legends of Somerset* (Bossiney, 1984)

Khatri, Vikas, *True Ghosts & Spooky Incidents* (Pustak Mahal, 2006)

Lee, Frederick George, *Glimpses in the Twilight* (Blackwood, 1885)

Llewelyn, Ken, *Flight into the Ages* (Felspin, 1991)

Ludlum, Harry, *Ghosts Among Us* (Janus, 1995)

MacGregor, Alisdair, *Ghost Book, The* (Hale, 1955)

Maple, Eric, *Realm of Ghosts, The* (Pan, 1964)

McEwan, Graham J., *Mystery Animals of Britain & Ireland* (Hale, 1986)

McKee, Alexander, *Into the Blue* (Granada, 1981)

McLaren, Calum, *Strange Tales of Scotland* (Lang Syne Publishers Ltd, 1982)

Michell, John & Rickard, Robert J.M., *Phenomena: A Book of Wonders* (Thames & Hudson, 1977)

O'Donnell, Elliot, *Dangerous Ghosts* (Consul, 1954)

Ogley, Bob, *Ghosts of Biggin Hill* (Froglets, 2001)

Paine, Brian & Sturgess, Trevor, *Unexplained Kent* (Breedon, 1997)

Redfern, Nick, *Three Men Seeking Monsters* (Paraview, 2004)

Robbins, Peter, & Warren, Larry, *Left At East Gate* (Marlowe, 1997)

Robson, Alan, *Grisly Trails & Ghostly Tales* (Virgin, 1992)

————, *Nightmare on Your Street: More Grisly Trails & Ghostly Tales* (Virgin, 1993)

Rutter, Gordon, *Paranormal Newcastle* (The History Press, 2009)

Shuker, Karl, *Dr. Shuker's Casebook* (CFZ Press, 2008)

Spencer, John & Anne, *Encyclopaedia of Ghosts & Spirits Vol.2* (Headline, 2001)

Taylor, Greg (ed.), *Darklore Vol.IV* (Daily Grail, 2009)

UFO: The Continuing Enigma (Reader's Digest, 1992)

Underwood, Peter, *Ghosts of Kent* (Meresborough, 1985)

————, *Ghosts of North Devon* (Bossiney, 1999)

Vallee, Jacques, *Passport to Magonia* (Contemporary Books, 1993)

Wales, Tony, *Sussex Ghosts & Legends* (Countryside Books, 1992)

Watson, Nigel, *Scareship Mystery, The* (Domra, 1999)

Whittington-Egan, Richard (ed.), *Weekend Second Book of Ghosts* (Associated Newspapers Group Ltd, 1978)

Wiltshire, Kathleen, *Ghosts & Legends of the Wiltshire Countryside* (Compton, 1973)

ISBN: 9780752461847

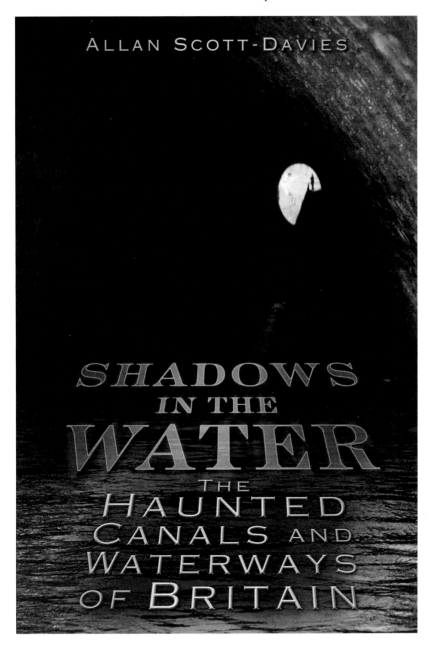

ISBN: 9780752455921

ISBN 978-0-7524-4746-9

Visit our website and discover thousands of other History Press books.
www.thehistorypress.co.uk